# AS IF WOMEN MATTER

Born on 25 March 1934 in Toledo, Ohio, Gloria Steinem is a writer, speaker and organizer whose work has been an organic part of the feminist revolution in the United States and other countries for the last forty years. She has been especially concerned with exploring the linkages between gender and race, caste and class, and between gender and violence. Gloria began her career in journalism and went on to co-found the *New York* and *Ms.* magazines. The latter is the only nationally distributed magazine for women which is owned and controlled by women.

Gloria's wide-ranging concerns and her passionate, insightful and witty voice are the hallmarks of her writing. Her essays have been collected in anthologies such as *Moving beyond Words: Age, Rage, Sex, Power, Money, Muscles: Breaking the Boundaries of Gender* (1995), *Revolution from Within: A Book of Self-Esteem* (1992) and *Outrageous Acts and Everyday Rebellions* (1983). In addition to being a prolific writer, Gloria is a board member of Equality Now, a global human rights group for women; and a co-founder and board member of the Women's Media Center, whose purpose is to name and change media bias against women. She is also the Chair of Apne Aap Women Worldwide, a grassroots anti-trafficking organization in India.

In recognition of her work and her achievements, Gloria Steinem was awarded the Presidential Medal of Freedom by Barack Obama in 2013.

\*

Ruchira Gupta, Founder-President, Apne Aap Women Worldwide, is an Emmy-winning journalist, feminist-activist and policymaker who has worked for thirty years to end human trafficking and empower marginalized women. She is also a Professor at New York University where she teaches the course, 'Human Trafficking as Gender-Based Violence', once a year.

Ruchira received the Clinton Global Citizens Award in 2009.

The Essential
# GLORIA STEINEM
Reader

Edited and introduced by
## RUCHIRA GUPTA

RUPA

Published by
Rupa Publications India Pvt. Ltd 2014
7/16, Ansari Road, Daryaganj
New Delhi 110002

*Sales centres:*
Allahabad Bengaluru Chennai
Hyderabad Jaipur Kathmandu
Kolkata Mumbai

Text copyright © Gloria Steinem 2014
Introduction and edition copyright © Ruchira Gupta 2014

Page 275 is an extension of the copyright page.

ISBN: 978-81-291-3103-4

First impression 2014

10 9 8 7 6 5 4 3 2 1

This edition is for sale in India, Nepal and Bangladesh only.

Typeset in Nebraska by SŪRYA, New Delhi

*To my lifetime friend,*
*Devaki Jain,*
*and to*
*Kamaladevi Chattopadhyay,*
*who inspired us both*
—Gloria Steinem

\*

*To my mother, who taught me to ask questions,*
*to my father, who taught me to look for answers in Movements,*
*and to Jyoti Singh Pandey,*
*whose courage is contagious.*
—Ruchira Gupta

# CONTENTS

# PREFACE

This book exists because my friend and colleague, Ruchira Gupta, thought that some of my writings over the years might be useful to the many women and men in India who are working for more empathy and equality—and far less violence—between women and men.

I hope with all my heart that you find some helpful fact or idea or companionship in these pages. My country, too, needs to bridge the distance between female and male human beings, and between 'masculine' and 'feminine' tasks that are really all human. Roles based on ideas of gender may be no more humane or inevitable than those based on race or caste or class or anything else that isn't earned or chosen.

Indeed, I've come to believe that the independent 'masculine' and the dependent 'feminine'—subject and object, active and passive—are just labels for universal human qualities. They may normalize inequality based on sex in the same way that stereotypes do for race, caste, class and other invented divisions.

But the important thing to remember is that female bodies are the means of reproduction, and so are doubly likely to be restricted when other divisions are at stake—which is why sexism and racism are so intertwined in my country, sexism and caste are so intertwined in yours, and why sex/race or sex/caste can only be uprooted together.

In most cases, gender inequality is what we experience first as children in our families, so we feel that those roles are natural, even good, and the domination of one gender by another seems normal. Even if we find such sex inequalities deplorable, we often think they are inevitable. After all, if we accept inequality within our own home and among the people we love, we'll accept it anywhere. But in the years when I was writing the essays in this book, studies of tribal societies were already proving that polarized gender roles were the best indicator of other forms of violence within that society, and also of the likelihood that it would use violence against outsiders. Anthropologist Geoffrey Gorer had shown that rigid sex roles characterized violent cultures, and a lack of sex-role rigidity characterized non-violent cultures.

Since then, *Sex and World Peace*, a 2012 book by Valerie Hudson and three other scholars, has documented current rates of violence against females in a hundred nations. It also documented rates of poverty, access to natural resources, degrees of democracy, and the influence of religion on the law.[1] The best predictor of violence within a country—and also of a country's willingness to use of violence against another country—was none of the usual suspects of poverty, natural resources, religion or democracy. *It was violence against females.*

As the authors explain: 'Those states that foster gender equality through laws and enforce those laws are less likely to go to war. They are less likely to use force first when in conflict... States do go to war over oil and scarce resources, among other things, but they are more likely to do so if the society has norms of violence rooted in gender inequality...'[2]

And if you're wondering where my country came out, it wasn't so great. As one of the few modern nations with no guarantee of women's rights in its Constitution, no national system of childcare or parental leave, no ratification of the Convention on the Elimination of All Forms of Discrimination against Women, and with high rates of maternal mortality, the US tends to let women fend for ourselves rather than guarantee rights. For instance, the women's movement worked long and hard to make domestic violence a crime, yet it's very under-prosecuted, rarely taken seriously enough to be prevented, and shelters are disappearing with budget cuts. Yet if you added up all the women who've been murdered by their husbands or boyfriends since 9/11—and then added up all the Americans killed in 9/11, in Iraq and in Afghanistan *combined*—more women have lost their lives to domestic terrorism.

As Hudson and her co-authors wrote as a challenge: 'You were taught that the clash of civilizations is based on ethno political differences, but did you know that the real clash of civilizations may instead be based on gender beliefs?'[3]

\*

Now, even more than when I wrote these essays, I understand why I wrote them. For instance, I look back on my research into Hitler's obsession with masculinity, and I see a gendered understanding of violence in the making. I re-read *The Politics of Food,* and think about genetically altered seeds and farmers in India committing suicide.[4]

I witness pornography spreading worldwide via the Internet, and I'm more aware of its difference from the erotic; from the playfulness and mutual pleasure of, say, the *Kamasutra.* I see the humour in imagining what would happen if men could menstruate—and it became proof of superiority—but I see the ultra-rich hiding in fortresses in both our countries, and I think, Not everything the powerful have is superior.

Now, the real Linda Lovelace has a movie, so more people know that she was a prisoner, but now I also know she died too young and was still suffering from internal injuries. I never imagined that the Playboy Clubs would be exported to India—here, the chain was rejected and closed in 1991—but at least I can offer my experience as a warning. I think about my essay, 'In Praise of Women's Bodies', and wish that we could look at real bodies instead of computer-altered images.

I still mourn for my mother's broken spirit and I still see many women who are living out the unlived lives of their mothers. Yet many mothers are using their talents in their own lives—and are setting their daughters free.

Most of all, I understand now the theme of violence against females which runs through these essays like a red thread. Perhaps for the first time in human history, women are no longer half the human race. Because of femicide in all its forms, the world sex ratio is 100 women to 101.3 men.

How did this happen? Partly because prejudice and violence

have been speeded up by travel and technology, also because refugees are mostly women and children, obviously because of sexualized violence in war zones, also because AIDS still kills far more women than men in Africa, and because of quiet and obscure deaths from female genital cutting, from children giving birth to children, from so-called honour killings—and so much more.

Some patriarchal ethnic groups and religions have tried to out-populate others by taking control of reproduction away from women, forcing child marriage, and forbidding contraception and abortion. As a result, pregnancy is now the number one cause of death among adolescent girls worldwide.

And in India, I needn't say that despite many good educational campaigns, bias towards sons and against daughters has created sex-selective abortion and has also led to the withholding of food and healthcare from girls. Worldwide, there is a Daughter Deficit and a Son Surplus. More girls have been killed in the last fifty years *because they were girls* than men have been killed in all the battles of the twentieth century combined.[5]

Finally, confining some women's bodies to reproduction—and punishing female sexuality—means that other women are confined only to sex. Prostitution is less the world's oldest profession than the world's oldest oppression. Wherever there is less equality for females, sex is more commercialized and compelled. A minimum of four million women and girls are bought and sold into the sex trade each year.[6] In my country, the average age of entry into prostitution is thirteen—often a runaway, throwaway and abused girl who is condemned to what she may call 'survival sex'.[7] There are also many women and girls trafficked from other countries. Added up globally, sex trafficking is an industry that has surpassed the drug trade in profitability and is second only to the arms trade. And added to that is labour trafficking of girls and women, often as domestics.

If the first step towards more equality and less violence is imagining it, we should study the first 95 per cent of human history on both our subcontinents. We both have remnants and some living examples of matrilineal cultures—not matriarchal, which would be simply reversing patriarchal and dominating men—but cultures of balance in which the paradigm was the circle. Before the arrival of Europeans from a continent of kings and patriarchs, women in the five hundred or so native cultures on what was known as Turtle Island had equal power, controlled their lives, controlled agriculture, governed reproduction with herbs and abortifacients, were responsible for agriculture, and for deciding questions of war and peace. They spoke languages like Cherokee which had 'he' and 'she', and no gendered pronouns.

In India before Europeans, colonialism and Christianity, there were matrilineal cultures from Kerala to the Himalayas, as there were in China and parts of Africa. Even now, I notice that the political demands of the Dalits, a group among the many who migrated from Africa, and preceded the caste system, now demand land for the landless and ask that it be registered in Dalit women's names.

Perhaps what we want once was here on both our lands.

*

Which leads me to my own past. It is hard to imagine myself arriving in India as an uncertain twenty-two-year-old, with far more idea of what I didn't want to do (stay home and get married) than what I did want to do (find the work I loved).

I didn't know that my two years here would shape my life, that I would learn organizing from the Gandhians who walked from village to village, as you will read in an essay here, 'The India That Shaped Me', and also meet women and men who would become the oldest continuous friends in my life. There is Devaki Jain—Devaki Srinivasen when I met her—my sister-writer, feminist organizer and Gandhian economist. Her late husband, Lakshmi Jain, a kind and great man who I greatly miss. There are other continuous heroes like Ela Bhatt, founder of the Self-Employed Women's Association of India (SEWA), and now for a decade, I've had the good luck to work and share travels with Ruchira Gupta, journalist and founder of Apne Aap, a grassroots movement to end sex trafficking. We first met in India in early 2007 when I came to see that work at the suggestion of a mutual friend—and one result was what she describes at the beginning of her introduction. Then at the end of that year, she and I were both at a long meeting in Nepal organized by Equality Now, a global group working for the rights of women and girls.

There, women's groups from countries as different as Cambodia and Kenya, Latvia and Peru, shared our work against sex trafficking. We each came to understand that we were not alone, and we learned from each other's organizing tactics and ways to empower survivors and their children. By the end, Ruchira and I had bonded. We discovered that we were both journalists who reported on injustices so great that just writing about them was no longer enough.

We're almost thirty years apart in age, and also separated by the different continents, languages and cultures of our birth, yet our lives and work are interwoven. Friendship is a country. And now she has brought me full circle with this book.

So I dedicate this book to her. And I also dedicate it to every woman and man in India who protested in the streets against sexualized violence, and turned tragedies into a global movement that is changing consciousness and laws for us all.

At the end of *Sex and World Peace*, there is an image that has stayed with me. The human race is a bird with two wings. As long as there is violence against females, one wing will be broken. Only when that wing is healed and strong can humans fly.

Then we all will soar.

# WHY THIS BOOK

On a humid pre-monsoon afternoon, a small group of women in the Delhi slum of Dakshinpuri stood listening to Gloria Steinem. She was speaking in English, there was a slight drizzle, and we were in a narrow lane surrounded by barking dogs, running children and screaming vendors. I was surprised to see that no woman left to go back to her urgent chores. Gloria had connected with them across language, religion, culture, class and national boundaries. She spoke about why she had had an abortion and why she had kept it a secret for a long time.

As her story unfolded, she took the women on a journey from the personal to the political and from the local to the global. She linked our inequalities with each other and to the power systems that control us. And she ended by telling the women: 'Remember you are not alone, you have sisters who are listening and standing by you in your struggle for equality in a country as far away as mine. All we have to continue to do is honour each other with the Truth.'

It was so simple that it sounded banal. But I tested the idea in my own meetings with circles of women in the coming years and found that when I spoke my personal truth to any group of women, we connected. Gloria had given me a valuable political tip at our very first meeting. This happened in February 2007, when she had come to see the workings of Apne Aap at the suggestion of an activist and mutual friend.

At the end of that year, Gloria and I met again at a long meeting in Nepal organized by Equality Now. Together, we decided to leave for Forbesgunge, my village in Bihar on the border with Nepal, to meet a group of Nat women organizing under the Apne Aap banner to resist inter-generational prostitution in their community.

As I stop now to think about why this trail-blazing feminist icon went with me in an auto-rickshaw to speak to a group of twenty women in Delhi, or gave up Jane Fonda's birthday party to sit in a circle of even less women in the red-light area of Forbesgunge, I remember two other political tips that she has shared with us:

'Nothing is capable of taking the place of the experience of being close, by direct contact, by being together; you have to listen...you have to know...you have to sit down eye-to-eye.'

And:

'When you do something, you don't know if it is big or small, only time will tell, but you have to do it as if it matters.'

Today, more than a hundred girls from the red-light areas of Forbesgunge are negotiating fathers who themselves have been raised to believe that their daughters should bring in money. They are supported by five hundred women who are risking punishment by pimps, customers and even the families they love, on behalf of their daughters and themselves. They have caused a caste commotion in our village by challenging the inevitability of their prostitution and they have done so in the most profound way—by first defying their own husbands and fathers at home, and then their communities and local authorities. The age-old caste and gender power structures are being uprooted together as the first four girls from this community have begun to study in a college in Patna. I had never imagined that our small effort would result in the shrinking of the red-light areas and the bustee brothels becoming real homes for the women inhabiting them.

Instead of trying to fit women into existing middle-class professions or working-class theory, Steinem's feminism assumes that women's experience should be the root of the theory. In 'Hitler and the Cult of Masculinity' Steinem writes, 'If we're to identify authoritarianism in all its forms, we must study a three-step progression of authoritarian units—the family, the nation, the very laws of God. If we grow callous in our earliest, most intimate world to a power difference among our own family members, how much easier is it to accept all other hierarchies? If one sex is born to greater power, then why not one race *(or in the Indian context—caste or religion)?* If women were allowed to marry and have children with men of their own choosing, how could race and class be kept "pure"? If a man is not allowed to dictate to a wife and children beneath him, how is he to tolerate the dictation he must accept from above?'

In 'The Masculinization of Wealth', she similarly links class and gender and describes how both rich and poor women are kept unequal to control both the means of production and reproduction so that the ruling-class inheritance system is kept in order, and so that these women can provide—and produce—cheap labour. And going again to the root of the problem, she emphasizes that not only are flexible roles more democratic, but also more natural.

In both her essays 'The Importance of Work' and 'If Men Could Menstruate', she not only highlights the fact that only what men do gets monetized and what women do does not, she also stresses that men need to play a greater role in child-rearing and women in bread-winning.

Gloria Steinem's radical belief goes beyond all other dominant political ideologies such as Socialism, Communism, Marxism, Capitalism and even those feminisms whose vision of equality is simply more equitable ways for women to fit into a system rather than the transformation of society itself.

In 'The India That Shaped Me', she mentions how she learned that 'radical' didn't have to mean big, violent, extremist or crazy—as American newspapers believed. Radical meant exactly what the dictionary said: going to the root, which she learned in the hands-on, organic, personal kind of activism while marching with Gandhian activists in the villages of Bihar to stop caste riots. Steinem's framework for transformation is rooted in Gandhi's advice of measuring our actions by their value to the least powerful, listening to them, and sitting eye-to-eye with them. She says that there is no competition of tears—suffering is suffering—so it's important to listen to each person's situation, whether it is a person of colour in the US or a person of low caste in India, or the more powerful in both countries who are cut off from community by cages of privilege.

For example, a white woman, at times, may be worse off than a black man; or an upper-caste girl in a Haryana village may be worse off than a Dalit man in Delhi—as well as vice versa. We must be open to listening so that the weakest can be identified and empathized with. In 'What is Self-Esteem?', she describes a revolution that starts with the individual but challenges all the contexts of power—race, caste, class, religion and gender. We each need to see what we ourselves have to gain when we are linked rather than ranked.

Linking the oppression of race, class, caste and gender, she analyses in the essays, 'Marilyn Monroe: The Woman Who Died too Soon', 'Romance versus Love', 'Erotica versus Pornography', 'Real Lovelace' and 'I Was a Playboy Bunny', how greed and profit drives the desire to control women's bodies. She exposes how the unmitigated sway of the market and the cult of masculinity has combined to commodify and destroy women.

In all her writings over forty years, she also offers hope in the stories of the women who have defied the worst of sexism, racism and authoritarianism in the US from within. I have chosen the most relevant of her essays for us in India today. We have valuable lessons to learn from Gloria's radical feminism.

What is harmful in the global north often gets sold to the global south—cigarettes, infant formula, harmful pesticides, genetically modified seeds, Playboy Clubs, pornography and development models designed to cut off empathy between the privileged and the marginalized. As Big Money and Big Arms collaborate across boundaries to promote a cult of masculinity, we, feminists of all colour, nationalities, race, caste and class must collaborate, too, so that we can challenge the structures which oppress us.

When I began contesting the AIDS control programme of the Bill and Melinda Gates Foundation, which was designed to protect male buyers from disease rather than protecting prostituted women and girls from male buyers, Steinem became my most powerful ally. Not only was she one of the few who were willing to stand up to such big money, but she also understood that the programme was designed top-down and had ignored the interests of that poorest and weakest girl. She wrote and spoke about how harm reduction without hard eradication entrenches the harm further and took it back to her deepest truth that the means are the end.

Walking through the red-light area of Sonagachi or lobbying in

Albany with New York State Assembly men for a change in the anti-trafficking law, our lives interwove into shared writing sessions, rallies, meetings, dinners, books, conversations, late night phone calls across continents, brainstorming and, sometimes, movies. A desk in her living room, across from where she wrote, became my writing desk and her guest room my New York home for years, just as my desk in Delhi still has her notes written on yellow paper—tucked away in drawers—left behind from her last visit.

With her, I have experienced how movements move and how immense our movement is. Such an adventure in experience happens only too rarely—where the sense of being an Indian or American is lifted off the mind and where the profoundly political is the simplest truth.

She taught me that there are always more than two choices. Even in resisting the Gates Foundation and the paradigm of sex-work which accepted the prostitution of poor and low-caste women as inevitable, she articulated a third way at the Jawaharlal Nehru University for the first time to penalize the johns, punish the pimps, brothel managers, recruiters and transporters and decriminalize the women. That speech is the basis of her essay on sex-trafficking in this book.

There is evidence of a third way of proceeding that is familiar to human experience—the remains of marketplaces, the remains of harbours, the sites of agoras and shrines, where the seats of old universities and academics are still in evidence, or the traces of trade routes have survived, such as the Silk Road, the Amber or the Saharan. In these places people encountered each other at every turn, exchanged thoughts, ideas and goods, traded and did business, made alliances and unions, found common aims and values. Gloria has helped feminists and men and women talk with each other across countries, generations, class, caste, race and other artificial boundaries in what she sees as the small spaceship—earth.

I have looked into the future with her, to the solidarity in dreams, in joy, in sorrow, in aspirations, and in hope. Her courage is contagious and, by editing this book, I hope to share Gloria's courage and hope with so many sisters across India when the movement is really moving!

# THE INDIA THAT SHAPED ME

The fall after graduating from college, I went to India on a year's fellowship. India was not only a place I'd always wanted to go to, but also an escape from a very kind and tempting man to whom I was engaged, but knew I shouldn't marry.

To my surprise, I found that I felt more at home and involved there than I ever had in any other country not my own. I stayed for another year doing freelance writing. In that diverse country that welcomes foreigners with the same equanimity that allowed it to absorb foreign cultures for centuries and yet remain unique, the students at the women's college of the University of Delhi accepted me as one of two Westerners to live there. They taught me to wear saris and were generally more instructive about India than was the curriculum, which was still shaped by the English system.

In the same period, I was also befriended by a group of gentle activists and intellectuals known as the Radical Humanists. From listening to their energetic analysing of world events, I learned that 'radical' didn't have to mean violent, extremist, or crazy, as the reading of US newspapers had led me to believe. It could mean exactly what the dictionary said: going to the root.

Though many Radical Humanists, women and men, had started out as members of the Communist Party of India when it was supporting the Indian Independence movement, they had left once the Party did an about-face during World War II and supported the British Raj—an evidence of its allegiance to Soviet needs rather than Indian members. Like many friends who were Gandhians, and who also were to show me new alternatives, these activists felt they had progressed beyond such Marxist tenets as 'the end justifies the means'.

Their experiences caused me to rethink my romance with Marxism, which had started in college when Joseph McCarthy's persecution of actual or imagined Communists made them seem admirable by comparison. As the Radical Humanists pointed out, the means we choose dictate the ends we achieve—so much so that one might more accurately say that 'the means are the ends'. M.N. Roy, one of their founders, wrote that 'the end justifies the means' and this eventually brought about the moral degeneration of the international Communist movement.[1]

As Gandhians explained, the goal was swaraj. Gandhi also used natural imagery: 'the means may be likened to a seed, the end to a tree'.[2]

I remember my first hands-on experience with activism that consciously reflected a future goal in its present tactic. I'd been travelling through south India on my own, having passed beyond the friendly chain of Radical Humanists in the north. As I made my way down the coast from Calcutta, I discovered that a Westerner in a sari was no more strange than someone from a distant part of India might have been, and that my English-with-a-little-Hindi was as useful (or useless) as some of the other fourteen major languages of India.

In the women's compartment of third-class trains and in public hostels, I found myself struggling to respond to the very un-British, thoroughly Indian habit of asking personal questions. In my case, this meant probing everything from why I wasn't married to whether I knew how to have fewer children—by methods their husbands couldn't discover.

When I went inland by a rickety bus to visit one of the ashrams started by Vinoba Bhave—a disciple of Gandhi who was asking village landowners to give part of their acreage to the poor—Bhave and most of his co-workers had already left; not on one of their usual pilgrimages to ask for land donations, but walking from village to village through Ramnad, a nearby rural area where caste riots had broken out. Government officials in faraway Delhi had responded by embargoing all news coming out of the area and closing it off in the hope that the burnings and the killings could be kept from spreading. Nonetheless, Bhave's teams had walked in on their own. Instead of asking people to stay in their houses, they were holding village meetings. Instead of a chain of vengeance, they were offering Gandhian non-violence. Instead of weapons, they were carrying only a cup and a comb, knowing that if villagers wanted peace, they would feed and house the peacemakers, thus becoming part of the process.

Their problem was that no woman was left in the ashram to join a last team of three. Men couldn't go into the women's quarters to invite women out to meetings, and if there was no woman at the meeting, other women were unlikely to come. The question was: Would I go with them? Bhave's co-workers assured me that I wouldn't seem any odder than others from outside the area. They themselves were trusted only because of their work in creating land trusts for the poor. Besides, part of their mission was to show villagers that people outside this isolated area knew and cared about what was happening to them.

For the next few days, we walked from one village to the next—sitting under trees for meetings in the cool of the early morning, walking during the heat of the day, and holding more meetings around kerosene lamps at night. Mostly, we just listened. There were so many stories of atrocities and vengeance, so much anger and fear that it was hard to imagine how it could end. But gradually, people expressed relief at having been listened to, at seeing neighbours who had been too afraid to come out of their houses and at hearing facts brought by Bhave's team, for the rumours were even more terrible than the events themselves. To my amazement, long and emotion-filled meetings often ended with village leaders pledging to take no revenge on caste groups whose members had attacked their group in a neighbouring village, and to continue meetings of their own.

Each day, we set off along paths shaded by palms and sheltered by banyan trees, cut across ploughed fields, and waded into streams to cool off and let our homespun clothes dry on us as we walked. In the villages, families shared their food and sleeping mats with us, women taught me how to wash my sari and wash and oil my hair, and shopkeepers offered us rice-cakes and sweet milky tea in the morning. I found that there was a freedom in having no possessions but a sari, a cup and a comb and, even in the midst of turmoil, peacefulness in focusing only on the moment at hand. I remember this as the first time in my life when I was living completely in the present.

Towards the end, when the violence had quieted down, my unseasoned feet had become so blistered that infection set in, and I hitched a ride in a bullock-cart back to the bus route, and to the ashram. But I ended those days with regret. I had also learned the truth of what I once disdained as an impractical and impossibly idealistic Gandhian saying: 'If you do something the people care about, the people will take care of you.'

From our team leader, a no-nonsense man in his seventies who had devoted his life to this kind of direct action—to tactics that were a microcosm of their goal—I also remember this radical advice: If you want people to listen to you, you have to listen to them. If you hope people will change how they live, you have to know how they live. If you want people to see you, you have to sit down with them eye-to-eye. Most of us have a few events that divide our lives into 'before' and 'after'. This was one for me.

When I finally travelled back home to my own country, these lessons didn't seem very portable. If 'radical' is often misunderstood now, consider how it sounded in 1958, with Eisenhower still president and fears of McCarthyite persecution still in the air.

At least at a visible level, there was no populist movement against the Cold War; no women's movement; not even an understanding yet that hunger existed in this country the US; and only a few groups working on such issues as the fallout from nuclear testing, plus civil rights events that had not yet become a movement. As for India, it hadn't yet appeared on this nation's media radar as anything other than a place of former British power and present poverty. Even the Beatles hadn't discovered India yet (indeed, there were no Beatles), and if I brought up India, an island of polite silence would appear in the conversation—and then the talk would flow right on around it.

I was in shock myself, for I was seeing my own over-developed country through the eyes of the underdeveloped world for the first time. In search of imagery for this revelation, I remember saying to all who would listen, 'Imagine a giant frosted cupcake in the midst of hungry millions.' What really ran through my head like a naïve mantra was: This can't last.

Because India had accustomed me to seeing a rainbow of skin colours, I was also realizing belatedly that in my own multiracial country, you could go snow-blind from white faces in any business area or 'good' neighbourhood. True, skin colour in India often carried the cruelty of caste, but a south Indian Brahmin might have darker skin than a north Indian Harijan, and since all had suffered collectively under British rule, there was at least a striving for a shared identity.

Furthermore, Indians described nuances of colour as unself-consciously as any other aspect of appearance. It made me realize that the deafening silence about colour in my own upbringing had not been polite, but just another way of saying that being anything other than white was impolite. I began to see how caste-divided this country was, how dishonest we were in discussing it, and how effective was this training that I had to experience a different society in order to see.

Sometimes my culture shock took surrealistic forms. In New York, where I had been sleeping on my friends' living-room floors while trying to find a job, I remember insisting on riding in the front seat with taxi drivers. My sense memory of sitting in an Indian tonga pulled by a man riding a bicycle or running between the staves—was so strong that I felt engulfed by the unacceptable experience of being driven by another human being. Of course, a Calcutta tongawallah had little to do with a New York taxi driver, but the images of the recent past were still imprinted on my eyes, and the world looked very different when viewed through them. I alternated between trying to explain what I'd experienced in India and leaving gatherings I couldn't handle because the contrast was too painful.

In other words, I must have been a terrible pain in the ass.

The more I became acclimatized to my own country, however, the more India began to seem like two years dropped out of my life—a time whose intensity and lessons I would never be able to match or make use of. Some of my trying to explain was really trying to catch what was slipping away. Though I attempted to work in student politics, it also didn't yet exist as a movement. I was far too broke and impatient to consider any graduate school.

Finally, I began to work as a freelance writer, but the assignments I could get as a 'girl reporter' often widened the gap between what I was working on and what I cared about. I was drawn to the civil rights and anti-Vietnam movements that were becoming public events by then, but they were not the assignments given to girl reporters. I found myself paying the rent with humour and advice pieces for women's magazines (while going to a school desegregation rally in Virginia or a civil rights march in Washington); writing about the mayor's wife or a fashion designer because I was impressed to get a freelance assignment from *The New York Times* (while lobbying for Peace Corps volunteers to go to communities in India); profiling actors, dancers and other celebrities for various magazines and newspapers (while organizing with writers and editors to refuse to pay that portion of our taxes going to the Vietnam war); and writing about the 'ins' and 'outs' of pop culture for *Life* (while trying to get César Chávez, a farm worker, labour leader and civil rights activist, and his new United Farm Workers on the cover of *Time* as protection against threats on his life from growers in California).

It wasn't that I disliked what I was doing. On the contrary, I liked Mary Lindsay, the mayor's wife, I loved writing satire for an *Esquire* campus issue or *That Was the Week That Was* on television, and I enjoyed learning about people while profiling them, from James Baldwin and Margot Fonteyn to Dorothy Parker and Truman Capote. But I never felt fully engaged, as if I were leading other than a derived life. Some of the tactics of those anti-Vietnam days made me feel more estranged than I had in India, for I had absorbed the idea that violent means are unlikely to reach a peaceful end—that ends and means are a seamless web—and this philosophy wasn't always guiding the most public events of the peace movement.

When *New York* magazine was founded—aided by a group of us who were to be its regular writers—this gap between work and interest narrowed somewhat. At least I could write about electoral politics, social justice movements and neighbourhood organizing in New York; all assignments that other magazines and newspapers usually gave to male reporters. But I was still a long way from the hands-on, organic, personal kind of activism I had glimpsed in India. Indeed, I had put it out of my mind.

In the movements of the 1960s, there was a saying: 'You only get radicalized on your own concerns.' That was to prove true again in the way feminism arrived in my life.

It wasn't the first brave, reformist variety of the mid-1960s that woke me up. Though I was old enough to be part of *The Feminine Mystique* generation, I wasn't living in the suburbs, wondering why I wasn't using my college degree. I'd ended up in the workforce many of these other women were then trying to enter.

Though college had taken me out of my blue-collar Toledo neighbourhood and made me a middle-class person, I shared the reaction of many working-class women and women of colour: I support women who want to get out of the suburbs and into jobs, I thought to myself, but I am already in the workforce and getting screwed. The women's movement isn't for me. Given the contrast between India and this country's share of the world's resources, I also had another reservation: sure, women should get a fair share of the pie, but what we really need is a new pie.

By the end of the 1960s, younger women were coming out of the civil rights and peace movements with similar feelings. They also had a new phrase, 'women's liberation', which addressed all women as a caste. Instead of integrating current systems, they were taking on the patriarchy and racism at their base. Instead of trying to make 'feminine' equal to 'masculine', they were joining all human qualities into a full circle that was available to everyone. At their speak-outs, I listened to stories of experience I, too, had known, but had never put into words.

When I covered as a reporter an early feminist hearing on abortion, I heard personal testimonies to the sufferings brought on by having to enter a criminal underworld. I had had an abortion too, but I'd been lucky enough to be in England, where laws were slightly less punishing. It was just after college, but I never forgot the weeks of panic before I found a doctor, or how it changed my life to be able to continue the trip to India that was then about to begin; yet I'd never spoken to anyone about this major experience in my life. Since one in three or four women had undergone an abortion even then, I began to wonder why it was illegal; why our reproductive lives were not under our own control; and why this fundamental issue hadn't been part of any other social justice movement. It was a time of epiphanies.

I remember sitting amazed in front of my television set watching Anne Koedt, Anselma Dell'Olio, Betty Dodson and other early feminists talk about sexuality on an obscure local show. It was the first time I'd ever heard women be sexually honest in public (it was rare enough in private) or take on Freud's myth of the vaginal orgasm (about which Koedt had just written an essay that was to become a classic).[3]

I started asking why women were supposed to have sex but not talk about it; why Freud got away with calling women 'immature' for failing to have a male-fantasy orgasm; and why the so-called sexual liberation movement of the 1960s had been mostly about making more women sexually available on male terms.

God may be in the details, but the goddess is in the questions. Once we begin to ask them, there's no turning back. Instead of trying to fit women into existing middle-class professions or working-class theory, these radical feminist groups assumed that women's experience should be the root of theory. Whether at speak-outs or consciousness-raising groups, 'talking circles' or public hearings, the essential idea was: Tell your personal truth, listen to other women's stories, see what themes are shared, and discover that the personal is political—you are not alone.

I'm not sure feminism should require an adjective. Believing in the full social, political and economic quality of women, which is what the dictionary says 'feminism' means, is enough to make a revolution in itself. But if I had to choose only one adjective, I still would opt for radical feminist. I know patriarchs keep equating that word with violent or man-hating, crazy or extremist—though being a plain-vanilla feminist doesn't keep one safe from such epithets either, nor does 'I'm not a feminist, but...'

Nonetheless, *radical* seems an honest indication of the fundamental change we have in mind and says what probably is the case: the false division of human nature into 'feminine' and 'masculine' is the root of all other divisions into subject and object, active and passive—the beginning of hierarchy. Since that division comes from the patriarchal need to control women's bodies as the means of reproduction—a control that racial 'purity' and caste and class systems are built on—digging out the 'masculine/feminine' paradigm undermines all birth-based hierarchies, and alters our view of human nature, the natural world and the cosmos itself. Just a few little things like that.

Everything comes together once we've found the work for which experience and temperament suit us. I've been travelling around this country every week for most of the last twenty-five years, working with many women and some men in the kind of direct-action organizing I first saw and was so magnetized by in India. Only recently have I understood the resonance between what I have been doing and that long-ago and long-buried turning point. I find the wisdom of our Ramnad team leader still holds true: You have to listen. You have to know. You have to sit down eye-to-eye.

As for the Gandhian adage: 'If you do something the people care about, the people will take care of you', I have to admit there is a big difference here. Walking from village to village could get you arrested, and having to pay for your own airline ticket is very different from hitching a ride in a bullock-cart.

But like other travelling feminists or organizers for other movements who bring hope in anything like a common-sense way, I do notice that the ticket clerk sometimes saves three seats across so I can sleep; flight attendants may slip me a healthier meal from first class; airport cleaning women stop to tell me about the latest woman candidate from their neighbourhoods; women, now able to mother other women, stock our car with spring water and apples; and even such brief contact as seeing women standing in highway toll booths yields good advice about the traffic or the weather. 'It's going to rain, honey,' one of them said kindly to me last week. 'Want to borrow my umbrella?' A movement is only composed of people moving. To feel its warmth and motion around us is the end as well as the means.

Even our faults can be useful if we're willing to expose them. Because I was scared to death of public speaking, for instance, I often began lectures by explaining that only the women's movement had given me a reason worth making a damn fool of myself, that I'd never spoken publicly at all until I was in my mid-thirties, and that if I could do it, anyone could. It was this fear that led me to speaking in teams in the beginning—which turned out to be a helpful tactic.[4] It's this fear now that makes me look forward to a discussion time in which the audience takes over and creates its own organizing meeting. Invariably the result is better than anything I, or any single speaker, could produce. In this way, I learned that being able to use all of ourselves, whether positive or negative, is a good sign that we're doing the right thing.

I've learned from the collective wisdom of these audiences, from the late-night groups that gather after meetings, individuals who stop me in the street to tell me stories of changes in their lives, people who write letters that should be books, populist researchers who send clippings with crucial passages marked, strangers who share what might be difficult to say to friends, and people in groups everywhere who are especially valuable as advisers about what I or others could be doing better. I've always been hooked on this 'found wisdom', as I've come to think of it.

When I went back to India almost twenty years after my student days, I realized it was a form of populist teaching to be preserved. I met with Indira Gandhi—then prime minister, though she had been a lonely and uncertain young woman when I first saw her—and she told me the story of her own third-class travels around India as a young mother in crowded women-only railway compartments like the ones I remembered. On learning that she had only two children, women invariably asked her: 'How did you do it?' And often: 'How can I keep my husband from knowing? How can I keep him from thinking I'll be unfaithful?'

As prime minister, she defied population experts who insisted that poor and illiterate women didn't want birth control, or couldn't understand it until they became literate, or would accept it only if their husbands approved. She instituted family planning programmes that were the first to offer women contraception in private. She also offered small financial rewards for men who agreed to be sterilized, and told health workers to explain to them that this way husbands would know if their wives were being unfaithful. Those measures were very controversial, but often more effective than the conventional ones. She received delegations of grateful women, and also criticism within her own country and in international circles for encouraging male sterilization. But the day we talked, she seemed unperturbed. She had never forgotten the words or the desperation of her populist women teachers.

On this same trip in the late 1970s, I was often told by academics, reporters and others in India's big cities that feminism was a Western phenomenon, that it had no roots in India. I later learned that, unknown to many in the cities, a movement called Stree Shakti Jagritti had been organizing conferences and padyatras, foot journeys, through rural India. Combining women's issues with the teachings of Gandhi and Vinoba Bhave, both of whom honoured their populist women teachers by saying that only awakening the inner strength of women could overcome India's obstacles, this movement had been working since the 1950s on everything from literacy campaigns to giving women small loans so that they could produce and sell vegetables or handicrafts, and wouldn't be forced into prostitution. At the time I was being told feminism was peculiar to the West, 10,000 members of this loose federation of women workers were marching from village to village, asking women about their problems, helping them to organize, offering the principles of self-strength and non-violence—just as we had done in a much smaller way two decades before. Though most of the funds and women came from the poor areas in which the work was being done, 75,000 women participated in the second padyatra.[5]

Now there is much more acknowledgment of the role of Indian feminist groups, urban as well as rural, in working for many forms of empowerment and against everything from sexual harassment in the workplace (often called eve-teasing in the Indian media) to the dowry murders that still take place when a husband or his family, wishing to acquire a second dowry, cause the 'accidental' death of his first wife. But the truth is that every country has its own organic feminism. Far more than Communism, Capitalism, or any other philosophy that I can think of, it is a grassroots event. It grows in women's heads and hearts.

It took me years to see the connections between discussions with Indian women in a third-class railway compartment and the feelings that finally gave me the courage to speak in public, or the links between walking in Ramnad and getting on planes to unknown places with Dorothy or Flo or Margaret—but they were there.

Now that I am finally retrieving the importance of India in my life, I think most of all of sitting on a New Delhi veranda in the 1970s, drinking tea with Kamaladevi Chattopadhyay, whose first name was—and is—enough to identify her in many countries of the world. Biographical dictionaries list her as 'freedom fighter, social worker, and writer'. In the 1950s, when I first met her, she was also in her fifties and already a legend for her leading role in the freedom struggle with Gandhi and Nehru—an activism for which she spent five years in British jails—and for her pioneering of the Indian handicraft movement. Our meeting was arranged by my oldest friend in India, Devaki Jain, because we wanted to seek Kamaladevi's advice. Since Gandhi's non-violent tactics were so well suited to women's movements around the world, we were thinking of studying his letters and writings, distilling what was most useful, and creating a kind of Gandhian-feminist handbook.

Kamaladevi listened patiently. Only at the end did she say, 'Of course Gandhi's tactics were suited to women—that's where he learnt them.' It was a sudden understanding that made us all laugh; one more instance of history lost, and then being attracted to what once was ours.

When I returned home, I lost track of Kamaladevi. I knew only that she had continued to travel the world into her eighties, helping other countries to preserve their creativity and culture in a handicraft industry, too, and also writing many books. But I always remembered this woman who taught us women's history over a cup of tea, while continuing to make history herself.

She died at the age of eighty-five on her way to make a speech, effective to the last. Devaki Jain wrote a moving tribute: 'I weep for her absence—a central support for realistic idealism... She made museums appear like bread or water—things without which one could not live.' She described how Kamaladevi, asked to join dignitaries on a podium and light a lamp celebrating the golden jubilee of the All India Women's Conference, had said just a year before she died, 'I have never gone onto a raised platform, it connotes hierarchy, distance.' As Devaki explained, 'She lit the lamp at the back of the hall, to the delight of the last rows.'[6]

—1994

# THE MASCULINIZATION OF WEALTH

In India, only five women feature in the list of the 100 richest individuals in India, according to *Forbes* magazine's index of 2013.[1] Of these, only three control their own wealth. Inordinate amounts of money are spent on lavish weddings between rich families but that same amount of wealth is never handed over to the bride to do with as she wishes.

Steinem examines the flip side of the feminization of poverty in this chapter, by analysing how men control wealth across class, race and caste. It makes the important point that women from both rich and poor families are equally unequal and while one group is tasked with producing heirs, the other group is tasked with producing cheap labour. Women from both classes are themselves cheap labour for their husbands and their families in different ways—women from the upper classes are home-managers, child-bearers, and public relations and secretarial executives for their husbands, while women from the poorer classes are homemakers, child-bearers, cooks, cleaners and additional bread-winners.

—Ruchira Gupta

Upper class men...are no more likely to be shaken in their positions as heads of their families than they are to be shaken in their positions as heads of society's economic institutions.[2]

—Susan Ostrander

Marx and Engels acknowledged that women's labour—in producing the labour force itself (reproduction) and in maintaining it (housewifery and motherhood)—was the underpinning of all economic activity. Having noted that, they went on to ignore it...otherwise, they would have wound up with a very different vision of the proletariat.[3]

—Robin Morgan

When I was growing up, the world seemed to be divided into rich people and the rest of us. The rich were magical families who went to country clubs and showed up in society columns; men who owned the factories in our industrial Midwestern city and women who gave dinner parties with real linen napkins; sons who played at college and tennis before joining their fathers, and daughters who always seemed to marry someone a little older, a little taller, a little richer than they, or, if they had no brothers, perhaps a son-in-law to join their father's business.

We were ordinary families whose names got in the newspapers only as part of an athletic team or an accident; men who worked in factories as long as they were able and women who cooked and cleaned for their own families if they were lucky, and for other families, too, if they were not; sons whose high-school years were a last fling before the assembly line, and daughters who got pregnant and married in that order or, if they were very ambitious, worked at the gas company until the first baby came.

It was a world of difference marked by possessions. Between Saturday night movies and winter vacations; weekly-pay envelopes and checking accounts; Easter outfits bought on the layaway plan and designer clothes ordered a season ahead; social security checks and stock dividends; kids who slept on sofa beds and children with nannies; in short, between an envious life and an enviable one. Because these symbols of class changed visibly from top to bottom, they seemed unnatural, perhaps unjust, and we resented them. Because male–female roles changed very little from their elegant dinner parties to our kitchen tables, they seemed natural, and very just indeed.

Were wives and daughters in these rich families the ultimate possession? We wouldn't have understood the question, much less asked it. As members of enviable families, they lived in the same pretty houses and drove in the same fancy cars, and that was enough to make us resent them.

In retrospect, I remember only one clue that such women might be less powerful, even a different class from their fathers and husbands, and so a little more like us. In my high school, girls dreamed out loud of marrying into this world of country clubs and fur coats. Of course this didn't happen, but in theory, a girl didn't need any special education or skills to be the wife of a powerful man. All she needed was the magic moment of being chosen. On the other hand, boys didn't dream out loud about becoming one of the factory owners. That would have been a betrayal of their fathers. Like enlisted men who would never think of becoming officers, they both envied and hated their superiors who ordered them into daily battle on the production line from the safety of their desks, fought against paying workers' compensation when one of them got mangled by a machine, and handed out layoffs with a callousness that only an equally tough union could handle. Besides, real men didn't wear suits and shuffle papers; they worked with their bands and used their strength—a bit of bluster that was also an admission that being a boss took a kind of training they didn't have.

After I became one of the very few from my high school to go to college—an exception that was due more to my mother's sacrifice and foresight than to my own—I noted but just accepted the differences between the rich young men and rich young women I was now seeing up close for the first time. At the women's college where I was, my wealthy classmates seemed a little apologetic for having 'daddyships' instead of the scholarships that marked achievers. In this intellectual school; for having money they couldn't have earned and didn't control; for living a lifestyle they were likely to continue by marrying a man from the same circles, since fear that a poor man might marry them for their money was like a cold wind on their hearts; and generally for carrying by accident of birth something as unfeminine as power.

On the other hand, rich young men seemed quite comfortable with the thought of dating and marrying women who were not as rich as they were. It was a power difference that only enhanced their male role. If the women's motives included something other than pure love, so what? These men, unlike their sisters, were not dependent on love for their sense of themselves, and buying a suitable wife wasn't that different from acquiring other things appropriate to their station. They drove expensive cars, spoke easily of assured futures, and—with a few exceptions born of social conscience or rebellion against their fathers—seemed comfortable with the idea that their family's power was just another attribute of their own. Indeed, even their rebellions took the form of choosing an unacceptable profession or political stance, not giving up or giving away their inheritance. If they married into a family of equal or greater wealth in a kind of corporate merger, that was okay too. I remember a young man who joked about the Securities and Exchange Commission giving permission for his wedding, such was the wealth that his fiancée was about to bring under his family's control. Neither he nor those of us listening gave a thought to the idea that she could be anything other than a conduit.

Some of the rich young women rebelled, too, but in a very different way. One eloped with a mechanic, fled her family's efforts to have him arrested for abducting a minor, and proved her love by being disinherited. Another scandalized the campus by going to a local nightclub, wearing a mink coat with nothing underneath, and dancing on a tabletop each Saturday night until the college finally expelled her. A third married a socially acceptable man, but one so much older that she could expect few sexual demands in the present and early widowhood in the future. ('It's a way of getting out of the house,' she explained, 'and after he dies, I'll be free.') In short, these rebels punished their families, but only in the most traditionally 'feminine' way. They punished themselves.

Most of my wealthy classmates conformed in the style of the day—by marrying men who had the profession we wanted but assumed we couldn't have on our own. One heiress from a literary family—who bore a resemblance to the actress Candice Bergen—married the heir and executive of a major publishing house. After much publicity for a country wedding that featured shampooed lambs in pink ribbons—like the perfect toy farm created for Marie Antoinette—this talented young woman was never heard from again. Several young women who had no brothers to take over the family business were encouraged to marry proper sons-in-law who could play this dynastic role. Even the very few women who were politically radical and had control of their own money didn't seem to have the confidence to give it away themselves. They married ambitious young radicals who published obscure magazines, contributed to political causes and candidates, started intellectual communities that pioneered everything except justice for women, or otherwise used their wives' family money to pursue goals of their own. Oddly, those men seemed to be accepted by their still poor radical colleagues—it was almost as if they had sacrificed themselves for the cause by marrying a rich woman. Meanwhile, the wives not only relinquished their power but seemed so guilty at ever having had it in the first place that they often lived and raised children under very difficult conditions of pretended poverty. They had paid for entry into an idealistic world that promised power to everyone except them.

The civil rights and anti-war movements of the 1960s did little to change or even challenge this pattern. If anything, those important political events reinforced a kind of populist Socialism that counted women as exactly the same class as their husbands or fathers, whether or not the women had any of the same power. Since rich wives and daughters were made to seem even more frivolous and less productive than rich men—by masculine standards that didn't include child-rearing and homemaking as work—the 1960s increased resentment of women in rich families for the majority of us who were not among them, and increased the isolation and guilt of those few who were. Besides, rich women could be ridiculed and condemned with far less fear of retribution than came from opposing men with real power. It was okay for male writers and revolutionaries, from Norman Mailer in *An American Dream* to Eldridge Cleaver in *Soul on Ice* to portray raping women from powerful families as a legitimate and manly way of fighting against the male adversaries they 'belonged' to.

Certainly, many activist women went along with all this. Those who had grown up poor could take pride in it at last, and perhaps those from well-to-do families felt they had to cheer most of all. Being accepted in a male-led movement was still the measure of political seriousness, and going along with ridicule or even hatred of one's own group was the admission price for some middle- or upper-class men too, but especially for women. Since feminist insight and mutual support were still a few years off—and since many white women identified with other powerless groups without knowing why, and many women of colour were asked to fight racism as if only male suffering mattered, supporting—these 'masculine' rebellions seemed to be the only game in town. I'm sure there were many women feeling hollow inside as they listened to anti-war Vietnam vets telling stories about rapes and bar girls, or to sex jokes about women that made us laugh in order to separate ourselves from the victim. Only in retrospect did I realize that women born to certain families had been made to feel shame twice over, not only by jokes and stories but by hostile rhetoric based on birth, not deed.

Though the violent writings of Cleaver, Mailer, and many others who seemed intent on imitating their adversaries made me supremely uncomfortable, I, too, tried not to admit this in public. In a world that still seemed class divided between the rich and the poor—but offered the same place to women in both—I always chose the poor. At least I could find one reliable piece of empathy. Besides, I was still fighting my own demons. If you've grown up in a house so ramshackle and unheated that you're ashamed to invite your friends over, it takes a long time to understand that your privileged friends may be ashamed to invite you home for the opposite reason. In college, I had a hint of my rich classmates' isolation when they asked me to teach them how to iron and mend their clothes (an autonomy so satisfying that they helped me with French grammar in return). But I still couldn't get past the fact that, unlike them, I had to earn money during the summer and would soon be completely on my own, a prospect that rapped into both my class and my female fears of being unable to do this. I hadn't yet learned that small sums earned were more empowering than large sums given, and so I continued to envy them.

Even in the 1970s, when many women began to realize that if idealistic movements like those against the Vietnam war and for civil rights weren't allowing women equal power, we needed women's liberation too, I didn't understand why women who earned a little money were more likely to use it in support of their sisters than were those who had inherited a lot. As a fund-raiser, I was being referred almost totally to women for the first time—especially by radical men, who assumed that, unlike any other social justice movement, this one should fund itself—and I was mystified to find that many of these women hadn't been approached as donors on their own before, or had only given to the same causes as their families, or didn't know how much money they had, or if they had enough control to write a cheque. To be honest, I didn't try to understand. It seemed more important to disprove the media's mischaracterization of feminism as a white, middle-class movement, and thus to phrase issues in a way that was least likely to touch the lives of the very women I was asking. So I talked about childcare (in ways that excluded women who had been raised too little by parents and too much by servants), or about reproductive rights for poor women (even if that meant disparaging women who could pay for illegal abortions but had risked their safety and health nonetheless), or about battered women (as if violence weren't just as frequent in well-to-do families, where women have money to flee, but society is even less likely to punish the barterer), or about equal pay (with little thought to women who were maintained on allowances in the midst of power and plenty and resented if they tried to get a paid job like everybody else). Obviously, all the issues being supported were crucial; but my exclusion, disparagement and lack of empathy were not. I realize now that I was still seeking approval from my radical male friends who behaved as if women's issues were frivolous and middle class—even though, statistically speaking, the women's movement was far more multi-class and multiracial than the anti-Vietnam, environmental, and most other movements had been.

In fact, I'm not sure that if a woman from a powerful family had been present at one of those feminist meetings of the 1970s, she would have felt more welcome than many of us had in the unfeminist, male-led groups of the 1960s.

Nonetheless, the lack of textbooks or reporting that explained our own experiences eventually forced us to turn to each other's lives as textbooks. The more I travelled during the 1970s and the 1980s and listened to women's stories, the more I learned about the problems of those who were supposed to have none. From the small towns of Alabama to the suburbs of Long Island, I met with women, especially the wives of powerful men, who had no work of their own (other than the job of homemaking, child-rearing and hostessing, which wasn't honoured as work) and identified emotionally with two other groups: prostitutes and domestics. In a glorified, socially approved way, that was the work those women felt they were doing. Their self-esteem was sometimes as low as or lower than those counterparts. Because it was harder for them to change employers, their feelings of dependence were higher, and so was their sense of being out of control of their lives; yet they were more likely to be envied than supported by other women. Given all that free-floating envy and resentment, they were also more likely than those at the bottom of the economic pile to assume that any problems must be their own fault, thus turning healthy anger into depression.

Most of the wealthy widows I'd heard so much about—the basis of the belief that 'women control the economy'—turned out to be conduits for passing power to children, especially to sons and sons-in-law. These widows had comfortable homes, good dental care, trips to exotic places, and other enviable benefits (though lifetimes of child-rearing and homemaking, if properly valued, could have earned some of these pleasures anyway), but the real money and decision-making powers were consigned to unbreakable trusts and to family trustees who were generally paternalistic, often condescending, and occasionally corrupt. I met only one widow, who was in control of her own financial life, and she had spent several hard years getting there—though the money in question had come from her family and her husband had taken over as a son-in-law. Generally, these widows had been left uninformed, untrained and scared to ask questions, much less mount challenges. 'If General Motors is going to pass through your womb,' as a more typical widow explained to me in one of those unforgettable 'clicks' of changing consciousness, 'they make damn sure you can't grab it on the way through.'

While speaking at a national convention of the Young Presidents' Organization (YPO), a group of executives who had become heads of large businesses before turning forty, I mentioned that though inheritance in general was certainly more destructive for the country than a meritocracy, its restriction to male relatives cut even that talent pool in half and thus made it twice as limiting. It was a minor point in a general speech about feminism, but it turned out to be the major controversy with that YPO audience; most of whom, I was surprised to discover, were the heads of family-owned companies. (One turned to a male friend of mine sitting next to him and, wrongly assuming him to be a YPO member, said only half in jest, 'You get the cross, I'll get the hood.') On the other hand, raising this subject also brought me invitations to private, late-night conversations with many YPO wives, especially those who would have inherited family businesses if their own fathers had not assumed only sons or sons-in-law could run them. They explained to me that: Because so few women were YPO members on their own (indeed, it had been de facto segregated for years, and I had been refusing to speak unless they called themselves the Young White Male Presidents, but a handful of women and black men had just been admitted), you could always tell the status of women in general at these meetings by their decreasing average age. Old wives were being traded in for new ones. 'Pretty soon,' as one explained, 'the wives will be younger than the Scotch.'

If the business was in your family, not your husband's, your marriage would last longer, mainly because the phrase 'till death do us part' took on a new meaning. Sons-in-law tended to get a divorce only *after* their powerful fathers-in-law died, and could no longer fire or disinherit them. Even after divorce, the ex-husband remained more likely to control the business than the woman to whose family it had belonged. 'It isn't women who sleep their way to power,' said one woman. 'It's sons-in-law.'

If you got divorced from a man who wasn't rich on his own or who didn't stay in a family business, he was likely to get a settlement: a lump-sum payment that wasn't conditional on good behaviour (for instance, it couldn't be withdrawn if he remarried), unlike the controlling monthly payments given to ex-wives. According to one of the wives who was a student of economics, the national total of these large settlements given to sons-in-law was greater in any given year than the total amount paid to women in the much-resented and publicized form of alimony. 'Besides, men can start their own businesses or live off the interest from a lump sum,' she explained. 'Women can't do that with alimony.'

We've read about rich girls who were victims of incestuous

relationships, from the fictional Nicole Diver in Fitzgerald's *Tender is the Night* to the real Edie Sedgwick as revealed in the 1970s or the son and daughter of J. Seward Johnson as made known in the 1980s—and innumerable others. Yet pre-feminism, a Freudian bias, eroticized incest as a fantasy of the victim, while class bias depicted it as an immorality of the poor. In fact, part of Freud's reason for abandoning his interest in the sexual abuse of children was society's hostility to the idea that so many abusers were solid patriarchs of the middle and upper classes, not to mention the possibility of Freud's reluctance to believe it of his own childhood. Though I know of no abuse study that has pinpointed families of inherited wealth and power, which may be one more way in which privileged children are assumed not to need attention, an overview of a variety of studies tells us that about one in three women (and one in seven men) have been sexually abused before the age of eighteen by someone with access to their households, and that 90 per cent of the abusers of both girls and boys are males. We also know that the greater the imbalance of power—between genders as elsewhere—the greater the abuse. In families where men are captains of industry and finance in the outside world, the internal power differences between men and women are extreme, and men's sense of being able to do no wrong is often greater than elsewhere. So is the reluctance of authorities to intervene. Furthermore, children are more likely to be isolated, cared for by servants who may be passing on their own abuse or acting out a resentment of wealth itself. Many observers believe that sexual abuse is *more* prevalent among families of inherited wealth and power than in the population at large—and I agree. In the 1980s, when the Ms. Foundation for Women started a group for women managing wealth, for instance, it was one of the first subjects discussed. Violence against women in general and sexual abuse in particular remain the issues women from wealthy families are most likely to single out when they contribute.

Even in the absence of any inequity or wrongdoing—and even with the best will in the world—there are still the problems of socialization and self-confidence that come from ladylike training in the upper classes. What happens, for instance, to a forty-five-year-old woman who has been shut out of self-sufficiency, has no training or experience at supporting herself by paid work, and feels dependent on a money source she doesn't control or understand? I never forgot going back to see women from my high-school neighbourhood who were about that age, and then going to my twenty-fifth college reunion. The contrast was startling. Most of the first group had supported themselves or helped to support their families—they had no choice. As a result, most had found professions, gone back to school, even run for local office, and generally discovered they could be self-sufficient and affect the world around them. In the second group, some of the most privileged—the same rich young women of whom I had once been so envious—were self-deprecating, lost and fearful of losing their looks or their husbands. They might have taken courses or acquired advanced degrees, but more as an end than a means. Generally, they seemed uncertain that they could be independent, much less have their own impact on the world. It echoed what I had seen in years of fund-raising.

By the mid-1980s, I had come to a conclusion I wasn't sure I should state out loud: There are many ways in which class doesn't work for women and some in which it's actually reversed.

Once I'd begun to look beneath the myth of class for women in families of inherited wealth, I noticed that it wasn't an unmitigated advantage for middle-class and upper-class women either. Take higher education and advanced degrees, for instance. They were simply expected to go to college, whether it was related to their own interest and career or not. There were times when I listened to privileged young women on campus and heard stories about lack of choice that sounded remarkably like my high-school classmates who had felt forced into clerical jobs or factories. Yet being told on all sides that they were fortunate had left them less prepared than my classmates to fight for themselves, or even to see the necessity. A study that followed a multiracial group of high school valedictorians through college was released in 1987. It found that intellectual self-esteem was about equal among females and males when they entered, but after four years, the number of young men who considered themselves 'far above average' had grown, while the number of women who did so had dropped to zero.[4] This was not related to grades, in which the women were equal or better, but apparently to the frequent invisibility of women in what they were studying, the rarity of women in authority in classroom or campus, more 'masculine' competition than 'feminine' cooperation in the academic atmosphere, and the approaching conflict between gender role and career role. One hopes that this disempowerment of women will change with a mainstreaming of women's studies and other reforms, but many women on campus are still left feeling there's something wrong with them.

There was also the lens of eating disorders through which to look at class. Anorexia and bulimia are almost unknown among the poor in this country, just as they are in the populations of poor countries. As Joan Brumberg reported in *Fasting Girls*:

> Ninety to 95 percent of anorectics are young and female, and they are disproportionately white and from middle-class and upper-class families.... The rare anorexic male exhibits a greater degree of psychopathology, tends to be massively obese before becoming emaciated, and has a poorer treatment prognosis. Moreover, the male anorexic is less likely to be affluent. Anorexia nervosa is not a problem among contemporary American blacks or Chicanos; neither was it a conspicuous problem among first-generation and second-generation ethnic immigrants such as Eastern European Jews. As these groups move up the social ladder, however, their vulnerability to the disorder increases. In fact, the so-called epidemic seems to be consistently restrained by age and gender but promoted by social mobility.[5]

In other words, those eating disorders that literally starve females out of all sexual characteristics, from breasts to menstruation, are almost totally restricted to social groups in which the 'feminine' role itself is the most restrictive, and to that time of life in which young girls are entering it. It's as if young women look at the dependent, decorative, lesser, ladylike role that awaits them, and unconsciously starve themselves out of it. Young women born into African American or white working-class families see less male/female power difference around them and behave accordingly. In the midst of the economic plenty of class, eating disorders are a political protest against the increased restriction of sexual caste.

Though this questioning of class was (and still is) an unpopular endeavour, it's evident the moment we look at women's individual experience instead of group myth. Here are an African American and a Hispanic woman interviewed by Linda Sanford and Mary Ellen Donovan for their classic *Women and Self-Esteem*:

> We lived in a very stable black neighborhood, and year after year my mother's friends would come over to talk, and as long as I sat quietly, I could listen. They sometimes talked about sex and orgasms and how you had to ask for what you wanted sexually. They also talked about their work when I grew up, not because I would *have to* but because it was a good experience. And moreover, it was wonderful to have your own money. My white, upper-class women friends told me they had a totally different experience. Although it was always assumed they would go to college, it wasn't assumed that they would work. Instead, their security was in getting a man to support them—even though they had skills to do it for themselves. I can't imagine being raised like that—so unsure of my future, putting time and energy into being prepared for something I wasn't expected to do.[6]

I didn't particularly like growing up in Harlem, but the one thing it did is teach me survival skills and I see that as a big advantage. I teach self-defense now and there is a world of difference between the urban Hispanic kids I teach and my classes that have some middle-class white women in them. I try to get them to make a fist and hit the punching bag, pretending it's an attacker, and most of them say, 'Oh, I could never do that.'[7]

Those educational, physical and social undermining are probably familiar to many women, but the very rich add more safeguards against woman's gaining control of real power. *Most* of them relate to depth training within the family—and nothing is more effective. At a 1990 conference of women managing wealth, I heard anthropologist Terry Odendahl, author of *Charity Begins at Home*, sum up her six years of research and interviews:

> The lives of most wealthy women are defined by family relationships, especially their roles as wives and mothers, but also as daughters and sisters and widows of rich men. Gender roles are much more rigid in the upper classes than they are in the

wider society.... Wealth is *not* a guarantee of authority. Women have less control over their assets.... Much of the money is in trusts and they just receive the income. Male attorneys and accountants are viewed as the culprits—keeping the money out of the hands of women. Usually, however, it is male family members who established the original trusts that limit the female beneficiaries' control over assets.... The modern women's movement affected most wealthy American women at least ten years later than it did women of the middle class.[8]

Even at that, more than a third of her interviewees had married into families of great wealth, and thus had escaped some of the training of those born into such families. But whether it was General Motors passing through one's womb, in the memorable phrase of my early informant, or a daughter who hears secrets of the establishment passed around the dinner table; whether it's an old-fashioned need to control women as the means of reproduction in order to keep the ruling class inheritance system in order—usually the task of first wives—or a modern need for what *Fortune* magazine called media-star hostesses or 'trophy wives'—usually second wives—the general truth is this: The closer women are to power, the weaker those women have to be kept.

This is not the same as the poor-little-rich-girl myth that is so much a part of our popular culture. That story is half of a double fantasy that the rich are unhappy and the poor are a jolly lot; a fantasy still well represented by such television staples as the *Dynasty* genre of melodramas about rich white families, and the various comedies about white ethnic and African American families of the poor or middle class. The political purpose is to convince us that the burdens of power are too great to seek, and the happiness of powerlessness is too great to leave, thus preserving the status quo. Looking at the lack of strength and power among women in families of inherited wealth has a purpose that is quite the opposite: upsetting the status quo and increasing those women's strength to seize power and redistribute it.

This rethinking of sexual caste versus social class is also not—repeat, not—intended to diminish the importance of everything money brings for women of wealth, from good healthcare and housing to travel, the arts, and time to enjoy them. A weakened body, a mind obsessed with survival, children who can't develop their intellectual capacity because of poor diets and violent schools: all these are tragedies of poverty that must never be minimized. They cause a person to suffer more—and millions more to suffer— than do such tragedies of dependency as unused strength, atrophied talents, and a circumscribed knowledge of the world.

Nonetheless, there is a clear continuum from the feminization of poverty to the masculinization of wealth. It's no accident that women and their dependent children are 92 per cent of those on welfare, and female-headed families make up most of the working poor, while the gender of those who control this country's great concentrations of wealth is even more uniformly male.[9] It's simply not possible to attack one ghetto without also attacking the other. The concentration of wealth is extreme. According to a 1987 report of *Forbes* magazine, for example, the total net worth of the four hundred richest people and/or families in the US—about half of whom have inherited wealth and almost all of whom are likely to pass it on to descendants—was $220 billion, more than enough to pay of the entire US budget deficit accumulated to that point.[10] To get an idea of how disproportionate this distribution is, a minuscule top 0.5 per cent of the country owns between 20 and 25 per cent of the wealth—a figure derived from taxes on estates worth $60,000 or more, and one that has remained relatively unchanged throughout this century.[11] One clear but undiscussed way of breaking up these hereditary concentrations is to seize and disperse them from within—a process that at least some women would be ready for, and a handful have begun. Therefore, it's in the interest of women at both ends of the spectrum to consider the class system *as women experience it*, not as women have been taught it—to see the ways it disguises and preserves a deeper system of sexual caste, and to explore how we might pool strengths and support one another for mutual benefit.

To do this, the range of women from poor to middle class have to go against class myth by trading envy of those above us for a recognition of our strengths. We are more likely to have the experience of supporting ourselves, and thus to discover our abilities and learn about the world. We may underrate the fact that we also have had to learn to run a household and navigate the shoals of daily life on our own. The men we live with are not accustomed to great power in the world, and they probably know we can earn at least half as much as they do. In other words, the imbalance of power between us and them may be painful, but it's not as extreme as at society's upper reaches. We need to look realistically at rich women, who have no excuse of necessity, the most common reason for anybody's discovery of confidence and capabilities, not even a responsibility for managing the family portfolio. A wealthy wife or daughter who tries to learn self-sufficiency by entering the daily work world may be resented, ridiculed or forced to conceal her background. The men she deals with intimately are accustomed to command, including female service, and their egos may be overblown by women who treat them like the pot of gold at the end of a marital rainbow, as well as by men in their sphere of power. Meanwhile, the dependent woman knows she could not earn a fraction of the family income if she were on her own, may worry about female competition for this gold-plated meal ticket, and often witnesses adulation of a man she knows to be very human indeed. Though she may start out loving her husband—or her father or her brothers—it's more difficult for love to survive years of such imbalance of power without the worm of resentment eating it away. Nor is it easy for a daughter who has seen what dependency has done to her mother.

But women in such families do have an intimacy and access to power. Otherwise, their rebellion would not be so dangerous that all the weaponry of gender roles and a patriarchal legal structure are brought into play. At the upper levels, it's patriarchy pure.

Our suffragist foremothers had a better understanding of these anomalies of economic class. For one thing, the laws about marriage and property were more obviously oppressive in their day, and there was less need for psychological seduction to keep women in line. When men could drink up their paychecks with no obligation to save even subsistence money for families, take children away from mothers without bothering to accuse them of anything, and legally beat their wives, providing they used a rod no bigger than a thumb (hence, 'rule of thumb'), there was less need for the sugar-coating of gender persuasion. Even Victoria Woodhull got considerable support for announcing: 'They say I have come to break up the family. I say amen to that with all my heart.' Susan B. Anthony shocked and alienated even abolitionists by offering shelter to the runaway wives of violent men, just as she did to runaway slaves. About the pain of dependency, with or without violence, she wrote: 'There is not a woman born who desires to eat the bread of dependence, no matter whether it be from the hand of father, husband, or brother, for anyone who does so eat her bread places herself in the power of the person from whom she takes it.'[12] There were also the constant reminders from black women in or newly out of slavery, with all the parallels that had made seventeenth-century slaveholders adopt the legal status of wives as the 'nearest and most natural analogy' for that of slaves, as Gunnar Myrdal wrote in *An American Dilemma*. The seduction of being a lady was the subject of Sojourner Truth's famous speech: 'That man over there says that women need to be helped into carriages…. Nobody ever helps me into carriages…. I could work as much and eat as much as a man—when I could get it—and bear the lash as well.'[13] As Elizabeth Cady Stanton wrote: 'The Negro's skin and the woman's sex are both [used as] *prima facie* evidence that they were intended to be in subjection to the white saxon man.'[14]

With all the parallels between sex and race to bind the abolitionist and suffragist movements into one drive for universal adult suffrage—until this unity was fractured by white liberal males who helped to get the vote for black males fifty years before women of all races, plus white women who then used racist arguments for their own 'educated' vote—there was a long and activist period in which consciousness of caste exceeded that of class. It was also the peak of European immigration, and thus a greater belief in class mobility. Women could see similarities in their female status across chasms of class and make alliances and be less seduced by a conventional, male-centred sense of class as a result. Only a handful of women had control over money, usually as widows or because of tolerant men in their family, but some acted on the unself-conscious connections with shop and factory girls, prostitutes and domestics that I was to hear upper-class wives dismissing privately a century later.

The most famous was Alva Belmont, a Southerner who had divorced a Vanderbilt, then married and been widowed by Oliver Belmont, a man of almost equal wealth. She paid many of the operating expenses of NAWSA (the National American Woman Suffrage Association), of which Elizabeth Cady Stanton and Susan B. Anthony were the first two presidents. In 1909, even before the Triangle fire had forced the country to face the truth of immigrant women's working conditions, she endorsed a strike of women shirtwaist workers and hired the Hippodrome in New York for a rally of eight thousand to support them. At the podium with her were Clara Lemlich and Rose Schneidermann, radical trade unionists who were Belmont's enemies by class. A shirtwaist manufacturer sued Alva Belmont and other suffragists for triple damages under the Sherman Act, accusing them of organizing an illegal boycott, but his action only created more publicity for this cross-class alliance. As an officer of the Women's Party during World War I, Belmont also opposed President Wilson's hypocrisy in saying that the nation was fighting for democracy, when the female half had none. It was a radical act in wartime, and one that supported workers' groups who were then saying that only an international ruling class would benefit from workers fighting each other.[15]

Though there were many tensions on the basis of class, some of these women's coalitions would be hard to match today. To organize working women's suffrage clubs in Connecticut, for instance, NAWSA hired the well-known socialist Ella Reeve Bloor, later known as 'Mother Bloor' of the Communist Party. The meetings she organized were held in halls rented and paid for by a niece of J.P. Morgan, a financier who headed the list of Socialism's enemies.[16]

In fact, suffrage might not have been put over the top had there not been a bequest of $2 million from a woman known as Mrs Frank Leslie (she had taken the name of her third husband after his death, for it was also the name of his publishing empire). It was money she had made by saving the failing magazines she had inherited. In the words of her will, this sum was left 'to Carrie Chapman Catt, leader of the cause of woman suffrage, to further that cause, so that all the women of this country will be able to live women's rights and shoulder women's responsibilities, so that for the women of the future all things will be possible'.[17] However, even a woman of her business acumen wasn't able to conquer the rich woman's bane of condescending lawyers and corrupt trustees. After her death in 1914, her lawyer, William Nelson Cromwell (the founder of the still famous law firm of Sullivan and Cromwell), spent two years contesting the purpose of her will, and thus cut the bequest in half by collecting $1 million in lawyers' fees from her estate. Nevertheless, the remaining half was finally used as she intended.

Of course, both Alva Belmont and Mrs Frank Leslie had lived relatively independent lives before marrying into wealth, and so had missed some upper-class conditioning. There were a few women born into powerful families who may have had less control over family wealth, but who lived in settlement houses with immigrant women, taught the knowledge of contraception they themselves had once been denied, established shelters where prostitutes could flee from pimps and corrupt police, and provided homes for newly arrived young working women who might otherwise have been forced onto the streets—just as teenage runaways are now.

In this modern wave of feminism, however, there are fewer places for women to come together across class boundaries, and no obvious institutions like the settlement houses where women lived together while doing feminist work. Though feminist groups often share an American denial of some of the deep effects of class, it's also true that a Marxist class analysis has entered the popular culture since the suffragist wave. Some of that insight has been especially valuable to women in helping us separate nature from nurture and appreciate the unlimited human diversity among us. In its absence, our suffragist foremothers often fell back into the biological determinism of arguing that women were more moral 'by nature'. But now we need a whole fresh look at what class means to women, and at the way caste and class intersect.

Anne Hess, an effective and compassionate activist, grew up with a stronger tradition of philanthropy, handed down by her great-grandfather Julius Rosenwald, of the Sears fortune, and by women within her family, than most women of wealth; yet she still remembers sitting silently in anti-war, women's liberation and black power meetings of the 1970s. 'We were the enemy,' she said, 'even though we were there as friends. More women than men are in the closet about their wealth, partly because they're drawn to other powerless groups, by their own experience as women, and then shunned by them.' Shad Reinstein, a woman from a family of relative wealth in her upstate New York community, remembers hearing a line from an anti-war song of the 1970s: 'We're going to rape the daughters of bankers.' 'It was harder to come out as a wealthy person, even though I was doing constructive things with my land and resources,' she said, 'than it was to come out as a lesbian.' When she moved to a different part of the country, she didn't use her given name or share her background until she had established herself as a working part of that community. These are the exceptions. Even though there are now a few groups of women of wealth around the country who are supporting each other in taking control of their money, breaking trusts, and initiating a new kind of philanthropy to empower women, it's still not easy to overcome the sexual caste system of families in which, for generations, only men have been socialized to power.[18] Jenny Warburg, the forty-one-year-old daughter of the German-Jewish banking family, was trained as a social worker and a photographer, but she didn't go on a retreat with women peers struggling with the same issues of wealthy families until five years ago. 'I was terrified of talking about money,' she explained. 'I didn't want to admit to myself that I had it, much less talk about it with anyone else. Growing up, I was embarrassed to have friends over to the house because of things like finger bowls.' None of this seemed to be as difficult for her brothers, who had very different expectations set for them and who were automatically given more power and credibility on the family foundation board. 'It took many years to be taken seriously on that board, even though I am the most politically active member and chaired a community foundation board for four years.' While she lobbies hard for the support of issues she cares about within her family foundation, emotional and economic ties to her family still make it difficult to seek out independent investment or legal advice.

The point is not to romanticize connections among women or to ignore class differences, but to figure out why many women in today's powerful families seem even less able than their foremothers to work on their own behalf, and to support other women who are doing so. Their giving and volunteering are more likely to support socially approved causes and organizations that do little to change women's lives; for example, statistics show that most widows keep on donating to their dead husbands' colleges while ignoring or giving less support to their own. When giving to their family's charitable priority of a local symphony, they rarely make that gift conditional on employing more women and people of colour as musicians; or to an art museum while challenging the absence of a diversity of women artists; or to a drug treatment programme while insisting there be more programmes for female addicts and addicted babies; or to political candidates according to their positions on issues of special importance to the female half of the country; or to Israel and other group causes while making sure that at least half of those dollars are going to women. In spite of the one-in-nine breast cancer rate that affects us all, fund-raisers for major cancer organizations say confidentially that they are surprised that women donors—including those giving very large gifts—rarely earmark their gifts for breast and other reproductive cancers, or even ask tough questions about where organizational resources are going.

Tracy Gary, a San Francisco activist who has used her own inheritance experience to become a pioneer organizer among women trying to gain control of family money for the empowerment of women, has done research showing that poor women actually give away a slightly larger percentage of their incomes than do women with incomes of $50,000 and more.[19] Looking at the human truth behind those statistics often reveals women of wealth who lack control of their own money, the self-confidence and knowledge to use it, or support from other women in gaining that confidence and control.

The first step as the support groups of women in wealthy families that are now spreading (and are listed in the endnotes), but we also need to develop more women's communities that are welcoming across class lines. The integration of some women into the mainstream—for which our foremothers fought and we continue the battle—has meant that we can buy entry and approval into male provinces; all the more so if we are willing to ignore our own interests. A woman with a cheque book is welcome in many places, but if she wants to be welcome *as herself*, with or without money, she needs to use that cheque book to attack the system of sexual caste. Yet if she wants to do this, how many feminist groups offer her understanding of her situation?

The vast majority of us who are not in powerful families must admit that we have not been very open to those who are. And I mean really open—not with preconceived ideas or envy or an effort to create guilt, but with honest questions and answers, and an understanding that we each bring a part of the mix that the other may need. Those of us who have the confidence and well-developed muscles that come from survival must recognize our worth and stop thinking that money would solve whatever problems we may have. In a way, we treat problems of women in rich families like those of the famous. It's the rare listener who isn't thinking: 'Oh, come off it, you really love it. How about trading places?' Yet fame is democratic enough to give some women, athletes, rock stars, and other members of 'out' groups a power they could have in no other way, while the internal workings of powerful families are often hierarchy in its most intimate form. It takes strength to challenge family traditions, powerful trustees and investment advisers, plus relatives who are also the country's rulers; or even to roll over in the morning and say to your husband that from now on, half of the family's charitable gifts are going to be distributed by you—and women in those situations need support.

What we all need, as adults or children, is at least one person who has confidence in us, so that we can have confidence in ourselves. We also need community. Women can become that for each other.

The good news is that, even with less encouragement than almost any other group, some women in powerful families are rebelling. In addition to those groups of women managing wealth who meet to support each other in many cities, there are individuals like Sallie Bingham, a sort of matron saint for rebellious women born into wealthy families. A playwright, short-story writer and novelist, she asked questions and raised challenges which eventually led to the sale in 1986 of the media properties that the Bingham family of Kentucky had owned for two generations, a conscious political rebellion against their patriarchal control as well as what she considered their mismanagement. Now she has started the Kentucky Foundation for Women to aid women in her area, and she also redistributes on her own about half a million dollars each year. ('I give out of rage,' she writes, 'rage that there is never an end to giving…rage that I didn't use to believe what I gave was mine.') Some of the women in such famous families as the Rockefellers have become active—in a setting where there was definitely no Rockefeller *Sisters* Fund—and are giving in new ways designed to empower the powerless. There is also Peg Yorkin, a longtime activist and theatre producer, who emerged from a thirty-year marriage to a television producer—which both had entered without inherited money—with enough to give a $10 million endowment in 1991 to the Fund for the Feminist Majority, a multi-issue action organization that she started with Eleanor Smeal, former president of the National Organization for Women. It is the largest grant to be given by a woman for advocacy on behalf of women as a group since Mrs Frank Leslie. Like her, she has become an inspiration to women whose marriages, and their own work within those partnerships, have given them resources to use on women's behalf.

They and many others have rebelled with very little support from their sisters. Imagine what could be done with that support. As I sit in meetings of the Ms. Foundation for Women and see brave women donors helping other women who are survivors of violence, especially sexual abuse in childhood—and yet are themselves still silenced about their own experiences by the powerful families from which they come—I realize how far we have to go. It is often a struggle to bring up the forbidden and unladylike subject of money in those families, much less subjects still more forbidden.

I think it will be women from the bottom of the class structure—with strength and a literal knowledge that 'money isn't everything'—who may be more able than middle-class women to welcome this personal and political connection to women at the top. I realized this again in 1990 while listening to the generosity of spirit with which Byllye Avery, founder and director of the National Black Women's Health Project, addressed a few women of inherited wealth. 'Women with wealth and women without wealth share a sense of isolation, alienation and powerlessness,' said this woman who had every reason to feel bitter and estranged. 'We feel this way no matter where we are...people like me need people like you, and people like you need people like me. Together, we make a wonderful whole.... We must look inside ourselves, take the risk to learn who we are and acknowledge all the pieces.'

Is the world of women so neatly divided into the rich and the rest of us? I no longer think so. Like art, revolutions come from combining what exists into what has never existed before.

—1994

# THE IMPORTANCE OF WORK

In rural India, 75 per cent of the workforce in agriculture is women whereas in trade, hotel, communication and other services, only 10 per cent of the workforce is women.[1] In urban India, 32 per cent of the workforce in construction, manufacturing, mining, domestic work is women, whereas in the trade, hotel, communication and other services, 59 per cent are women.[2] Ninety four per cent of the women in the workforce are part of the unorganized sector and just 6 per cent are in the organized sector as per the estimate of the National Commission on Self-Employed Women.[3]

According to the Gender Gap Index 2012, India stands 123rd out of the 135 countries surveyed.[4] The gender pay gap varies across Indian states. Women in Uttarakhand earned 9 per cent less than men, whereas women in Bihar earned 63 per cent less than men.[5]

Surprisingly, women who attained educational qualification below the 10th standard earned 9.37 per cent less than men, whereas women with professional qualifications such as CA/CS/ICWA or equivalent earn 44.25 per cent less than their men counterparts.[6] Women employed in the accommodation and food service activity and industry earned 4.19 per cent less than men whereas those employed in the arts, entertainment and recreation industries earned 41.17 per cent less than men.[7]

The increased visibility of women in the urban workspace of coveted service sector jobs has led to a violent backlash. In 2012 alone, working women were raped in a lift in Goa, in an abandoned mill compound in Mumbai, on a bus when returning home after watching a movie in Delhi, and while giving a job exam in Haryana. However, no amount of violence is going to push women back. They have discovered their voice and courage.

—Ruchira Gupta

Towards the end of the 1970s, *The Wall Street Journal* devoted an eight-part, front-page series to 'The Working Woman'—that is, the flood of women into the paid-labour force—as the greatest change in American life since the Industrial Revolution.

Many women readers greeted both the news and the definition with cynicism. After all, women have always worked. If all the productive work of human maintenance that women do in the home were valued at its replacement cost, the gross national product of the US would go up by 26 per cent. It's just that women, especially white women, are now more likely than ever before to leave the poorly rewarded, low-security, high-risk job of homemaking (though we're still trying to explain that it's a perfectly good one and that the problem is male society's refusal both to do it and to give it an economic value) for more secure, independent and salaried jobs outside the home.

Obviously, the real work revolution won't come until all productive work—including child-rearing and other jobs done in the home—and men are integrated into so-called women's work as well as vice versa. But the radical change touted by *The Wall Street Journal* and other media is one part of that long integration process: the unprecedented flood of women of all races into salaried jobs; that is, into the labour force as it has been male-defined and previously occupied by men. We are already more than 41 per cent of it—the highest proportion in history. Given the fact that women also make up a whopping 69 per cent of the 'discouraged labour force' (that is, people who need jobs but don't get counted in the unemployment statistics because they've given up looking), plus having an official female unemployment rate that is substantially higher than men's, it is clear that we could expand to become half of the national workforce by 1990.[8]

Faced with this determination of women to find a little independence and to be better paid and honoured for our work, experts have rushed to ask: 'Why?' It's a question that is rarely directed at male workers whose basic motivations of survival and personal satisfaction are taken for granted. Indeed, men are regarded as 'odd' and therefore subjects for sociological study and journalistic reports only when they *don't* have work—even if they

are rich and don't need jobs, or are poor and can't find them.
Nonetheless, pollsters and sociologists have gone to great expense
to prove that women work outside the home because of dire
financial need or, if we persist despite the presence of a wage-
earning male, out of desire to buy 'little extras' for our families, or
even out of good old-fashioned penis envy.

Job interviewers and even our own families may still ask salaried
women the big 'Why?' If we have small children at home or are in a
job regarded as 'men's work', the incidence of such questions
increases. Condescending or accusatory versions of 'What's a nice
girl like you doing in a place like this?' have not disappeared from
the office or the factory.

How do we answer these assumptions that we are 'working' only
out of some pressing or peculiar need? Do we feel okay about
arguing that it's as natural for us to have salaried jobs as for our
husbands—whether or not we have young children at home? Can
we enjoy strong career ambitions without worrying about being
thought 'unfeminine'? When we confront men's growing
resentment of women competing in the workforce (often in the
form of such guilt-producing accusations as 'You're taking men's
jobs away' or 'You're damaging your children'), do we simply state
that a decent job is a basic human right for everybody?

I'm afraid the answer is often no. As individuals and as a
movement, we tend to retreat into some version of the tactically
questionable defence: 'Women work because we have to.' It's a
phrase that has become one word, one key on the typewriter—an
economic form of the socially 'feminine' stance of passivity and
self-sacrifice. Under attack, we still tend to present ourselves as
creatures of economic necessity and familial devotion. 'Women
work because we have to' has become the easiest thing to say.

Like most truisms, this one is easy to prove with statistics.
Economic need is the most consistent work motive—for women as
well as men. In 1976, for instance, 43 per cent of all women in the
paid-labour force were single, widowed, separated, or divorced,
and working to support themselves and their dependents. An
additional 21 per cent were married to men who had earned less
than ten thousand dollars in the previous year, the minimum then

required to support a family of four. In fact, if you take men's pensions, stocks, real estate, and various forms of accumulated wealth into account, a good statistical case can be made that there are more women who 'have' to work (that is, who have neither the accumulated wealth, nor husbands whose work or wealth can support them) than there are men with the same need to work. If we were going to ask one group 'Do you really need this job?' we should ask men. But the first weakness of the whole 'have to work' defence is its deceptiveness. Anyone who has ever experienced life on welfare or any other confidence-shaking dependency knows that a paid job may be preferable to the dole, even when the handout is coming from a family member. Yet the will and self-confidence to work on one's own can diminish as dependency and fear increase. That may explain why—contrary to the 'have to' rationale—wives of men who earn less than three thousand dollars a year are actually less likely to be employed than wives whose husbands make ten thousand dollars a year or more.

Furthermore, the greatest proportion of employed wives is found among families with a total household income of twenty-five to fifty thousand dollars a year. This is the statistical underpinning used by some sociologists to prove that women's work is mainly important for boosting families into the middle or upper middle class. Thus, women's incomes are supposed to be used for buying 'luxuries' and 'little extras': a neat double-whammy that renders us secondary within our families and makes our jobs expendable in hard times. We may even go along with this interpretation (at least, up to the point of getting fired so a male can have our job), because it preserves a husbandly ego-need to be seen as the primary breadwinner, and still allows us a safe 'feminine' excuse for working.

But there are often rewards that we're not confessing. As noted in *The Two-Career Couple* by Francine and Douglas Hall: 'Women who hold jobs by choice, even blue-collar routine jobs, are more satisfied with their lives than are the full-time housewives.'[9]

In addition to personal satisfaction, there is also society's need for all its members' talents. Suppose that jobs were given out on only a 'have to work' basis to both women and men—one job per household. It would be unthinkable to lose the unique abilities of, for instance, Eleanor Holmes Norton, the distinguished chair of the Equal Employment Opportunity Commission.[10] But would we then be forced to question the important work of her husband, Edward Norton, who is also a distinguished lawyer? Since men earn more than twice as much as women on the average, the wife in most households would be more likely to give up her job. Does that mean the nation could do as well without millions of its nurses, teachers and secretaries? Or that the rare man who earns less than his wife should give up his job?

It was this kind of waste of human talents on a society-wide scale that traumatized millions of unemployed or underemployed Americans during the Depression. Then, a one-job-per-household rule seemed somewhat justified, yet the concept was used to displace women workers only, create intolerable dependencies, and waste female talent that the country needed. That Depression experience, plus the energy and example of women who were finally allowed to work during the manpower shortage created by World War II, led Congress to reinterpret the meaning of the country's full-employment goal in its Economic Act of 1946. Full employment was officially defined as 'the employment of those who want to work, without regard to whether their employment is, by some definition, necessary. This goal applies equally to men and to women'. Since bad economic times are again creating a resentment of employed women—yet also creating more need for women to be employed—we need such a goal more than ever. Women are again being caught in a tragic double bind: We are required to be strong and are then punished for our strength.

Clearly, anything less than government and popular commitment to this 1946 definition of full employment will leave the less powerful groups, whoever they may be, in danger. Almost as important as the financial penalty is the suffering that comes from being shut out of paid and recognized work. Without it, we lose much of our self-respect and our ability to prove that we are alive by making some difference in the world. That's just as true for the suburban woman hostess as it is for the unemployed steel worker.

But it won't be easy to give up the passive defence of 'we work because we have to'.

When a woman who is struggling to support her children and grandchildren on welfare sees her neighbour working as a waitress, even though that neighbour's husband has a job, she may feel resentful; and the waitress (of course, not the waitress's husband) may feel guilty. Yet unless we establish the obligation to provide a job for everyone who is willing and able to work, that welfare woman may herself be penalized by policies that give out only one public-service job per household. She and her daughter will have to make a painful and divisive decision about which of them gets that precious job, and the whole household may have to survive on only one salary.

A job as a human right is a principle that applies to men as well as to women. But women have more cause to fight for it. The phenomenon of the 'working woman' (that is, salaried woman) has been held responsible for everything from an increase in male impotence (which turned out, incidentally, to be attributable to medication for high blood pressure) to the rising cost of steak (which turned out to be due to high energy costs and beef-import restrictions, not women's refusal to prepare the cheaper, slower-cooking cuts). Unless we see a job as part of every citizen's right to autonomy and personal fulfilment, we will continue to be vulnerable to someone else's idea of what 'need' is, and whose 'need' counts the most.

In some ways, women who do not have to work for simple survival, but who choose to do so nonetheless, are on the frontier of asserting this right for all women. Those with well-to-do husbands are dangerously easy for us to resent and put down. It's easier still to resent women from families of inherited wealth, even though male heirs generally control and benefit from that wealth. (There is no Rockefeller Sisters Fund, and no J.P. Morgan & Daughters. Sons-in-law are the ones who really sleep their way to power.) But to prevent a woman whose husband or father is wealthy from earning her own living, and from gaining the self-confidence that comes with that ability, is to keep her needful of that unearned power and less willing to disperse it. Moreover, it is to lose forever her unique talents.

Perhaps modern feminists have been guilty of a kind of reverse snobbism that keeps us from reaching out to the wives and daughters of wealthy men; yet it was a few such women who refused the restrictions of class and financed the suffragist wave of revolution.

For most of us, however, 'women work because we have to' is just true enough to be tempting as a rationalization. But if we use it without also staking out the larger human right to a job, we will never achieve that right. We will always be subject to the false argument that independence for women is a luxury that can be afforded only in good economic times. Alternatives to layoffs will not be explored, acceptable unemployment will always be used to frighten those with jobs into accepting low wages, and we will never remedy the real cost, both to families and to the country, of dependent women and a massive loss of talent.

Worst of all, we may never learn to find productive, honoured work as a natural part of ourselves and as one of life's basic pleasures.

—1979

# THE POLITICS OF FOOD

Of the 111 million teenage Indian girls in India, 45 per cent are undernourished.[1] According to the UNICEF Global Report Card on Adolescents 2012, 47 per cent of adolescent girls aged fifteen to nineteen in India are underweight, with a body mass index of less than the prescribed level of 18.5.[2] The reasons cited for this deficiency are discrimination, son-preference and the low value placed on girls.

However the chief minister of Gujarat, Narendra Modi, has stated in an interview to *The Wall Street Journal* that the craze for beauty among young women is the reason for malnourishment among women in Gujarat.[3] According to the National Family Health Survey, over 41 per cent of Gujarat's children under the age of three are underweight while over 55 per cent of Gujarati women in the 15–45 age group are anaemic.[4]

Steinem's essay in 1980 about who gets how much food and why, is relevant even now across cultures and countries, highlighting the commonalities of our inequalities.

—Ruchira Gupta

For much of the female half of the world, food is the first signal of our inferiority. It lets us know that our own families may consider female bodies to be less deserving, less needy and less valuable.

In many poor countries, mothers often breastfeed sons for two years or more, especially when other food is scarce or uncertain. Daughters are usually nursed for less than half that time.

What happens in the mind of a girl child who is denied her own mother's body, or in the mind of her brother who is not?

In India, like other countries where the poor must make painful choices, female infanticide is often carried out by the denial of scarce food and healthcare. Its practice is so common that a ratio of only 80 females to 100 males is the norm in some parts of the country.

Economists say that scarcity increases value, but that rule doesn't seem to hold when the commodity is female. Mothers of daughters, no matter how poor their health, are expected to bear more and more children until they have sons. Families of bridegrooms go right on demanding dowries from the families of brides. If someone pays the price of scarcity, it seems to be the women themselves. Brides may be kidnapped from neighbouring areas. The childbearing burden of a woman may be increased because her husband's brothers have no wives.

The cultural belief in a female's lesser worth goes so deep that many women accept and perpetuate it. 'Food distribution within the family arises from the deliberate self-deprivation by women,' concludes a 1974 study of nutrition in India, 'because they believe that the earning members (and the male members who are potential earning members) are more valuable than those who do domestic work and the child-rearing, which they consider devoid of economic value.'

What happens to the spirits of women who not only deprive themselves, but police the deprivation of their daughters?

Even in this wealthier, luckier country, we may know more than we admit. Black slave women and indentured white women were advertised as breeders or workers, and also as assets who would eat and cost less than males. The hardworking farm women of the frontier served men and boys more plentifully and first, yet the toll of their own hard work and child-bearing was so great that the two-mother family was the average family: most men married a second time to replace a first wife who died of childbirth, disease or overwork.

Within our own memories, there are wives and daughters of immigrant families who served meals to fathers and brothers first, sometimes eating only what was left on the men's plates. Right now, some homemakers still save the choice piece of meat for the 'man of the house' or 'growing boys' more often than for their growing daughters—or themselves.

Millions of women on welfare eat a poor and starchy diet that can permanently damage the children they bear, yet their heavy bodies are supposed to signify indulgence. Even well-to-do women buy the notion that males need more protein and more strength. They grow heavy on sugar or weak on diets while preparing good food for their families. Does a woman alone prepare a meal differently for a male guest than for another woman—or for herself? Perhaps food is still the first sign of respect—or the lack of it—that we pay to each other and to our bodies.

Of course, women have always rebelled. We can guess that from knowing ourselves. We can also guess it from the elaborate, punitive systems that exist to punish female rebellion.

In many areas of Africa and Asia, strict taboos reserve the most valued sources of energy and nourishment for males. Red meat, fish, poultry, eggs, milk, even some fruits and vegetables—each is forbidden to females in some parts of the world. The explanation of these taboos may be a euphemism (that eating red meat will make women 'like men'), or it may play on women's deepest fear (that drinking milk will destroy a woman's value by making her sterile), but these cultural restrictions go very deep. Some women students from Africa observe them even after years of living in Europe or America. Others report anxiety and nausea when they first force themselves to eat an egg or an orange.

With or without taboos, food itself may be used as punishment or reward. In many cultures, husbands and fathers ration out food from family storerooms to which they guard the key. Wives are accountable not only for what they eat, but for children, extended family and servants as well.

Even in wealthier societies, wives may be disciplined or rewarded with the treat of 'eating out', or given a strict family food budget that holds them accountable for the whole household. In times of inflation, women may be expected to stretch the shrinking food dollar with impossible ingenuity.

When world food prices skyrocketed in the 1970s, a study of families in Great Britain showed that 75 per cent of husbands made no increase in the housekeeping money they allowed their wives. No wonder food has become a primary source of identity for women.

Some cultures go beyond external controls. In tribal societies of Ethiopia, a young girl's entry into womanhood and marriageability is marked by the pulling of several crucial teeth, a ritual performed in the name of beauty that serves to make eating, especially much-coveted meat, permanently difficult. A gap-toothed smile is regarded as feminine. So are the heavy ankle bracelets a female is bound with at puberty. (Think of the bound feet of the upper-class women of China.) In the same tribes, male decoration is confined to body-painting or hair matted with clay and braids—nothing that restricts movement, eating, or freedom.

To deprive females of equal nourishment increases the male food supply, and decreases the energy for rebellion among wives and daughters. But like all oppression, it is dangerous in the long run—to everyone.

Poorly nourished women give birth to less healthy children, males as well as females. Even cultures that selectively reward pregnant women with better feeding rarely make up completely for the damage already done in the name of sexual politics. In extreme cases, high infant mortality, poor brain development and protein-deficiency diseases are the results of poor maternal nutrition. None of these is any respecter of gender.

We don't have to look far from our own doors to find infant mortality rates and protein deficiency that surpass those in almost any other industrialized country. The US is producing generations of an impoverished underclass; yet political resistance to food stamps, adequate welfare payments, even feeding programmes confined to infants and pregnant or breastfeeding women continues to increase. So does resistance to the job-training programmes, childcare centres and penalties for sex discrimination in the workplace, all of which would allow women to better support themselves and their children.

The short-term goal of saving money is cited in all of the above cases; yet that goal is rarely mentioned when discussing the many billions of dollars spent on the military. A dead certain, immediate loss of human talent is simply considered less important than a possible future loss of military superiority.

It makes you wonder, is the fear of independent women so

great, consciously or unconsciously, that our 'pro-family' leadership will choose female dependency over the country's long-term self-interest? Do they maintain the example of poor women—or any women who can't survive without the goodwill and protection of men—as a constant reminder to keep us all in line?

Surely women can learn from the politics of food that arguments of enlightened self-interest aren't enough. Sometimes only rebellion will do.

Facts persuade us of the need to rebel.

*The Myth.* Males need more and better food because they do more work.

*The Fact.* According to the United Nations, females do one-third of the paid work in the world, and two-thirds of all work, paid and unpaid. In industrialized societies like the US, homemakers work harder than any other class of worker: an average of 99.6 hours a week. In Latin America, females make up at least 50 per cent of the agricultural labour force, and as much as 90 per cent in Africa and Asia. In many societies like our own, most women have two jobs, inside the home and outside it, while most men have only one.

*The Myth.* Given the famine and malnutrition suffered by much of the world, it is diversionary to focus on how food is distributed. The first and only question should be how to create more food.

*The Fact.* The earth already produces enough food to nourish all of its inhabitants. The politics of distribution is the major reason for hunger and starvation. As the Swedish Nutrition Foundation and other international study groups concluded years ago, the use of food and starvation as a political weapon is even more destructive than bacteriological warfare or other weapons that affect all people equally, precisely because withholding nutrition afflicts pregnant women, nursing mothers and children preferentially.

*The Myth.* There is no consistent attitude towards females. Some cultures like plump women while others prefer thin ones. It's all a matter of personal preference and style.

*The Fact.* What is rare and possessed only by the powerful is envied as a symbol of power. Thus, poor societies with little food produce an ideal of feminine beauty that is plump and available only to the rich. Pashas, African chieftains and American robber barons sometimes force-fed or otherwise fattened up their women as testimonies to their wealth. In more fortunate societies where women become plump on starch and sugar if nothing else, thinness and delicacy in women are rare and envied. Nonetheless, the common denominators are weakness, passivity and lack of strength. Rich or poor, feminine beauty is equated with subservience to men. Lower-class women, who have to do physical labour and develop some degree of strength, are made to envy this weakness. Middle Eastern peasant women envied and imitated the protection and restriction of the veil that began with women who were the possessions of upper-class men. American farm and factory women may envy the thinness and artifice of rich women. To those who have the double role of working for a salary and raising children, life as a child-bearer and hostess for a well-to-do man may look desirable by comparison.

Freedom can only be imagined. But thanks to the contagious ideas of feminism, imaginations are working overtime.

Poor women are demanding the practical means to control the endless births that endanger their health, and improved maternal and infant nutrition to make those fewer children healthier and more likely to survive. This major focus of women in poorer, agricultural countries is also important among the poor inside wealthy, industrialized countries like this one. We may know, for instance, that most poor women in the US still don't have access to adequate contraception and safe abortion. But do we know that African doctors training here have diagnosed kwashiorkor, the disease that produces the yellow skin and bloated bellies of African famines, in our own inner cities?

Middle-class women are beginning to cultivate fitness and strength. Bodybuilders, everyday joggers, tennis champions and Olympic athletes have begun to challenge the equation of beauty with weakness. Even upper-class women are less likely to cultivate the hothouse delicacy that testified to male protection.

All women need strength—health, muscles, endurance—if we are to literally change the world.

Do we think of this as we imagine beauty? Or crave empty

calories? Or pass our politics of food on to children and younger sisters?

It will take a lot of nourishment to grow the world's longest revolution.

—1980

# IN PRAISE OF WOMEN'S
# BODIES AGAIN

Nudity has been celebrated in India through both male and female sculptures which are prominently displayed in the most sacred of our spaces—our temples. In fact, it is only with British colonialism and imported Western values that a Victorian morality has been imposed on our understanding of nudity and the female body. When upper-class women began to wear blouses underneath their saris during the British Raj, they were considered risqué. Today, some priests are draping statues of Shiva and Parvati with dhotis and saris, artists are being attacked for painting nude women and some college principals have even tried to issue edicts against the wearing of jeans by women to protect them from rape.

On the other hand, the fashion industry imposes a hyper-sexuality on women who are trying to belong by dressing up not for their own satisfaction but for the display and edification of men. Both are inhibiting women in different ways.

Steinem's 1980 essay talks about how women have started understanding and celebrating their own bodies in spite of imposed conservative or market values.

—Ruchira Gupta

How long has it been since you spent a few days in the intimate company of women: dressing and undressing, talking, showering, resting—the kind of casual togetherness that seems more common to locker rooms of men?

For me, high-school gym class came the closest. But that was during the repressive 1950s, when even the most daring of us hid behind our towels and others were so insecure about our bodies' adolescent changes (or the lack of them) that we went through group showers with our underwear on, or endured the damp discomfort of gym suits under our clothes so we never had to undress at all.

By the time we got to college, I suppose we must have been more grown-up and open. Nonetheless, sports for women, still 'unfeminine', became anti-intellectual as well. Two good excuses to avoid most situations of casual nudity among women, and thus to go right on concealing the imperfect bodies on which we secretly thought our worldly worth depended.

So I found myself belatedly having a basic, human, comforting experience that should have been commonplace in my life long ago. Thanks to a few days spent at an old-fashioned spa in the company of ninety or so other women, I discovered a simple, visceral consciousness-raising that was just as crucial as the verbal kind. Like many basic experiences women are encouraged to miss, it brought both strength (through self-acceptance) and anger (why didn't I know this before?).

It's a truism, for instance, that a few clothes are more shocking than none. But for women especially, bras, panties, bathing suits and other stereotypical gear are visual reminders of a commercial, idealized feminine image that our real and diverse female bodies can't possibly fit. Without those visual references, however, each individual woman's body can be accepted on its own terms. We stop being comparatives. We begin to be unique.

Nobody commented on these events, of course. They just happened. The more hours and days we spent together, moving between the locker room and exercise classes or pool and sauna, the less we resorted to the silky wisps or formidable elastic of our various underwear styles. Nudity was fine. Exercise leotards were also okay. They coated the body comfortably instead of chopping it up into horizontal strips. But gradually, skinny bikinis, queen-size slips, girdles and other paraphernalia begin to disappear from our bodies and our lockers, like camouflage in a war we no longer had to fight.

'I've always loved fancy lingerie,' said one woman, 'but it's beginning to look weird to me.'

'That's why my husband likes black garter belts,' said a Rubenesque woman in a towel. 'They look the *most* weird.'

'Did you ever hear the story about Judy Holliday?' asked a woman peeling off a sweaty leotard. 'When she went for a movie interview, the head of the studio started chasing her around the desk. So she just reached into her dress, pulled out her falsies and handed them to him. 'Here,' she said, 'I think this is what you want.'

'My God,' said a big-breasted woman who, by *Playboy*'s standards, should have been very happy. 'If only I could do that!'

Gradually there was also less embarrassment about appendectomy scars, stretch marks, Caesarean incisions and the like. Though I had always resented the anthropological double standard by which scars are supposed to be marks of courage and experience on a male body but ugliness on a female one, I began to realize that I had been assessing such wounds in masculine terms, nonetheless. Duelling scars, war wounds, scars-as-violence, tribal scars as painful initiations—those images were part of the reason I had assumed such marks to be evidence of violence on men as well as on women.

But many of women's body scars have a very different context, and thus an emotional power all their own. Stretch marks and Caesarean incisions from giving birth are very different from accident, war and fight scars. They evoke courage without violence, strength without cruelty, and even so, they're far more likely to be worn with diffidence than braggado. That gives them a moving, bittersweet power, like seeing a room where a very emotional event in our lives once took place.

There were other surgical scars that seemed awesome to me, too, but not as evocative as those from childbirth. How do women survive even the routine physical price of skin stretched to its limit? After one Caesarean birth, where do some women find the courage to attempt one or several more?

True, there are tribal societies that treat women who give birth like honorary male warriors, but that is paying too much honour to war. Childbirth is more admirable than conquest, more amazing than self-defence and as courageous as either one. Yet one of the strongest, most thoughtful feminists I know still hides in one-piece bathing suits to conceal her two Caesarean scars. And one of the most hypocritical feminists I know (that is, one who loves feminism but dislikes women) had plastic surgery to remove the tiny scar that gave her face character.

Perhaps we'll only be fully at ease with ourselves when we can appreciate scars as symbols of experience, often experiences that other women share, and see our bodies as unique chapters in a shared story.

To do that, we need to be together unself-consciously. We need the regular sight of diverse reality to wear away the plastic-stereotypical-perfect image against which we've each been taught to measure ourselves. The impossible goal of 'what we should look like' has worn a groove in our brains. It will take the constant intimacy of many new images to blast it out.

So, from my belated beginnings, I write in praise of diverse women.

A cheerful, seventyish woman with short white curls held back by an orange ribbon, wearing a satiny green leotard that hugs her gently protruding stomach like a second skin. From her, I learn the beauteous curve of a non-flat stomach. I also learn that a great-grandmother can touch her toes with more flexibility than I can, and leave me panting in aerobic-dance class.

A small, sturdy, young masseuse with strong hands who dreams of buying a portable massage table so that she can start a business of her own. 'My boyfriend's grandmother has arthritis real bad,' she explains, 'but I massage her hands every day to stop the pain.' She also has insomniac clients she massages into drug-free sleep, and clients with painful knots of tension she relaxes through direct pressure. We agree that if everyone had one good massage a day, there would be fewer wars. From her, I learn there can be sisterly satisfaction, not subservience, in serving other women's bodies.

Two women friends who speak only Spanish, and whose arrival causes uncertainty among locker mates who speak no Spanish at all. From them, we soon learn that the language of bodies and gestures is universal.

A perfectly egg-shaped woman who sits upright and serene in

the nude sunbathing area every day. From her, I learn beyond doubt that only the female curves of breasts and stomach make the Buddha image believable.

A beautiful, tall, slender young woman whose legs dangle from her torso, scarecrow-like, as she leaps in exercise class. Older, stouter women are much more graceful in their movements and, God knows, more in time with the music. From her, I learn that beauty may be skin-deep, but natural rhythm is deeper.

A fiftyish locker-room attendant, under five feet tall, who jogs five miles every morning, and explains, 'My husband used to go with me but he had to stop, the cold air froze his lungs.' We are discussing the need for this spa to offer judo or some other self-defence class, and she agrees. Why? Because she was attacked in the parking lot by a six-foot-tall man with a cement block in his hand, yet she fought him off with self-defence tactics that included a hard blow to the groin. From her, I learn that a small woman can be to a big man what a bullet is to Jell-O.

A new, no-nonsense athletic director who is trying hard to persuade traditional women clients that there's more to fitness than the tape measure and the scale. Since the spa management is still convinced that men are interested in fitness and health, but women want beauty and pampering, she is relieved when I complain to the management that men in the same spa get cardiovascular and muscle-flexibility tests while women have to request them and pay extra. From each other, we re-learn the activist value of pressure from both outside and inside any system.

A tall, calm, dark-haired mother and her tall, calm, dark-haired daughter who talk together about their mutual profession of social work. Mostly they seem companionable without needing to talk. A woman's body has given birth to a friend.

A tough, witty criminal lawyer who wants to figure out how to use her legal talents to advance other women. In nudity, she relaxes enough to gift us with an epigram: 'Most men want their wives to have a jobette.'

A no-nonsense young beautician who gives a pore-cleaning facial and a discourse on cosmetic surgery at the same time. 'I've seen all kinds of scars—breast implants, chin tucks, facelifts, eyelid tucks. There was a woman in here who had such a bad eyelid job that she couldn't close her eyes.' I wait to hear some resentment of rich women with little to do but revise their faces, but I am wrong. 'Poor things,' says the beautician, digging away expertly. 'I wouldn't trade places for any amount of money.' More silence. 'I'm only planning to have a chin tuck myself.'

A few women who sit quietly in the steam room, each immersed in a cloud of vapour, her own muscle pains and her own thoughts. Two newcomers arrive and get help from veterans of a day or two. 'Start on the first bench—it gets hotter as you go up.'

'Use this ice for your forehead.'

'Don't stay more than five minutes the first time.' Together, we make a small misty world of diverse sizes, shapes and colours: a quiet place that cares about the welfare of strangers. The steam that surrounds us seems to communicate our thoughts.

'It's nice that you can come here by yourself or with a group of women,' says a voice from the mist.

'And not feel like a nut,' finishes another.

'I thought I'd be embarrassed,' says a young voice. 'I've never been with a bunch of women like...like *this* before.'

Laughter comes from the steamy Buddha in the comer. 'Honey,' she says, 'what you see is what you get.'

When I return home, caffeine-free, sugar-free and relatively healthy, I ask a few much younger women about their experiences of seeing women's bodies. I had assumed this generation would be more at ease than mine, but the spa's younger guests have shaken my faith. From random answers, I learn that although no one is wearing underwear into the shower anymore, this non-verbal form of consciousness-raising still isn't an accepted part of younger women's lives.

'There's no real place where we can be together like that,' says a high-school student thoughtfully. 'Sports aren't important, and I don't know anybody who goes to the gym or to a steam bath. It just doesn't happen.'

Meanwhile, two editors have reminded me that an evening in a Turkish bath in Jerusalem turned out to be one of the high points of a feminist tour of Israel that *Ms.* magazine organized a few years ago. It created an unexpected bonding among strangers at the beginning of the tour—'instant sisterhood'—and a realization of the beauty of women's bodies on their own terms. The few women who had missed that evening felt they were one step behind the group's intimacy for the rest of the trip.

I had listened to this same story when the tour group came home, but I hadn't really heard it. Like other basic experiences, this one is better absorbed than described.

But now I know: I know that fat or thin, mature or not, our bodies wouldn't give us such unease if we learned their place in the rainbow spectrum of women. Even great beauties seem less distant, and even mastectomies seem less terrifying, when we stop imagining them and see them as they really are.

Changing the artificiality of media images would help, but that isn't enough. Like the children who were shown photographs of women and men doing non-traditional jobs—women welding, for instance, and men diapering babies—but reversed those roles in their memories within a few weeks, we only retain a complete image when we experience it completely. A one-dimensional remedy can't cure a three-dimensional wrong.

Now, like the teenage heroine in the movie *Gypsy*, who is aware of her body only after she becomes a stripper, too many of us experience female bodies, our own and others, in social settings and private bedrooms, only when they are most isolated, artificial, self-conscious and on display for men or conventional judgement.

A little natural togetherness would show us the Family of Woman, where each of us is beautiful and no one is the same.

—1980

# MARILYN MONROE:
# THE WOMAN WHO DIED TOO SOON*

If Marilyn Monroe were alive today, she would have been ninety years old. Almost fifty-five years after her death, the influence of this great, powerful, unconfident movie star; this whispering, simpering, big-breasted, childlike sex goddess, stretches both forward and backward. We can empathize with her efforts at self-education and her rebellion against her own image of being more body than mind.

When a well-known astrologer innocently asked if she, as a Gemini, knew that she had been born under the same sign as Rosalind Russell, Judy Garland and Rosemary Clooney, Marilyn looked him straight in the eye and said: 'I know nothing of these people. I was born under the same sign as Ralph Waldo Emerson, Queen Victoria and Walt Whitman.'

As more women are declaring our full humanity—now that we are more likely to be valued for our heads and hearts, not just the bodies that house them, Steinem asks the question: Could we have helped Marilyn survive?

As one watches the frustrations of Silk Smitha in the movie *Dirty Picture* or reads about the suicide/murder of Parveen Babi, Divya Bharti, Reema Kapadia and Jiah Khan we have no answers.

—Ruchira Gupta

'What I really want to say: That what the world really needs is a real feeling of kinship. Everybody: stars, labourers, Negroes, Jews, Arabs. We are all brothers... Please don't make me a joke. End the interview with what I believe.'

---

*I would like to thank *Ms.* co-founder and editor, Harriet Lyons, whose idea this was.

'I knew I belonged to the public and to the world, not because I was talented or even beautiful but because I had never belonged to anything or anyone else.'

—Marilyn Monroe

Saturday afternoon movies—no matter how poorly made or incredible the plot—were a refuge from my neighbourhood and all my teenage miseries. Serials that never ended, Doris Day who never capitulated, cheap travelogues, sci-fi features with zippers in the monster suits: I loved them all, believed them all and never dreamed of leaving until the screen went sickeningly blank.

But I walked out on Marilyn Monroe. I remember her on the screen, huge as a colossus doll, mincing and whispering and simply hoping her way into total vulnerability. Watching her, I felt angry, even humiliated, but I didn't understand why.

After all, Jane Russell was in the movie, too (a very bad-taste version of *Gentlemen Prefer Blondes*), so it wasn't just the vulnerability that all big-breasted women seem to share. (If women viewers prefer actresses who are smaller, neater—the Audrey Hepburns of the world—it isn't because we're jealous of the zaftig ones as men suppose. It's just that we would rather identify with a woman we don't have to worry about, someone who doesn't seem in constant danger.) Compared to Marilyn, Jane Russell seemed in control of her body and even of the absurd situations in this movie.

Perhaps it was the uncertainty in the eyes of this big, blonde child-woman; the terrible desire for approval that made her different from Jane Russell. How dare she expose the neediness that so many women feel, but try so hard to hide? How dare she, a movie star, be just as unconfident as I was?

So I disliked her and avoided her movies, as we avoid that which reflects our fears about ourselves. If there were jokes made on her name and image when I was around, I joined in. I contributed to the laughing, the ridicule, the put-downs, thus proving that I was nothing like her, nothing at all.

I, too, got out of my neighbourhood in later years, just as she had escaped from a much worse life of lovelessness, child abuse and foster homes. I didn't do it, as she did, through nude calendar photographs and starlet bits. (Even had there been such opportunities for mildly pretty girls in Toledo, Ohio, I would never have had the courage to make myself so vulnerable.) Yes, I was American enough to have show-business dreams. The boys in my neighbourhood hoped to get out of a lifetime in the factories through sports; the girls, if we imagined anything other than marrying a few steps up in the world, always dreamed of show-business careers. But after high-school years as a dancer on the Toledo show-business circuit, or what passed for show business there, it seemed hopeless even to me. In the end, it was luck, an encouraging mother and a facility with words that got me out; a facility that helped me fake my way through the college entrance exams for which I was totally unprepared.

But there's not much more confidence in girls who scrape past college boards than there is in those who, like Marilyn, parade past beauty-contest judges. By the time I saw her again, I was a respectful student watching the celebrated members of the Actors Studio do scenes from what seemed to me two very impressive and highbrow plays (Arthur Miller and Eugene O'Neill were to be served up that day). She was a student, too, a pupil of Lee Strasberg, leader of the Actors Studio and American guru of the Stanislavski method, but her status as a movie star and sex symbol seemed to keep her from being taken seriously even there. She was allowed to observe, but not to do scenes with her colleagues.

So the two of us sat there, mutually awed, I think, in the presence of such theatre people as Ben Gazzara and Rip Torn, mutually insecure in the masculine world of High Culture, mutually trying to fade into the woodwork.

I remember thinking that Strasberg and his actors seemed to take positive pleasure in their power to ignore this great and powerful movie star who had come to learn. Their greetings to her were a little too studiously casual, their whispers to each other about her being there a little too self-conscious and condescending. Though she stayed in the back of the room, her blonde head swathed in a black scarf and her body hidden in a shapeless black sweater and slacks, she gradually became a presence, if only because the group was trying so hard not to look, to remain oblivious and cool.

As we filed slowly out of the shabby room after the session was over, Marilyn listened eagerly to the professional post-mortem being carried on by Ben Gazzara and others who walked ahead of us, her fingers nervously tracing a face that was luminous and without make-up, as if she were trying to hide herself, to apologize for being there. I was suddenly glad she hadn't participated and hadn't been subjected to the criticisms of this rather vulturous group. (Perhaps it was an unschooled reaction, but I hadn't enjoyed watching Strasberg encourage an intimate love scene between an actor and actress, and then pick them apart with humiliating authority.) Summoning my nerve, I did ask the shy, blonde woman in front of me if she could imagine playing a scene for this group.

'Oh, no,' Marilyn said, her voice childish, but much less whispery than on the screen, 'I admire all these people so much. I'm just not good enough.' Then, after a few beats of silence: 'Lee Strasberg is a genius, you know. I plan to do what he says.'

Her marriage to Arthur Miller seemed quite understandable to me and, I think, to other women, even those who were threatened by Miller's casting off a middle-aged wife to take a younger, far more glamorous one. If you can't be taken seriously in your work, if you have an emotional and intellectual insecurity complex, then marry a man who has the seriousness you've been denied. It's a traditional female option—far more acceptable than trying to achieve that identity on one's own.

Of course, Marilyn's image didn't really gain seriousness and intellectuality. Women don't gain serious status by sexual association any more easily than they do by hard work. (At least, not unless the serious man dies and we confine ourselves to being keepers of the flame. As Margaret Mead has pointed out, widows are almost the only women who are honoured in authority.) Even Marilyn's brave refusal to be intimidated by threats that she would never work in films again if she married Miller, who was then a 'subversive' called to testify before the House Un-American Activities Committee, was considered less brave than Miller's refusal to testify. Indeed, it was barely reported at all.

Perhaps she didn't take her own bravery seriously, either. She might be giving up her livelihood, the work that meant so much to her, but she was about to give that up for marriage anyway. As Mrs Arthur Miller, she retired to a Connecticut farm and tried to limit her life to his solitary work habits, his friends and his two children. Only when they badly needed money did she come out of retirement again, and that was to act in *The Misfits*, a film written by her husband.

On the other hand, the public interpretation was very different. She was an egocentric actress forcing one of America's most important playwrights to tailor a screenplay to her inferior talents: that was the gossip-column story in the US and in Europe. But her own pattern argues the case for her. In two previous marriages, to an aircraft factory worker at the age of sixteen and later to baseball star Joe DiMaggio, she had cut herself off from the world and put all her energies into being a housewife. When it didn't work out, she blamed herself, not the role, and added one more failure to her list of insecurities. 'I have too many fantasies to be a housewife,' she told a woman friend sadly. And finally, to an interviewer: 'I guess I am a fantasy.'

*The Misfits* seemed to convey some facets of the real Marilyn: honesty, an innocence and belief that survived all experience to the contrary, kindness towards other women, a respect for the life of plants and animals. Because for the first time she wasn't only a sex object and victim, I also was unembarrassed enough to notice her acting ability. I began to see her earlier movies—those few in which, unlike *Gentlemen Prefer Blondes*, she wasn't called upon to act the female impersonator.

For me, as for so many people, she was a presence in the world, a life force.

Over the years, I heard other clues to her character. When Ella Fitzgerald, a black artist and perhaps the greatest singer of popular songs, hadn't been able to get a booking at an important Los Angeles nightclub in the 1950s, it was Marilyn who called the owner and promised to sit at a front table every night if he allowed Ella to sing. The owner hired Ella, Marilyn was faithful to her promise each night, the press went wild and, as Ella remembered with gratitude, 'After that, I never had to play a small jazz club again.'

Even more movingly, there was Marilyn's last interview. She

pleaded with the reporter to end with, 'What I really want to say: That what the world really needs is a real feeling of kinship. Everybody: stars, labourers, Negroes, Jews, Arabs. We are all brothers... Please don't make me a joke. End the interview with what I believe.'

And then she was gone. I remember being told, in the middle of a chaotic student meeting in Europe, that she was dead. I remember that precise moment on 5 August 1962—the people around me, what the room looked like—and I've discovered that many other people remember that moment, too. It's a phenomenon usually reserved for the death of family and presidents.

She was an actress, a person on whom no one's fate depended, and yet her energy and terrible openness to life had made a connection to strangers. Within days after her body was discovered, eight young and beautiful women took their lives in individual incidents clearly patterned after Marilyn Monroe's death. Some of them left notes to make that connection clear.

Two years later, Arthur Miller's autobiographical play, *After the Fall*, brought Marilyn back to life in the character of Maggie. But somehow this Maggie didn't seem the same. She had Marilyn's pathetic insecurity, the same need to use her sexual self as a way of getting recognition and feeling alive. But, perhaps naturally, the play was about Miller's suffering, not Marilyn's. He seemed honestly to include some of his own destructive acts. (He had kept a writer's diary of his movie-star wife, for instance, and Marilyn's discovery of it was an emotional blow, the beginning of the end for that marriage. It made her wonder: Was her husband exploiting her, as most men had done, but in a more intellectual way?) Nonetheless, the message of the play was mostly Miller's view of his attempts to shore up a creature of almost endless insecurities; someone doomed beyond his helping by a mysterious lack of confidence.

To women, that lack of confidence was less mysterious. Writer Diana Trilling, who had never met Marilyn, wrote an essay just after her death that some of Marilyn's friends praised as a more accurate portrayal than Miller's. She described the public's 'mockery of [Marilyn's] wish to be educated'; the sexual awareness that came only from outside, from men's reactions, 'leaving a great emptiness where a true sexuality would have supplied her with a sense of herself as a person with connection and content'. She questioned whether Marilyn had really wanted to die, or only to be asleep, not to be conscious, through the loneliness of that particular Saturday night.

Trilling also recorded a feeling of connection to Marilyn's loneliness felt by so many strangers ('especially women to whose protectiveness her extreme vulnerability spoke so directly'), so much so that we fantasized our ability to save her, if only we had been there. 'But we were the friends,' as Trilling wrote sadly, 'of whom she knew nothing.'[1]

'She was an unusual woman—a little ahead of her times,' said Ella Fitzgerald. 'And she didn't know it.'

Now that women's self-vision is changing, we are thinking again about the life of Marilyn Monroe. Might our new confidence in women's existence with or without the approval of men have helped a thirty-six-year-old woman of talent to stand on her own? To resist the insecurity and ridicule? To stop depending on sexual attractiveness as the only proof that she was alive—and therefore to face ageing with confidence? Because the ability to bear a child was denied to her, could these new ideas have helped her to know that being a woman included much more? Could she have challenged the Freudian analysts to whom she turned in her suffering?

Most of all, we wonder if the support and friendship of other women could have helped. Her early experiences of men were not good. She was the illegitimate daughter of a man who would not even contribute for her baby clothes; her mother's earliest memory of her own father, Marilyn's grandfather, was his smashing a pet kitten against the fireplace in a fit of anger; Marilyn herself said she was sexually attacked by a foster father while still a child; and she was married off at sixteen because another foster family could not take care of her. Yet she was forced always to depend for her security on the goodwill and recognition of men; even to be interpreted by them in writing because she feared that sexual competition would make women interviewers dislike her. Even if they had wanted to, the women in her life did not have the power to protect her. In films, photographs and books, after her death as well as before, she has been mainly seen through men's eyes.

We are too late. We cannot know whether we could have helped Norma Jean Baker or the Marilyn Monroe she became. But we are not too late to do as she asked. At last, we can take her seriously.

—1972

# WHAT IS SELF-ESTEEM?

Courage is contagious. The rape of Jyoti Singh Pandey on 16 December 2012 has set fire to the dry tinderbox of centuries of patriarchy. Young women and men are out on the streets of India, asking for more safe spaces for women. Kavita Krishnan, a student leader of this movement, has expressed the mood in the slogan: 'Bekhauf Azaadi—Life Without Fear'.[1] 'Women want the freedom to be not just daughters and mothers and wives but to be able to go out at midnight and buy a cigarette without fear,' is what she said to a huge rally outside Parliament.

No amount of violence is driving women back. They have discovered their voice and courage, by standing up for others and themselves they have found their inner strength—their self-esteem.

Woman after woman has been speaking up about the right to work, to earn a living, study, stay at home or earn a livelihood without fear. Recently, an intern has reported against a judge and a journalist against her editor for sexual assault. The editor's daughter has heroically stood by the journalist and challenged the father.

—Ruchira Gupta

'The notion of giving something a name is the vastest generative idea that was ever conceived.'[2]

—Susanne K. Langer

The Plaza Parable
'The mind is its own place, and in itself
Can make a Heav'n of Hell, a Hell of Heav'n'

—John Milton

As I write this, I'm still the same person who grew up mostly in a Midwestern, factory-working neighbourhood where talk about 'self-esteem' would have seemed like a luxury. In my memory of those times and that place, men were valued by what they did, women by how they looked and then by what their husbands did, and all of life was arranged (or so we thought) from the outside in.

This experience of living among good people who were made to feel 'ungood' by an economic class system imposed from above—people who often blamed themselves for hard times they had done nothing to deserve—left me with a permanent resistance to any self-help book or religion or psychological theory that tells us we can solve all our problems on our own. So did a later realization that sexual and racial caste systems are even deeper and less in our control than class is. After all, we know that if children are treated badly enough for long enough, they come to believe they are bad people. As adults, we often try to rationalize the world by asking what we did to deserve some instance of bad luck, violence, humiliation or even illness.

As Susan Sontag wrote in *Illness as Metaphor*, many theories of disease 'assign to the luckless ill the ultimate responsibility both for falling ill and for getting well'.[3] And we often accept this, for it gives us an illusion of control. As Princeton mayor Barbara Boggs Sigmund protested in *The New York Times* shortly before she died of the cancer that she had been courageously battling for years, 'We humans would rather accept culpability than chaos...'[4]

That's why to this day, if I were forced to choose between 'Bread and Roses'—the dual demands of nineteenth-century women millworkers who organized one of this country's first strikes—I still would start with 'bread' (and warmth and physical safety and a roof over everyone's head) before moving on to self-knowledge, self-expression, and other 'roses'. I still would baulk at phrases like 'She [or he] just has a self-esteem problem,' as if this were something an individual chose to have.

But not until some time in my thirties did I begin to suspect that there might be an internal centre of power I was neglecting. Though the way I'd grown up had encouraged me to locate power almost anywhere but within myself, I began to be increasingly aware of its pinpoint of beginning within—my gender and neighbourhood training notwithstanding.

And with this awareness, I gradually began to notice that many of the people I had been brought up to envy and see as powerful— mostly men from groups who were supposed to be the givers of approval—actually had the other half of the same problem I was experiencing. I had been raised to assume all power was outside myself, but they had been raised to place power almost nowhere but within themselves. Often, they were suffering, too. Just as the fantasy of no control was the enemy of my self-esteem, the fantasy of total control was the enemy of theirs. For both of us, the goal should have been a point of balance in between: a back-and-forth between the self and others, uniqueness and unity, the planned and the accidental, our internal selves and the universe. As wise women and men in every culture tell us: The art of life is not controlling what happens to us, but using what happens to us.

Like all great oaks, this understanding began with a very small acorn.

It was the late sixties, those days that were still pre-feminist for me. I didn't question the fact that male journalists with less experience than I were getting the political assignments that were my real interest. Instead, I was grateful to be writing profiles of visiting celebrities—a departure from the fashion and family subjects that female reporters were usually given—and this included an interview that was to take place over tea in the Palm Court of the Plaza Hotel.

Because the actor was very late, I waited while the assistant manager circled disapprovingly and finally approached. 'Unescorted ladies,' he announced loudly, were 'absolutely not allowed' in the lobby. I told him I was a reporter waiting for an arriving guest who couldn't be contacted any other way—an explanation that sounded lame even to me. The manager escorted me firmly past curious bystanders and out the lobby door.

I was humiliated: Did I look like a prostitute? Was my trench coat too battered—or not battered enough? I was anxious: How was I going to find my subject and do my work? I decided to wait outside the revolving door in the hope of spotting the famous actor through its glass, but an hour passed with no success.

Later, I learned that he had arrived, failed to see me, and left. His press agent called my editor to complain that I had 'stood up' his client. The actor missed his publicity, the editor missed a deadline, and I missed a cheque that I needed to pay the rent. I also blamed myself for not figuring out how to 'get the story' and worried about being demoted permanently back to the ghetto of 'women's interest' articles I was trying to escape.

By coincidence a month or so later, I was assigned to interview another celebrity who was also staying at the Plaza. To avoid a similar fiasco, I had arranged to meet this one in his suite, but on my way through the lobby, I noticed my former nemesis standing guard. Somehow, I found myself lingering, as if rooted to the spot—and sure enough, the manager approached me with his same officious speech. But this time I was amazed to hear myself saying some very different things. I told him this was a public place where I had every legal right to be, and asked why he hadn't banished the several 'unescorted men' in the lobby who might be male prostitutes. I also pointed out that since hotel staff were well known to supply call girls in return for a percentage of their pay, perhaps he was just worried about losing a commission.

He looked quite startled—and let me stay. I called my subject and suggested we have tea downstairs after all. It turned out to be a newsworthy interview, and I remember writing it up with more ease than usual and delivering it with an odd sense of well-being.

What was the lesson of these two incidents? Clearly, the assistant manager and I were unchanged. I was even wearing the same trench coat and freelancing for the same publication. Only one thing was different: my self-esteem. It had been raised almost against my will—by contagion.

Between those two interviews, a woman doctor had made a reservation for herself and a party of friends at the Plaza's Oak Room, a public restaurant that was maintained as a male-only bastion at lunchtime on the grounds that female voices might disturb men's business meetings. When this woman was stopped at the Oak Room door for being the wrong gender of 'Dr', as she knew she would be, her lunch group of distinguished feminists turned into a spirited sidewalk picket line and held a press conference they had called in advance.

Now, I also had been invited to join this protest—and refused. In New York as in most cities, there were many public restaurants and bars that either excluded women altogether or wouldn't serve 'unescorted ladies' (that is, any woman or group of women without the magical presence of one man). Certainly, I resented this, but protesting it in the Oak Room, a restaurant too expensive for most people, male or female, seemed a mistake. The only remedy was a city council ordinance banning discrimination in public places, and that would require democratic support. Besides, feminists were already being misrepresented in the media as white, middle class, and frivolous, a caricature that even then I knew was wrong: the first feminists I had heard of in the sixties were working-class women who broke the sex barrier in factory assembly lines, and the first I actually met were black women on welfare who compared that demeaning system to a gigantic husband who demanded sexual faithfulness (the no-man-in-the-house rule) in return for subsistence payments. If groups like those were not publicized—and if well-to-do women who lunched at the Plaza were—I feared this new movement's image would become even more distorted.

As it turned out, I was right about tactics and the media's continuing image of feminism: 'white middle class' did become like one key on the typewriter of many journalists (though polls showed that black women were almost twice as likely to support feminist changes as white women were).[5] But I was very wrong about women's responses—including my own. For instance: By the time of that demonstration at the Plaza, I had already picketed for civil rights, against US involvement in Vietnam, and with migrant farm workers, often in demonstrations that were far from tactically perfect; so why was I suddenly demanding perfection of women? When blacks or Jews had been kept out of restaurants and bars, expensive or not, I felt fine about protesting; so why couldn't I take my own half of the human race (which, after all, included half of all blacks and half of all Jews) just as seriously?

The truth was that I had internalized society's unserious estimate of all that was female—including myself. This was low self-esteem, not logic. Should a black woman demonstrate for the right to eat at dime store lunch counters in the South, where she was barred by race, and then quietly leave when refused service at an expensive New York restaurant on account of sex? Of course not. The principle—and, more important, the result for one real woman— was the same. But I had been raised to consider any judgement based on sex alone less important than any judgement based on race, class, or anything else alone. In fact, if you counted all groups in the world other than white women, I was valuing just about everybody more than I valued myself.

Nonetheless, all the excuses of my conscious mind couldn't keep my unconscious self from catching the contagious spirit of those women who picketed the Oak Room. When I faced the hotel manager again, I had glimpsed the world as if women mattered. By seeing through their eyes, I had begun to see through my own.

It still would be years before I understood the seriousness of my change of view. Much later, I recognized it in 'Revolution', the essay written by Polish journalist Ryszard Kapuscinski, who describes the moment when a man on the edge of a crowd looks back defiantly at a policeman—and when that policeman senses a sudden refusal to accept his defining gaze—as the imperceptible moment in which rebellion is born. 'All books about all revolutions begin with a chapter that describes the decay of tottering authority or the misery and sufferings of the people,' Kapuscinski writes. 'They should begin with a psychological chapter—one that shows how a harassed, terrified man suddenly breaks his terror, stops being afraid. This unusual process—sometimes accomplished in an instant, like a shock—demands to be illustrated. Man gets rid of fear and feels free. Without that, there would be no revolution.'[6]

But even then, this moment in a hotel lobby was my first inkling that there is a healthier self within each of us, just waiting for encouragement. It's such a common experience of unexpected strength that we have ordinary phrases for it: 'I surprised myself,' or 'In spite of myself.' In *The Red and the Black*, Stendhal called this inner self 'a little friend'.[7] In Alice Walker's *The Color Purple*, Celie writes letters to a strong friend called God, but she is also writing to the strength within herself.[8] Children create imaginary playmates, and athletes, musicians and painters strive to free this true and spontaneous self in their work. Meditation, prayer, creativity—all these are ordinary ways of freeing an inner voice. It's a feeling of 'clicking in' when that self is recognized, valued, discovered, esteemed—as if we literally plug into an inner energy that is ours alone, yet connects us to everything else.

To put it another way: I began to understand that self-esteem isn't everything; it's just that there's nothing without it.

### Self-Esteem Is Personal: An Inner Child of the Past

Until recently, I thought I had built a brick wall between myself and my childhood. I valued those early years for making me an optimist (nothing could ever be that bad again) and a survivor (learning how to cope has its advantages). Then I put their memories and feelings behind me.

Of course, I did notice that small things made me feel irrationally sad or depressed—for instance, any story about a mother and daughter on their own, certain landscapes, or the sound of a radio in an empty room—but I just avoided them. When bigger things made me feel self-pitying but defiant—feeling rootless and proud of it, for example, or giving money away but then feeling deprived— I assumed they were the inevitable results of my conscious, rational decisions to remain free, unencumbered, with no possessions to possess me.

I continued in this way for decades while pressures grew. I worked for a magazine I loved and a movement that had given me life. I organized and travelled and lectured; I campaigned and raised contributions and solicited ads to keep the magazine going; I turned my apartment into a closet where I changed clothes and dumped papers into cardboard boxes; and I only once in twenty years spent an entire week without getting on a plane. But at home or away, I often woke up with sweaty palms and pounding heart, worried that I was going to mess up some public event, fail to find enough money to pay the printer and meet the payroll, or otherwise let down this movement that meant as much to me as it did to millions of other women.

After the first five or six years, I had become aware that I was usually doing over again things I already knew how to do and often saying things I'd said before—that I was reacting more than acting—

but I also knew that no matter what happened, I could always keep on functioning. It was part of my survivor's skills, my childhood defiance. If there had been an Olympic team for just functioning, I would have been on it. Later, as economic times got tougher for magazines in general and ours in particular, and inevitable backlashes greeted women's advances, I felt pressure to do more and more. When my friends asked about my state of mind or emotions, I made them laugh—and despair—by turning Plato on his head. 'The examined life,' I explained, 'is not worth living.'

Then one evening after a lecture on the road, a woman in the audience recommended a book, *Your Inner Child of the Past.*[9] She described it with such conviction that I went out and bought it.

Of course, I wasn't interested in self-knowledge, just research—or so I thought. In this case, I needed insight for a book of essays I was writing about Marilyn Monroe, especially about her childhood as Norma Jean Baker.[10] The author, Hugh Missildine, a child psychiatrist, had identified the most common sins and excesses of child-rearing—overindulgence, neglect, perfectionism, sexual abuse, and so on—and then described each one as it manifested itself in later life. Because Marilyn's story of being sexually abused as a little girl had been disbelieved by other biographers, I was looking to Missildine for confirmation of my belief that Marilyn's lifelong inability to value herself as anything other than a sexual being was a classic result of sexual abuse in childhood.

Even more than obvious abuse, however, the hallmark of Marilyn's earliest years had been neglect. Boarded out as a baby by a mother with severe emotional problems of her own, Marilyn had been so neglected that as a little girl, she believed she was invisible. When her mother was committed to a state mental institution, Marilyn was sent to an orphanage. Only the early maturing of her body and the attention it attracted made her feel 'visible' and convinced her that she did indeed exist. It was this division between an internal, worthless self and an external, sexually valuable self that would haunt her for the rest of her short life. Missildine's text described some of the typical results of the kind of neglect Marilyn had experienced: a lifelong search for nurturing, wanting to belong yet feeling a perpetual outsider, trying to make fathers out of husbands and lovers, using sex to get childlike warmth and approval, and neglecting one's own welfare because neglect feels familiar, like home. These were all problems Marilyn herself described. As Missildine wrote: 'Many such people, particularly women, are drawn into theatrical and movie work because... When you're a nobody, the only way to be anybody is to be somebody else.'[11] It was almost as if he had met Marilyn Monroe; certainly, she had said almost exactly those words.

Such extremes of childhood neglect—and of response in adulthood to that neglect—were clearly Marilyn's, not my own. I read them feeling interested and safe. But soon, this slender, simple little book was describing more ordinary results of neglect—among those with alcoholic, ill, or absent parents, for example—that gave me a jolt of recognition. 'The childhood of persons who suffered from neglect,' wrote Missildine in his matter-of-fact way, 'usually reveals a father who somehow wasn't a father and a mother who somehow wasn't a mother.'[12]

Well, my mother had suffered spells of depression, delusions, and long periods as an invalid both before and after I was born. My father had taken care of her until I was ten or so and seemed old enough to replace him. Then my parents separated, and my mother and I lived on our own. Though my parents always made me know that they loved me, and treated me as well as or better than they treated themselves—all very different from the degree of neglect Marilyn had suffered—they still hadn't been able to be real parents much of the time. Basics like regular school attendance, clean clothes, a bedtime, enough money to pay bills and, after I was ten, any kind of consistent parenting at all, had gone the way of my father's wandering lifestyle. After their divorce, my mother's frequent depressions and need for a caretaker had reversed our roles. Since I always knew they were doing the best they could, I didn't allow myself to be angry—and thus just buried my feelings about what I had missed.

For the first time, I began to wonder what was behind the wall between me and my childhood, and if it hadn't seeped into the present in spite of all my bricks and mortar.

I remembered longing to escape the littered, depressing, rat-infested house where I lived alone with my mother; yet I had recreated an upscale, less dramatic version of it in my own apartment with cardboard boxes, stacks of papers and long absences.

I remembered worrying as a child about our lack of money and my father's penchant for borrowing it; yet I had saved nothing of what I earned, couldn't resist giving money away, never planned for the future, and often ended up with a familiar feeling of being neglected, deprived and insecure.

I remembered feeling sad about navigating life by myself, working after school, worrying about my mother, who was sometimes too removed from reality to know where she was, or who I was, and concealing these shameful family secrets from my friends; yet I had chosen to work by myself as a freelancer, and then to do a parallel kind of caretaking for a magazine and a movement. Now as then, I turned away sympathy with jokes and a survivor's pride. In both cases, I was turning away from a well of neediness that I feared would swallow me up if I admitted it.

The parallels were so obvious that even I began to see that I was repeating the painful, familiar patterns of home. In spite of my insistence that I'd put the past behind me, that free will and the realities in which I found myself were the only shapers of my life, it just wasn't so.

I began to follow clues backward. Why was the sound of a radio so depressing, though television and records were not? Because the radio had been the only sound in the house where I lived with my mother. Why couldn't I give myself security and a pleasant place to live in? Because they hadn't been given to me as a child. Why didn't I ask for help from people who would have freely given it? Because they hadn't been there in the past. Why had I lived my life so that I would be ready to leave any place at any time, even if I didn't actually do it? Because that was the way I had protected myself against getting attached to places as a vagabond child.

It may be obvious that we continue to treat ourselves the way we were treated as children, but I lived a diverse and seemingly aware life for more than forty years without figuring it out. I suspect many other people have, too. Only becoming conscious of old and unchosen patterns allows us to change them and even so, change, no matter how much for the better, still feels cold and lonely at first—as if we were out there on the edge of the universe with the wind whistling past our ears—because it doesn't feel like home. Old patterns, no matter how negative and painful they may be, have an incredible magnetic power—because they do feel like home.

This repetition begins to diminish the moment we're aware of its source, and the more we heal the past so we can respond to the present. As the twelve-step Alcoholics Anonymous-type programmes say, 'Dig it out or act it out.' Though we may repeat some sequence of events and feelings in different ways before they gradually dissolve, at least now the point of power is no longer in others who made decisions for us, but in ourselves. I don't know whether Marilyn made connections between past and present or not: between her lost father and the 'fathers' she kept marrying; between the invisible child she once was and her imprisonment in a very visible image that Hollywood had concocted. Perhaps the patterns went too deep, or perhaps there was too much reward for not changing in a world that paid and praised her for staying helpless and childlike. She died before feminism made clear that women have every human possibility, and even before people like Missildine were beginning to write about the inner child. Whether she could have become strong enough to go back and be a parent to her own sad child of the past, we'll never know. But her life story has helped others, if not herself. Certainly, her often repeated plea to be taken seriously reached out to me, made me want to write about her, and thus gave me the great gift of seeing the echoes of her life in my own.

Each of us has an inner child of the past living within us. Those who needed to build no walls have access to that child's creativity and spontaneity. Those who had to leave this crucial core behind can tear down the walls, see what the child needed but didn't have, and begin to provide it now. The more we do this, the more we know that we are worth it.

And that we always were.

## Self-Esteem Is Self-Discovery:
## Gandhi, Marilyn Murphy, and Others

When I was living in India on a fellowship after college, a kind Indian friend took me aside and suggested I might consider saying 'South Asia', 'Southeast Asia' and the like, instead of the 'Near' and 'Far East'. It was the first time I'd ever realized that 'Near' and 'Far' assumed Europe as the centre of the world.

Ever since then, I've noticed that the process of discovering and esteeming a true self is remarkably similar for a person or a race, a group or a nation. When women began to call themselves 'Mary Jones' instead of 'Mrs John Smith', for example, they were doing the same thing as formerly colonized countries that stopped identifying themselves in relation to Europe. When India and England continued their Commonwealth and other relationships after India's independence, one might say that, as George Sand once suggested men and women do, they had broken the marriage bond and reformed it as an equal partnership. When 'Negroes' became 'blacks' and then 'African Americans' in the US, it was part of a long journey from the humiliation of slavery to a pride of heritage. When I myself started to say 'we' instead of 'they' when speaking of women, it was a step toward self-esteem that was at least as important as identifying with one's true ethnic heritage. It was also my Declaration of Interdependence.

No matter who we are, the journey towards recovering the self-esteem that should have been our birthright follows similar steps: a first experience of seeing through our own eyes instead of through the eyes of others (for instance, the moment when an Algerian first looked in defiance at a French soldier, or when a woman stops being defined by the male gaze); telling what seemed to be shameful secrets, and discovering they are neither shameful nor secret (from the woman who has survived childhood sexual abuse to the man whose bottomless need for power hides weakness); giving names to problems that have been treated as normal and thus have no names (think of new terms like homophobia, battered women, or Euro-centrism); bonding with others who share similar experiences (from groups of variously abled people to conferences of indigenous nations); achieving empowerment and self-government (from the woman who has a room and income of her own to the nation that declares its independence); bonding with others in shared power (think of democratic families, rainbow coalitions, or the principles of the United Nations); and finally, achieving a balance of independence and interdependence, and taking one's place in a circle of true selves.

In this spirit of comparing journeys not usually seen as comparable, I've combined two stories that aren't as different as they seem.

Marilyn Murphy was forty-three years old before she began to see the world in colour instead of, as she later wrote, 'in gradations of grey'. Not that she had known what was missing. Growing up as the first of five sisters in a Catholic Irish/Italian working-class family in New York City, she had assumed that, if she couldn't see colour, it wasn't there. She went through all the expected girlish stages, from sneaking on lipstick when the nuns weren't looking to fantasizing about being a nightclub singer in a sequinned gown. When an experience did stand out in this grey world, she wasn't sure why. After her union-organizer father had moved the family to Tulsa, Oklahoma, for instance, she saw a sign in a local bus: 'Colored—Sit in the Back'. It burned into her consciousness, so that forever after, she could remember the sick feeling in the pit of her stomach; yet as a white person, she was not supposed to feel this.

At eighteen, she chose motherhood over convent life, the only two options she remembers being conscious of, and by twenty-five, she was the mother of four children. But she continued to feel a mysterious identity with any group or person having a hard time, and this led to one of her many differences with her husband, who ridiculed her attempts to 'do something' by calling her 'Crusader Rabbit'. So she kept living an expected life, trying to see herself through the eyes of others, even dieting her comfortable body down to the shape society said it was supposed to be, with diet pills prescribed by her obstetrician. Only when she was thirty-three and her three daughters and one son were old enough to be more self-sufficient did she enter a junior college near her new home in California where her husband began taking courses, too. Even then, she worried about his resentment of her new interest, so she studied in the bathroom or at night when he was asleep. When she was elected Student of the Year, he put up a large homemade sign declaring her Wife of the Year. Then he told her that it no longer pleased him for her to go to college, that she could finish out the semester—but no more. But somehow, her first personal success had given her the courage to rebel, and by the time she was thirty-five, she was divorced, living on and off welfare with her children, and trying to finish college part-time.

When the women's liberation movement began, she read each book, pamphlet and essay that came her way. Patriarchy and men in power reminded her of racism and whites in power, which began to explain her feelings. If women's position in the home and the world wasn't natural, she hadn't been so wrong to identify with other groups in trouble after all. When her English professor made clear that only men's conflicts were the proper themes of great literature, she decided she was definitely a feminist. In 1969, when Florence Howe, later to become founder of the Feminist Press, came to speak, she inspired Marilyn's first political action: as part of a group trying to get women writers included in the English department curriculum, Marilyn agitated and organized. At the time, she considered herself a heterosexual feminist, and when she met lesbian feminists, they seemed to her 'unstable'. Their love relationships were not as long as she was accustomed to thinking partnerships should be.

Since she had challenged society's assumptions about women, she began to challenge her own assumptions, too. Perhaps without economic and social pressure to stay in marriages that weren't mutually rewarding, she thought, many heterosexual women's relationships wouldn't be so 'stable' either. For all the suffering of living in a way that society didn't legally bless or even admit, perhaps lesbians were not less stable—just more free.

Curiosity has a way of telling us what we need to know. By 1975, Marilyn had separated from a second husband. She was beginning to understand the soul-killing depth of male dominance and could no longer imagine living with a man. Nonetheless, her conscious mind still assumed she was destined to be, as she put it at the time, 'that least happy of women—a heterosexual feminist who wants to be sexual, but can't speak to a man without a growl'. Then, to her surprise, she fell irresistibly, head-over-heels in love with another woman.

Suddenly, she began to feel an inexplicable sense of rightness and naturalness, as if she was finally living her own life. The world seemed open and 'free-form', unlike her heterosexual past in which everything had 'rules, guidelines, customs and traditions', as she put it. Lesbians suffered from living outside society, but that meant they invented their own society as they went along. Like so many people who discover their true self, she had the odd sensation of suddenly seeing the world in colour, the reverse of many people who become depressed and feel their surroundings fade to grey. As she later wrote:

> I feel about Lesbianism as if I spent forty-three years being colour blind.... At first the sight of the primary colours intoxicated me. I still am, but now I am able to see an ever-widening spectrum. I run around saying, 'Look at all the varying shades of green. How brilliant! How subtle!' Some women, having seen colour all their lives, are not impressed. 'Big deal,' they say. 'I've seen some shades of green that were positively disgusting.'
>
> In my next life when I am a Lifelong Lesbian, I may be blasé about my good fortune, too, though I do not really think so.[13]

She didn't stay with that first lover, but she did form a loving partnership with another 'Lifelong Lesbian', as Marilyn would say. In 1976, they were among the founding mothers of Califia Community, named for the goddess of the once-united land of Mexico and California. For a decade, she helped to organize and run week-long women's retreats on the hard subjects of class, race, homophobia, divisions of age, ethnicity, appearance and able-bodiedness—all the divisions that keep women from working together. About four thousand women passed through these Califia sessions over ten years, and they continue to play crucial roles in keeping women's groups around the country together, in spite of all the societal pressures trying to break them apart.

As for Marilyn herself, she now travels around the country, speaking, working as a conference-organizer with her long-time lover and colleague, Irene Weiss, creating new feminist projects with their vast network of activists and friends, and also visiting Marilyn's seven grandchildren. Since 1982, she has written warm and wise columns that, in *The Lesbian News* and in book form, have helped many other women find their true selves. It is from these essays—along with our telephone talks from her stops around the country—that her words here are taken. One of her chief hopes is to help establish bodily integrity as a fundamental human right: a legal umbrella that would guarantee women's right to make sexual choices without punishment, the right to reproductive freedom, protection for poor women against being used as surrogate mothers, for poor people against pressure to become sources of transplants and transfusions for the well-to-do—all the ways in which bodies are owned or exploited. It would make clear, once and for all, for both women and men, that the power of the state stops at our skins.

Most recently, she has come to see incest and other childhood sexual abuse as, in her words, 'a preverbal sexual terrorism that breaks the female spirit, and makes women continue to believe terrible things will happen to them if they tell men's secrets'. Neither the new spirit of freedom in Eastern Europe or the older democracy here will mean anything, she believes, as long as 'a three-year-old child can't find protection in our courts of law'. It's one of the many sources of anger that make her refuse to become 'mellow' and insist on 'growing old ungraciously'.

Marilyn's spiral of self-esteem began, in the time-honoured phrase of the lesbian and gay cultures, with 'coming out'. Our sexuality is such a deep, spontaneous and powerful part of our core identity that the conscious or unconscious need to falsify it is a little death. But concealing any part of our true self is a partial death, too. The act of 'coming out' has been invested with such honesty and courage by so many millions of women and men that it has become a paradigm for discovering a true self. Whether our inner truth is a false childhood shame or a true talent, a group identity or a unique one, we all need to 'come out' as who we really are.

## Gandhi's Transformation

About being called 'Mahatma', the Great One, Gandhi wrote in his autobiography, 'Often the title has deeply pained me; and there is not a moment I can recall when it may be said to have tickled me.'[14] His hope and his heart were with average people and ordinary actions. 'I have not a shadow of a doubt that any man or woman can achieve what I have,' he insisted.[15] Only if we remember his life before he became the man we know can we learn what he wanted to teach.

Mohandas K. Gandhi was born into a family who were grocers by caste at the peak of the British Empire, in an India that was even then in its second century of domination. As a boy, he memorized such sayings as:

> Behold the mighty Englishman
> He rules the Indian small,
> Because being a meat-eater
> He is five cubits tall.

Later, as a teenager, he himself would secretly eat meat for a year, though this meant lying to his family and violating his own morals, even having nightmares about tortured animals; all because he hoped to become superior like the English. Nonetheless, he remained so unconfident that he went home directly from school every day 'lest anyone should poke fun at me'.

At thirteen, he married a girl of his own age by their parents' arrangement, as was the custom, and did his best to dominate her, as a proper husband should. When she was too spirited to obey, he became both jealous of her sexually and envious of her strength. He himself was still afraid to sleep in the dark. When he once went to a brothel, he was so shy that the prostitute lost patience and asked him to leave. 'I felt as though my manhood had been injured,' as he wrote later, 'and wished to sink into the ground for shame.'[16] He ascribed even his mediocre accomplishments as a student to luck. 'I had not any high regard for my ability,' as he later explained. 'The least little blemish drew tears from my eyes. When I merited, or seemed to the teacher to merit, a rebuke, it was unbearable for me.'[17]

After graduating from high school, he went on to college with a vague idea of becoming a doctor, but failed every course. Only the financial help of an older brother, plus his young wife's willingness to sell her jewellery, paid for his decision to go to London, where a barrister's degree was notoriously easy to earn and would allow him to put that magical phrase, 'England-returned', on his calling card. But once in that cold and unfamiliar country, he was so ashamed of his ignorance of English manners, his embarrassingly homemade suits, and his inability to recite in class that he sometimes went hungry out of reluctance to ask for vegetarian food. Determined to learn the secrets of English superiority, he moved in with a family, bought Bond Street pinstripes and high collars he could ill afford, and even took lessons in French, the violin and the fox-trot. As he would later admit, he 'wasted a lot of time and money trying to become an Englishman'. Even the Bhagavad Gita was encountered for the first time when two English brothers asked for his help with reading it in the original Sanskrit, though Gandhi himself was more skilled in English. Only his continuing ineptitude made him give up his social lessons, sell his violin, and retreat to cheap rooms where he did his own cooking. Gradually, he began to feel more comfortable, as if his failures had been the signals of a true self. Though he maintained his proper English suits for many years, he also began to call his shyness his 'shield', for it kept him away from pursuits that felt false and also forced him into a simplicity of speech.

Once he was back in India after finishing his studies, however, even his London degree couldn't make him a success at practising law. Finally, he took an assignment in South Africa, and there, his willingness to learn bookkeeping and his fear of conflict combined to produce his first success: a negotiated settlement in a financial lawsuit. It was his second discovery that what seemed a weakness in one context could also be strength in another. 'My joy was boundless,' he wrote. 'I had learned to find out the better side of human nature and to enter men's hearts...to unite parties riven asunder.'[18] Flushed with his first success at twenty-seven, he brought his wife and sons to live with him in a large English-style house with servants, a perquisite he had insisted upon as part of his job, and asked that they adapt to this 'civilized' (that is, European) way of eating, sitting in stiff-back chairs, and dealing with servants, even though it made them supremely uncomfortable. But one day on a train, Bond Street cutaway, first-class ticket and all, Gandhi ran afoul of the colour bar and was thrown off in the dust. It was a rude awakening. No matter how successfully he assumed a false self, he realized, his skin colour would always humiliate him, and make him 'a coolie' in the eyes of white South Africans. Once that shock was absorbed, he decided that if he were going to be dishonoured as an Indian, he would live as an Indian. Moreover, he would live simply in order to be truly independent. After a racist barber refused to cut his hair, for instance, he began to cut it himself. In order to be free of the need for servants, he began to wash, starch and iron his high-collared shirts himself.

But Western writers like Ruskin, Thoreau and Tolstoy instructed even this rebellion. It was as if Gandhi needed their theories to support his own values that had begun with vegetarianism and continued in a non-hierarchical view of all life forms. But unlike many revolutionaries, this support for non-violence made him realize that adopting violent means would be an imitation of his adversaries. Though he challenged the hierarchy of skin colour on behalf of Indians only and not the black majority of South Africans, he did become a leader who was known for his ability to bring people together and negotiate with the powerful. He adopted the traditional Indian dress, founded a small experimental community in which no person turned another into an inferior as a servant, and won many dignified and successful battles for Indian rights in South Africa.

After almost twenty years of practising law and social reform, he returned at forty-five to the disunity that was India in 1915. He was something of a hero, but he also looked at the struggling independence movement with new eyes. It would have to unite Indians across many barriers to be successful. There were fourteen major language areas, with at least as much cultural diversity as in Europe, seven major religions with hundreds of caste and other divisions within them, and an economic ladder that stretched from millions of impoverished villagers to the heads of 562 princely states who lived more opulently than (but at the pleasure of) the British Raj. At the same time, the few Indians who went to a university learned more about England than India, and even the leaders of the movement for independence were urban and English-educated. Many Indians had come to believe in Indian 'disorder' versus European 'order', in Indian backwardness versus British excellence, and in their own inability to unify versus the tradition of The Crown. Often, they trusted the British more than they trusted each other. It was a colonized mentality that imprisoned this vast subcontinent more effectively than any army.

Gandhi began to travel in rural India and to call on the urban independence leaders to do the same. He campaigned for the unifying dignity of basics for everyone, whether this meant asking rich Indians to give up jewellery and possessions, or giving poor ones the fundamentals of life for the first time. Everyone was to wear homespun khadi in defiance of British laws against weaving, which were a way of creating a market for their own manufactured cloth, and to practise civil disobedience to other unjust laws. All castes were to be respected as one, all religions as one. He literally turned the hierarchy on its head, not by giving orders but by himself making the bottom rung of the standard of living. He led by example. Even his surprising choice of the Salt Laws as a subject for civil disobedience was meant to unify. Salt was the one staple used more by the poor, who sweated it away by work in the sweltering heat, than by the middle class and rich; yet all Indians were forced to purchase salt from the British instead of harvesting it free from the ocean.

For the first time, there was a movement that began in the villages, not in a British-educated top layer of leaders. A large and populist women's movement had also been struggling for most of a century against such customs as child marriage and sati (the immolation of widows), and Gandhi learned from it and adopted many of its culturally non-violent methods. (Indeed, Gandhi included women to an unprecedented degree, yet also submerged many women's issues—for instance, family planning, which he opposed in favour of abstinence—thus leaving much to be done by an independent women's movement in years to come.) Even the Harijan, or 'untouchable', caste was included, and so were the British themselves. Instead of denying the humanity of the oppressor, Gandhi appealed to that humanity. Though long years of British and also post-Independence Indian religious violence challenged his methods of passive resistance, when the British left peacefully after two hundred years of domination, the world learned a new possibility from this first case of a nation that gained its independence without war. It was an object lesson in ending a cycle of colonial violence, and also in self-esteem. Without self-esteem, the only change is an exchange of masters; with it, there is no need of masters.

As for Gandhi himself, he continued to date his life as 'before' and 'after' what he called 'my experiments with truth'; that is, his efforts to give up a false self and learn to trust a true one. Having experienced the humiliation of hierarchy, he eliminated hierarchy, stopped identifying with the oppressor, and in so doing, discovered an important secret: A leader cannot raise a people's self-esteem by placing himself above them.

Nineteenth-century India or the twentieth-century US, a cultural monolith or a sexual one, freeing a country or freeing female minds and bodies: the lives of Mohandas Gandhi and Marilyn Murphy are very different in detail yet very similar in shape. Both spent half their lives trying to live as a false self, both found their strength only when they followed an inner voice, both taught by example, and both worked to unite people across boundaries. Sometimes, even their provinces are now seen as parallel. The female half of the world is often described as a Third World country: low on capital, low on technology, and labour-intensive, with female bodies controlled as the means of reproduction. It is a psychic nation unifying for a common dream of independence, just as India became a geographical one.

I think if Marilyn Murphy had met Gandhi, she would have recognized a kindred revolutionary. I hope he would have, too. Perhaps when you and I are feeling discouraged, we can think of a radical lesbian feminist as an obedient housewife or Mahatma Gandhi trying to foxtrot in a Bond Street suit, and know that we can find a true strength, too.

**Self-Esteem Is Physical: The Women of Ahmedabad**

In modern India, the women who sell vegetables in the street, roll cigarettes or weave baskets for sale while they nurse their babies, carry construction materials on their heads in human chains at building sites, and perform a thousand other individual, piece-work jobs are called 'self-employed women'. They are the bottom rung of the labour force, but their work is indispensable. In addition to making and distributing many small products, they also mend and resell cooking pots, collect paper from offices and garbage dumps, and pound used nails straight enough to be used again: a human recycling system in a country where everything is used many times.

Not only are they the poorest of India's workers, they are also subject to the special punishments of living in a female body. Girl children are considered so much less valuable than boys that two-thirds of the children who die before age four are girls—the result of infanticide, plus saving scarce food and medical care for boys. Girls are so much less likely to be sent to school that the national female literacy rate is less than half that for males (among these workers, often much less), and their humanity is so minimally acknowledged that killing a wife in order to take another wife—and get another dowry—is one of the major sufferings addressed by the women's movement.

In a world that so devalues them, they have little reason to value themselves—which is why there is so much to learn from their successes.

For years, journalists and government officials in industrial cities like Ahmedabad have been condemning the fact that women do such hard physical labour—but nothing changed. Then in 1971, a young Gandhian labour organizer named Ela Bhatt did something new: she asked the women themselves what they wanted.

As it turned out, they had long been amused and angered by experts with soft hands who said that women shouldn't do such work. It helped feed their families and gave them a small measure of independence, and they were not about to give it up. What they wanted were better conditions in which to do it: safe places to leave their children in; higher wages for their handmade or recycled products and construction jobs; an end to the bribes they had to pay the police for the privilege of selling their wares in the street; and relief from moneylenders who charged murderous interest rates for the few rupees they borrowed to buy vegetables or raw materials each morning and then paid back at the end of each day. Finally, they wanted a secure place to keep their few rupees from husbands who otherwise considered women's earnings their own.

But even as they wished for these things, they also said nothing could be done. They had no faith in each other, no trust in Ela Bhatt, no reason to believe in change. Who would listen to poor and illiterate women?

By the time I first met Ela and some of these women in Ahmedabad in 1978, their Self-Employed Women's Association, whose acronym SEWA also means 'service', was about six years old. They had exposed the corruption of police who demanded bribes, started childcare centres and infant crèches, and even persuaded the Bank of India to let them open a special branch for their small loans and hard-won savings. They themselves pounded the streets for members, put two improvised teller windows in a small room, and literally created a bank. (The problem of illiteracy had been overcome by putting a photograph of each woman on her passbook. 'Maybe we can't read,' as one of them explained with a smile, 'but we can think.') To the surprise even of Ela Bhatt's sponsors, a Gandhian textile workers' union that had considered these women too passive and disparately employed to organize, they were doing better than many more educated workers in traditional unions.

What made the difference? First, an organizer who had lived the problems of being a woman herself, and who listened to each woman as a sister. For the first time, they felt worth listening to. Second, their mutual support and their small but growing list of successes when dealing with corrupt police and dishonest employers. As a lawyer and a skilled organizer, Ela knew the importance of both listening and explaining new alternatives in using demonstrations, the media, and even the courts.

But Ela Bhatt herself thought there had been one crucial turning point. After the work of forming SEWA, Ela suggested the founding group celebrate by taking a holiday together. The women had never done anything separate from their families and children before, but other workers took holidays. Why shouldn't they?

After a discussion, they decided to visit Hindu holy places that were nearby, but farther from home than most of these women had ever been. After much planning and preparation to free them from family obligations, which was not easy to do even for a few hours, Ela hired a rickety bus and they set off.

Everything was fine until they neared a temple that could be reached only by boat. Menstruating women were not allowed in temples, and inevitably, some of the women had their periods. They were sure that if they crossed the river, the boat would capsize to punish them for defying tradition, and since they couldn't swim, everyone would drown.

By appealing to every emotion from curiosity to defiance, Ela finally convinced them to get in the boat and consign themselves to the wide river and fate. They crossed—and nothing happened. After placing their offerings of fruit and flowers in the temple, they crossed back again—and still nothing happened. For the first time in their lives, they had defied the rules that denigrated them—and they had won.

Somehow, everything was connected to that first defiance and victory. If women's bodies were not so 'unclean' and inferior after all, perhaps their work was not so inferior either.

Now, a dozen years later, SEWA is the most powerful women's trade union in India, and one of the largest in the world, with independent grassroots organizations in nine other regions. It offers revolving loan funds to help women farm, set up small businesses, and carve out a small security in a system that offers little hope to those at the bottom. As for Ela Bhatt, she is consulted by the World Bank on grassroots economic development and served for a while in the Indian Parliament. But at heart, she is an organizer and still spends most of her time helping to develop strength and leadership among poor women.

SEWA itself has become a model of self-help and economic empowerment for women throughout the Third World. And even in our own industrialized nation, SEWA is often mentioned as an example to follow wherever poor or otherwise powerless women gather to organize.[19]

But these least valued of women should inspire anyone, anywhere, female or male, who is devalued so deeply that inferiority seems to be inherent in the reality of her or his own body—whether for reasons of race or appearance, disability or age, or anything else.

If feelings of unworthiness are rooted in our bodies, self-esteem needs to start there.

—1992

# ROMANCE VERSUS LOVE

Steinem argues in this essay that as romance has its source in an incompleteness of self, it is unlikely to turn into love: the neediness and low self-esteem of the lovers is the worst adversary of anything deeper and more lasting. She speaks about the commodification of love in the Valentine Day industry, the love of reading romances by readers who are yearning for a wholeness and escape from their feeling of incompleteness. She quotes Simone de Beauvoir who wrote, 'Genuine love ought to be founded on the mutual recognition of two liberties; the lovers would then experience themselves both as self and the other.'[1]

—Ruchira Gupta

Romance. A tale in verse, embodying the adventures of some hero of chivalry.… A fictitious narrative in prose of which the scene and incidents are very remote from those of ordinary life.

Love. That disposition or state of feeling with regard to a person which…manifests itself in solicitude for the welfare of the object, and…delight in his [sic] presence.

—*The Oxford English Dictionary*

## I. UNLEARNING ROMANCE

'I cannot live without my life! I cannot live without my soul!'

—Heathcliff

'Nelly, I am Heathcliff!'

—Catherine

What do you remember about the story of *Wuthering Heights*, whether from the novel, the classic movie, or the myth that has become a part of our culture?

I remember the yearning of two people to be together—and the intensity, the merging, the loss of boundaries when they were. There was an obsessiveness and a sense of fate about these two lifelong lovers that made even the romantic yearnings of Romeo and Juliet seem pale.

In Emily Brontë's novel, their romance begins when they are children. From the moment Heathcliff, a dark-skinned urchin found wandering the streets of Liverpool, is rescued and brought home as an adopted servant by little Catherine's father, they are soul mates. But divided as they grow up by chasms of class and race, their union as adults seems so impossible that Catherine agrees to marry a kind and wealthy neighbour. Humiliated by her idea that marriage to him would 'degrade' her, Heathcliff runs away to sea, and Catherine nearly dies from a fever that is an almost literal lovesickness. By the time a newly prosperous Heathcliff returns three years later, it is too late: Catherine has married Edgar Linton. Heathcliff rages, swears vengeance, and marries Linton's sister to get control of her property and to spite the family—but Catherine knows she is the cause of all this suffering. Torn between her alter ego and her kind husband, and also pregnant, she falls ill but lives long enough to give birth to a daughter.

It's one of the departures of this novel that its heroine dies halfway through it. We then see almost twenty years of Heathcliff raging, mourning and trying to control everything Catherine ever touched. When he finally succeeds, he seems to will himself to die, as if this obsession had been the only thing keeping him alive. At his request, he is buried next to 'my Cathy' at the edge of the moors where they once roamed happily as children, with the facing sides of their coffins cut away so nothing will separate them for eternity.

When this magical novel was first published under the pen name of Ellis Bell in 1847, English critics were shocked by its intimate, romantic focus; a departure from the big canvas, many characters and broad issues that characterized the Victorian novel. When the author was revealed to be the reclusive daughter of a country clergyman, a woman who had died at thirty from consumption and what we would now call anorexia, and who had little experience of life apart from what she had gleaned from voluminous reading, there began generations of scholarly efforts to understand how such a woman could have produced this masterful novel—the first in English, one critic was to say a century later, 'which invites the same kind of attention that we give to Macbeth'.[2] The most fervent part of the search was for the man who was the model for the passionate, brooding and very 'masculine' Heathcliff.

Some literary investigators theorized that Emily Brontë must have carried on an affair with one of her father's curates, almost the only unrelated men around, though there was no evidence for it. Others thought that, like her contemporary Charles Dickens, she had observed a variety of lives around her, copied down character names from gravestones, and stitched together a novelistic quilt from scraps of reality. Still others assumed that Heathcliff's excesses had been copied from Emily's tormented brother, Branwell, who died young from an excess of gin and opium. Whatever his source in reality, many called her an immoral woman for including such a character as Heathcliff in her novel at all. As one scholarly introduction to *Wuthering Heights* admitted: 'Those critics who feel compelled to "explain" a work of art by tracing it to its origins and who assume that the imagination simply adds up experiences in the external world are ill at ease with this novel.'[3]

Only when the most recent wave of feminism brought a less traditional view of women's inner lives into the mainstream of criticism did there begin to be a body of scholars who believed *Wuthering Heights* could have come from one isolated woman's imagination. Long ago, she had given us a major clue when she said, in the guise of Catherine, 'I am Heathcliff.' Emily Brontë was both the capricious, suffering girl who could not escape the restrictions of a female life, and the dark, adventurous, rebellious outsider. Like each of our true selves, her nature was both 'masculine' and 'feminine', but unlike most of us, she lived in such isolation that, far from being handicapped, she seems to have preserved more of that wholeness. Growing up outside schools and conventional society, choosing to be reclusive even by the standards of her own isolated family, she was free to commune with nature on the moors, to turn inward, to learn from an inner universe. Though she read a great deal—novels, poetry, and the many political journals her father brought into the house—she missed the social training that convinces women we must not identify with men—and vice versa.

As her older and more gregarious sister, Charlotte Brontë, explained about both Emily and their younger sister, Anne, who also died young: 'Neither Emily nor Anne was learned; they had no thought of filling their pitchers at the wellspring of other minds; they always wrote from the impulse of nature, the dictates of intuition.'[4]

But it was in Emily that 'masculine' and 'feminine' seemed most perfectly blended; Emily who was the most creative of a gifted family; and Emily in whom Charlotte, herself to become the author of *Jane Eyre* and other classic novels, found endless fascination. 'In Emily's nature,' Charlotte wrote, 'the extremes of vigour and simplicity seemed to meet. Under an...unpretending outside, lay a secret power and fire that might have informed the brain and kindled the veins of a hero.'[5] This fascination began the moment Charlotte found Emily's secret stash of poems and persuaded her retiring sister to let them be published under a pseudonym. As Charlotte later explained, 'Something more than surprise seized me—a deep conviction that these were not common effusions, or at all like the poetry women generally write. I thought them condensed and terse, vigorous and genuine. To my ear, they had also had a peculiar music—wild, melancholy, and elevating.'[6] Her obsession with Emily's enigmatic strength and independent spirit continued long past her sister's death from consumption. After watching Emily hasten her demise by refusing to eat, a means she had often used to gain control over her otherwise dependent life, Charlotte wrote: 'Never in all her life had she lingered over any task that lay before her.... She made haste to leave us. Yet, while physically she perished, mentally she grew stronger.... I have seen nothing like it; but indeed, I have never seen her parallel in anything. Stronger than a man, simpler than a child, her nature stood alone.'[7]

A few years later, when *Wuthering Heights* became popular enough to be reissued in a new edition, Charlotte wrote a preface in which she tried to disarm its critics by first joining their disapproval of its tortured hero ('Whether it is right or advisable to create beings like Heathcliff, I do not know: I scarcely think it is'), then defending her sister by explaining, 'The writer who possesses the creative gift owns something of which he is not always master—something that, at times, strangely wills and works for itself.' Heathcliff, she makes clear, is 'a man's shape animated by demon life'. That demon lived within her quiet sister, who 'rarely crossed the threshold of home'.

Charlotte also defended Emily for endowing Catherine's husband with such 'feminine' traits as 'constancy and tenderness'.

'Some people will think these qualities do not shine so well incarnate in a man as they would do in a woman, but Ellis Bell [Emily's pseudonym] could never be brought to comprehend this notion: nothing moved her more than any insinuation that the faithfulness and clemency, the long-suffering and loving-kindness which are esteemed virtues in the daughters of Eve, become foibles in the sons of Adam.'

Clearly, Emily believed in the presence of all human qualities in both men and women. At the very end of the novel, when Catherine's daughter marries a cousin raised by Heathcliff, thus uniting the two families he had sought to divide and destroy, the union seems to symbolize Emily's hope for future wholeness in both women and men. The romance between Catherine and Heathcliff had been the result of an inner void within each of them, and the story tells of their impossible effort to fill it with the body and soul of the other. Indeed, in Heathcliff, Emily created the perfect vision of a self in which the 'masculine' is totally bereft of the 'feminine': energetic, focused, strong-willed, controlling, even violent, unable to empathize beyond his own boundaries or to love without possessing. Catherine embodied the fate of the 'feminine' without the 'masculine': vulnerable, diffused, too connected, more aware of the needs around her than of her own. In Emily herself, of course, there were both; yet this unity was forbidden. The bond between the lovers who were born of her imagination, as poet and theorist Adrienne Rich has written, 'is the archetypal bond between the split fragments of the psyche, the masculine and feminine elements ripped apart and longing for reunion'.[8]

No wonder the romance of *Wuthering Heights* endures—as do

romantic myths in almost every culture. Indeed, the more patriarchal and gender-polarized a culture is, the more addicted it is to romance. These myths embody our yearning to be whole.

No wonder romance so often begins at a physical distance or across a psychic chasm of class and race, and thrives on death and separation.[9] Projecting our lost qualities onto someone else can be done more easily from a distance.

No wonder romance grows weaker with closeness, dailiness and familiarity. No one can be or give to us the rest of our unique self.

No wonder many women need romance more than men do. Since most human qualities are labelled 'masculine', and only a few are 'feminine'—and even those are marginalized—women have an even greater need to project life-giving parts of themselves onto another human being.

No wonder that, while it lasts, romance brings such an explosive feeling of melting, merging and losing boundaries. We are making love to the rest of ourselves.

Do you fall in love when you're feeling vulnerable or not so good about yourself? When you fall out of love, do you 'crash', as if you had been on a drug? Have you noticed that friendship, shared values, working together, almost anything is more likely to lead to a lasting love than the usual romance—yet you still find yourself thinking this romance will be different? Are you waiting to make basic decisions in your life because those should be determined by a future partner? If you already have a partner, do you spend more time thinking about pleasing and/or improving him or her than pleasing and/or improving yourself? When you're not in a romance, are you prone to too much eating or drinking or other addictions? If the person you are in love with would only change or solve his or her problems, do you feel your problems would be solved, too? Do you feel a 'rush' of adrenaline and power when a coveted person agrees to go to bed with you (more usual for men) or professes love for you (more usual for women)? In general, is your sense of well-being determined more by the state of your love life than by your own life?

If you can answer yes to any of those questions—as so many of us can—then you are still playing a role in some version of the classic script in which romance blooms at a distance, bursts into obsession, and then diminishes into ordinariness—or perhaps unrequited pain. In the true sense of the word's root, *addicere*, 'to give oneself up' or 'to devote or surrender oneself to something habitually or obsessively', romance can become an addiction, and this cycle can repeat itself again and again. That twelve-step programme originated by and for alcoholics, and then expanded to include many other addictions, has now been adapted by those addicted to sex and romance.

But like other addicts, many of us are still in denial: we still believe we can find the rest of ourselves in a foreign substance; that is, in the body and mind of another person. But we didn't invent this dilemma.

Think about it: On the one hand, each of us is born with a full circle of human qualities, and also with a unique version of them. On the other hand, societies ask us to play totalitarian gender roles that divide labour, assign behaviour, provide the paradigm for race and class, and are so accepted that they may be seen as part of nature. Societies have been so intent on creating an elaborate difference where none exists that in many languages, even inanimate objects are genderized; thus, one kind of pen may be 'feminine' (la plume) and another 'masculine' (le stylo). Yet despite all of these pervasive efforts to categorize and limit everyone and everything, the little boy who is ridiculed for crying 'like a girl' doesn't stop feeling sad, he just buries that emotion; and the little girl who is punished for wilfulness as a 'tomboy' just takes that spirit underground. Later, since both have been told that some parts of themselves are appropriate only to the 'opposite sex', they will look for them in other people. In search of inner wholeness, they will try to absorb and possess someone else as Catherine and Heathcliff did—and as you and I probably have done, too.

This polarization of 'feminine' and 'masculine', this internal mutilation of our whole selves, would be cruel enough if its effects went no further, but the two halves aren't really 'halves' at all. Male dominance means that admired qualities are called 'masculine' and are more plentiful, while 'feminine' ones are not only fewer but also less valued. Thus, boys as a group have higher self-esteem because they are literally allowed more of a self and because the qualities they must suppress are less desirable, while girls as a group have lower self-esteem because they are expected to suppress more of themselves and because society denigrates what is left. Once adolescence and hormones hit, this lack of a true self in both sexes, this feeling of being incomplete and perhaps also ashamed of parts of oneself that 'belong' to the opposite sex, combines with society's intensified gender expectations to make many of us construct a false social persona—in a big way. The boy who has been allowed to retain more than the usual amount of self-esteem by his upbringing may resist this tendency, or only pretend to conform; especially if he has an adult model to follow, support for some 'unmasculine' talent, or perhaps a racial, sexual, or other status that strengthens an 'outsider' identity. The girl with exceptional self-esteem may get away with such 'masculine' qualities as assertiveness and tomboyish behaviour—after all, imitation is the sincerest form of flattery, so it's more okay for girls to imitate boys than vice versa—as long as she compensates by becoming a female impersonator in romantic and other social areas. But with low self-esteem, both males and females are likely to seek refuge and approval in exaggerated versions of their gender roles, and thus to become even less complete as they grow up. Inflexibility, dogmatism, competitiveness, aggression, distance from any female quality or person, homophobia, even cruelty and violence, become the classic gender masks of low self-esteem in men. Submissiveness, dependency, the need for male approval, the fear of conflict, self-blame, and an inability to express anger are classic gender masks of low self-esteem in women.

This means that, with low self-esteem, men and women grow more polarized and have more suppressed parts of themselves to project onto others. They then become the objects of an affair, romance, 'falling' in love—all the words we instinctively use to describe the addictive 'rush' and withdrawal of adrenaline that is so different from the steady well-being of love. In a survey of four hundred US psychiatrists by 'Medical Aspects of Human Sexuality', for instance, the majority reported that both women and men with low self-esteem were more likely to be promiscuous, to have difficulty finding fulfilment in sexual relationships, and to be less likely to fall deeply in love.[10] Even among women and men with healthy self-esteem, a temporary setback or insecurity can increase the appeal of romance, whether it's the scared young man going off to war who falls in love with someone he's only known a few days, or the scared pregnant woman who falls in love with her obstetrician. Indeed, any strong gender trigger may create a romantic chimera for a while, from the woman who gets a crush on a man because he leads masterfully on the dance floor, to the man who falls in love with a secretary who is being paid to support him.

In her novel *The Company She Keeps*, Mary McCarthy described this phenomenon in her heroine: 'Now for the first time she saw her own extremity, saw that it was some failure in self-love that obliged her to snatch blindly at the love of others, hoping to love herself through them, borrowing their feelings, as the moon borrowed light. She herself was a dead planet.'[11]

Playwright Sherwood Anderson confessed the same thing from a man's point of view: 'I've never been able to work without a woman to love. Perhaps I'm cruel...I'm like an Irish peasant taking potatoes out of the ground...I take from her. I know damned well I don't give enough.'[12]

But if romance has its source in an incompleteness of self, it's unlikely to turn into love: the neediness and low self-esteem of the lovers is the worst adversary of anything deeper and more lasting. As Linda Sanford and Mary Ellen Donovan report in *Women and Self-Esteem*, low self-esteem is perhaps the single greatest barrier to intimacy. It makes a woman 'terrified of letting someone get too close lest they discover the real her and reject her.'[13] And, of course, men experience the same terror, and often an added fear that dependence on a woman or the discovery of 'feminine' feelings within themselves will undermine their carefully constructed façade of manliness.

Obviously, jealousy also springs from these feelings of inadequacy and incompleteness. It increases as self-esteem diminishes. The more incomplete we feel, the more obsessed we become with owning someone on whom we've projected all our missing qualities, hence the more jealous we become. Yet gender masks of low self-esteem also make us feel more interchangeable with any other woman or man.

This cycle of gender roles, low self-esteem, romance, jealousy, lack of love and intimacy, even lower self-esteem, more exaggerated gender roles, and so on, can be dangerous in every way. As four family therapists found in a study of abusive relationships, it is precisely when men and women conform to traditional roles most rigidly that abuse is most likely to occur. In their words: 'Abusive relationships exemplify, in extremis, the stereotypical gender arrangements that structure intimacy between men and women generally.'[14] And, of course, this violence also has the larger political purpose of turning half the population into a support system for the other half. It polices and perpetuates gender politics by keeping the female half fearful of the moods and approval of the male half. In fact, patriarchy requires violence or the subliminal threat of violence in order to maintain itself. Furthermore, the seeming naturalness of gender roles makes male/female violence seem excusable, even inevitable. As G.H. Hatherill, Police Commander of London, put it: 'There are only about twenty murders a year in London and not all are serious—some are just husbands killing their wives.'[15]

Romance itself serves a larger political purpose by offering at least a temporary reward for gender roles and threatening rebels with loneliness and rejection. It also minimizes the very anti-patriarchal and revolutionary possibility that women and men will realize each other's shared humanity when we are together physically for the sexual and procreative purposes society needs. Finally, it privatizes our hopes and distracts us from making societal changes. The Roman 'bread and circuses' way of keeping the masses happy—and the French saying that 'marriage is the only adventure open to the middle class'—might now be updated. The circus of romance distracts us with what is, from society's point of view, a safe adventure. When it fails, we blame only ourselves.

Perhaps the greatest testimony to the power of this 'feminine/masculine' romantic paradigm is that even same-sex couples are not immune to it. Though lesbians and gay men often create more equal partnerships that opposite-sex couples would do well to learn from—especially now that both feminism and the gay movement have challenged old gender roles—we are all living in the same culture, and most of us were born into families where this pattern was assumed to be the only one. Sometimes, gender roles produce an exaggerated version known as doubling, in which two men together may become twice as aggressive, unempathetic, unavailable for intimacy but promiscuous about sex; or two women together may become twice as passive, dependent on one another, and focused on intimacy, with or without sex. For all the internal and external sufferings of same-gender couples in a biased culture, however, at least society doesn't polarize the partners when they leave home every day, and that in itself allows more freedom to explore new forms of balance.

In short, the internal wholeness that allows one to love both one's self and another, freely and joyously, is hard to find anywhere. On the other hand, the personal wreckage caused by romantic obsession is a feature of our everyday landscape. We have only to open a newspaper in any country of the world to read about someone who has been murdered, beaten, or imprisoned in what is known as a 'crime of passion'. In more than twenty years of speaking on campuses here and in other countries, for instance, I've yet to find one where, within the memory of current students, there wasn't at least one young woman murdered by a jealous lover. Statistically, the man most likely to physically attack or even murder a woman is not a stranger, but someone to whom she is romantically attached. The most dangerous situation for a woman is not an unknown man in the street, or even the enemy in wartime, but a husband or lover in the isolation of their own home. Though women mainly become violent in self-defence or in defence of their children, the power of romantic obsession is so great—and women are so much more subject to it—that even 'feminine' non-violent conditioning can be overcome. When women do commit violent crimes, they are even more likely than a man's to be attributable to romance rather than to economics, whether that means the rare crime in which a woman kills out of jealousy or the more frequent one in which a woman is an accessory to a crime initiated by her husband or lover.

What's wrong with romance is neatly summed up by the Valentine's Day 1991 statistics given to me by a judge in Tennessee.

In his county courthouse that services Knoxville and its environs, there were, on that one day, thirty applications for marriage licences, sixty applications for divorce, and ninety applications for orders of protection against violent spouses.

Will self-esteem cause the withering away of romance? Yes—but only in its current form. After all, romance is one additional very important thing: the most intense form of curiosity. If we weren't so needy, so full of illusions about a magic rescue, so hooked on trying to own someone—in other words, if the conscious goal of romance were stretching our understanding of ourselves and others, and not, as it was for Catherine and Heathcliff, looking for the completion of our souls—romance could be a deep, intimate, sensual, empathetic way of learning: of seeing through someone else's eyes, feeling with their nerve-endings, absorbing another culture or way of life from the inside, stretching our boundaries, and bringing into ourselves a wider view of the world. If there were equality of power and high self-esteem among women and men, or between two lovers of the same gender, both could have the pleasure of learning and of teaching in this all-five-senses way— without feeling incomplete, angry or abandoned when romance has run its course.

In the meantime, romance remains among the experiences most written about but least understood. But it's beginning to be demythologized and taken more seriously. Psychologist Charlotte Davis Kasl compares its symptoms ('mood swings...distortions of reality') to those of manic-depressive disorders.[16] In many cultures it is 'a sacred form of insanity, as sacred as cows are in India', as family therapist Frank Pittman has written.[17] Like every other kind of illness, romance tells us a lot about what is lacking in us—and what to do about it. If, for example, we think about episodes from our own personal romantic histories, we can learn what we're missing, and then consider what we need to do to grow and change. I've contributed a memory of mine in the hope that it will lead you to meditate on one of your own.

Like Heathcliff as a lost child and Catherine as a six-year-old, or like Dante who fell in love with the real Beatrice when both were only eight, children, too, are vulnerable to romance. They're too young for sex and hormones to have much to do with it, but not too young to be restricted by gender and so begin to yearn for wholeness. I remember spending second-grade recesses watching a kind, quiet, dark-haired boy as he ran in the cold with no mittens and a hand-me-down coat. It's the first time I remember feeling 'in love', and we exchanged serious Valentines. Only now do I understand that I was watching a part of myself race across that playground reserved for boys while girls played quietly by a wall, or that his poverty made him an outsider, and therefore someone I could identify with. Only now do I notice that this first romance came just after a teacher had insisted I could not possibly have written my Thanksgiving poem because its refrain (something like 'Not only for the dead but for the living') was too 'adult'.

I realize that I kept on falling in love with men who were outsiders, particularly those doing work I longed for myself but assumed I could only do by helping them. I also fell in love with their families, since I was longing for parents, too. Fortunately, I chose kind men with good hearts who loved me back—whether due to good luck or the self-respect my mother had tried to instill in me—and so we remained friends even after the intensity of romance was gone. In this way, I proceeded through college and beyond, trying on the name and life of each man I thought I might marry—thought I would have to marry eventually if I was to be a whole person—and acquired one of women's survival skills: getting men to fall in love with us, a form of self-protection that is also a female version of men's sexual conquering. (I'm sure that, as long as shopping and romance are two of women's few paths to a sense of power and well-being in this culture, both will continue to be addictive—and for the same reason.) But since we really believed then that a husband would decide the rest of our lives, marriage became a decision almost impossible to make. If it closed off all other decisions, then it was like a little death. I'll definitely get married, I kept thinking, but not right now. There's this one thing I want to do first... Fortunately, feminism came along to help me and millions of others try to become ourselves, with or without marriage; to understand, in the brilliant phrase of some anonymous feminist, that we could 'become the men we wanted to marry'. I realized that everyone didn't have to live the same way, and this led to a more personal discovery: I was happy. If life is what happens while we are making other plans, I had found work I loved and a chosen family of friends while I was waiting for a mythical future.

But sometimes in the middle of life, as Dante said, we come upon 'a shadowed forest...dense and difficult'. That's where I found myself at the end of my forties. Having chosen a particularly insecure, stretched-thin kind of life in a movement trying to change the oldest power difference, but with relatively little power to do it, I had spent most of two decades getting on a treadmill of travelling, organizing, fund-raising, lobbying, working on *Ms.* magazine, and generally doing a triage of emergencies every morning—then falling off the treadmill into bed every night only to get back on it the next day. Though I was privileged to be working in this movement that had given me life and friends I loved, I had less and less time to replenish lost energy—or even to pick up my drycleaning. Pressure is cumulative. In retrospect, I was redoing the grisly experiment in which a frog, dropped in hot water, jumps out and saves itself; but a frog put in water that is heated very gradually stays there and boils to death. After many years in varying kinds of hot water, I was well on my way to becoming the second frog.

Into this time of exhaustion came a man different from others I had known. Instead of working in fields where progress was measured by change in people, he lived in a world where progress was measured in numbers and things. Contrary to my habit of keeping former lovers as chosen family, which seemed odd to many people, his alienation from women who had been his important romances seemed odd to me. Unlike other men in my life, who were as interested in my work as I was in theirs, and who took as much pleasure in finding books, articles or movies that I might like as I did in doing the same for them, this man answered questions about his own life and childhood, but didn't know how to ask them of someone else.

On the other hand, he had traits I found magnetic. For one thing, he had enormous energy and a kind of Little-Engine-That-Could attitude towards his work that I found very moving. Being work-obsessed, too, he didn't mind all my travelling and crazy schedules. For another, he made every social decision (via his staff), so all I had to do was show up, look appropriate, listen, relax at dinners, dance, laugh at his wonderfully told jokes—whatever was on his agenda. I found this very restful. Since I had been helplessly recreating my caretaking pattern left over from childhood, he seemed the perfect answer: someone I couldn't take care of. For a third, he was miserable and said he wanted to change his life, to use his considerable power in new and creative ways. Since I was hooked on helping people change as a way of proving that I was alive and valuable, a man who said he was miserable was irresistible. Finally, I was just so…tired. When I arrived at the airport late one night to find that he had sent a car, its sheltering presence loomed out of all proportion. Remember the scene in *Bus Stop* when Marilyn Monroe, a desperate singer in a poor café, wraps herself in the warm, rescuing sheepskin jacket of her cowboy lover? Well, that was the way I felt sinking into that car.

So I reverted to a primordial skill that I hadn't used since feminism had helped me to make my own life: getting a man to fall in love with me. As many women can testify, this is alarmingly easy, providing you're willing to play down who you are and play up who he wants you to be. In this case, I was aided by my travel and his work and social schedule, which left us with little time to find out how very different we were. And also by something I didn't want to admit: a burnout and an erosion of self so deep that outcroppings of a scared sixteen-year-old had begun to show through. Like a friend who lost weight and, with the burning away of her body fat, re-experienced an anaesthetic that had been stored in it from an operation years before, I had lost so much energy and hope that I was re-experiencing romantic rescue fantasies that had been forgotten long ago.

The only problem was that, having got this man to fall in love with an inauthentic me, I had to keep on not being myself. Thus, I had to ignore the fact that the cost of a casually purchased painting on his wall was equal to what I had come up with for movement groups in years of desperate fund-raising—and was by a famously misogynist artist at that. I had to suppress the thought that his weekend house cost more than several years' worth of funds for the entire women's movement in this country—and maybe a couple of other countries besides. If I was to be his companion, I had to ignore how obliterated most of my chosen family felt in the company and conversation he enjoyed; indeed, how marginalized they made me feel, too. If I was to be properly appreciative for the advice he gave to me and some of the women I worked with—advice I'm sure he thought of as helpful—I had to forget that, like a gourmet recipe for people with no groceries, it had no practical application. Indeed, even the laughter we first so delightfully shared turned out to be generated by very different senses of humour: his centred around jokes he collected in a notebook and recited wonderfully, complete with ethnic accents; mine was improvised and had a you-had-to-be-there perishability.

I'm sure you know what's coming. So did all my friends. But it took me much longer. Having for the first time in my life made a lover out of a man who wasn't a friend first—my mistake, not his, since I was the one being untrue to myself—I had a huge stake in justifying what I had done. When he supported the same policies and hierarchies that I was working to change, I thought: Nobody said we had to have the same views. When I told him about a trip I'd made to raise a few thousand dollars for a battered women's shelter that was about to close down, and he in the next breath celebrated an unexpected six-figure cheque that, he joked, would buy a good dinner, I said to myself: It's not his fault he can't empathize—and besides, everyone can change. When a small inner voice began to miss the comfort and eroticism that comes with empathy and sensuality, I thought: If I treat him as I want to be treated, this can change, too. In other words, I made all the classic errors of romance, including one I'd never made before: loving someone for what I needed instead of for what he was. Far from being a light in my Dantesque 'shadowed forest', this relationship became a final clue that I was really lost.

I got lonely and depressed—and then more lonely and more depressed. When I finally tried to voice these feelings that I'd been having all along but not voicing, he got mystified—and then angry. But there's something to be said for hitting bottom: as with swimming, it may be the only way to propel oneself back up again. To quote Dante, let me 'retell the good discovered there'.

After two years, when my last bit of energy and faith in my own judgement was fast disappearing, I finally got down past the scared sixteen-year-old and came to a clear childhood voice that actually said, 'Are you going to condemn yourself to this?' It was such a surprise that it made me laugh. Of course, my well-socialized adult self ignored it for quite a while—but it was the beginning.

Slowly, I began to realize that there might have been a reason why I was attracted to someone so obviously wrong for me. If I had been drawn to a man totally focused on his own agenda, maybe I needed to have an agenda of my own. Finally, I began to make time to write. If I had felt comforted by the elaborate organization of his life, maybe I needed some comfort and organization in my own. Therefore, I enlisted the help of friends to take the stacks of cardboard boxes out of my apartment and started the long process of making it into a pleasant place to live. I even began to save money for the first time in my life. If I had been drawn to simple-minded fun and dancing, maybe I should get off the treadmill and ask myself the revolutionary question: What do I enjoy? Finally, I interrupted my triage of emergencies and started taking the initiative to do a few things I loved. If I had glossed over the world's most obvious differences in values (for instance, he advocated trade with a government I got arrested for protesting against), maybe I should have a more realistic idea of what distances I could bridge. I began to focus my energy on what I might be able to do—and to question why I was so often drawn to attempting what I couldn't. Finally, if I had been interested for the first time in my life in a man who really didn't know what other people were thinking or feeling, perhaps I had to face the fact that I had the usually 'feminine' disease of being empathy-sick—of knowing other people's feelings better than my own. It was a crucial signal that I needed to look inward for solutions instead of outward—a change of which this book is a part.

And perhaps most of all, if I had fallen in love with a powerful man, I had to realize that I was in mourning for the power women need and rarely have, myself included.

I don't mean to make this a neat ending. Romances don't have them. I had deceived him by deceiving myself, and I'm still working on what I learned. But I do know that I chose an opposite as a dramatic example of what I missed in myself. Even allowing for my dissembling, perhaps that's what he was doing, too.

Clearly, romance can arrive with all its obsession whenever we're feeling incomplete, at any age or station of life—and as I can testify, even when we know better. We hurt both ourselves and other people when we become who they want us to be instead of who we really are. Nonetheless, the prospect of getting unhooked from this obsession sometimes creates as much anxiety as giving up any addiction: Where will that 'rush' of excitement come from? Who will we become?

I think the truth is that finding ourselves brings more excitement and well-being than anything romance has to offer, and somewhere, we know that. Think of the joy of self-discovery: solving a problem, making a bookcase, inventing a dance step, losing oneself in a sport, cooking for friends, writing a poem—all by reaching within for a vision and then making it real. As for who we will be, answer is: We don't know; we are on the edge of history. But we do know that growth comes from saying yes to the unknown.

Donna Jensen, a friend and an expert on how we relate to one another—in couples, families and organizations—gave me this list of past excesses and the golden mean that is the future:

'Masculine' Extreme
Wholeness
'Feminine' Extreme
Domineering
Creative
Victimized
Angry
Relaxed
Depressed
Dictates
Invites
Begs or schemes
Knows everything
Curious
Knows nothing
Arrogant

Attentive
Shut down, numb
Out of touch with one's own feelings
Draws self-wisdom from feelings
Overwhelmed by one's own feelings
Unwilling to show weakness
Flexible
Unwilling to show strength
Ignores own mistakes or blames others
Learns from mistakes
Makes excuses or obsesses about mistakes
Feels superior
Feels equal
Feels inferior

When the choice is so clear, who wouldn't say yes to a whole self in the centre?

To figure out more personally what you need to do to get there, try this exercise:

Write down—in whatever order or form they come to you—all the things you want in an ideal lover.

You have just described the rest of yourself

## II. LEARNING LOVE

'I have now been married ten years.... I am my husband's life as fully as he is mine.... To talk to each other is but a more animated and an audible thinking.'

—*Jane Eyre*

Charlotte Brontë felt so close to Emily that the tragically bad notices for *Wuthering Heights* kept her from enjoying the generally good ones for her own first novel, *Jane Eyre*, published only a few months later. For her part, Emily was such a private person that she talked almost only with Charlotte. And talk they did. Each evening after supper while pacing around the parlour table 'like restless wild animals', they discussed their own writing projects and their revolutionary theory of the novel. As poets, they wanted to go beyond the realistic observation of events that had been the novel's mainstay thus far ('more real than true', as Charlotte once said of Jane Austen), and try for poetic power in language and psychological revelation in narrative. These long nightly talks between two immensely talented sisters still in their twenties, as critic Q.D. Leavis was to observe more than a hundred years later, 'led to the novel's becoming the major art form of the nineteenth century'.[18] But here the similarity between these two women ended. In spite of sharing everything from parentage to professional dreams, and even with the uncommon influence each had upon the other, these two women had such different inner lives—and from them, created such different characters and ideas of love and power— that they are still among the best testimonies to the unique self in each of us. Unlike Emily's protagonists, Charlotte's never searched for romantic completion through others; and unlike Emily's only novel, Charlotte's didn't end with the hint that love was a subject for the distant future. In *Jane Eyre* as in her other novels, Charlotte made self-completion the goal, the struggle to preserve an independent spirit the underlying tension, and loving oneself the only path to loving others. 'One of the impressive qualities of Charlotte Brontë's heroines, the quality that makes them more valuable to the woman reader than Anna Karenina, Emma Bovary, and Catherine Earnshaw combined,' as Adrienne Rich wrote, 'is their determined refusal to be romantic.'[19]

Of course, this may come as a surprise to many who saw the romance-addicted Hollywood version of *Jane Eyre.* It filtered out all but the novel's central episode—and distorted even that. What's left is the barest plotline of a poor young governess who falls in love with her rich employer, discovers he has concealed a mad first wife in the attic, runs away because there can be no legal marriage, and then returns after the wife has been conveniently killed in a fire that also blinds the man, thus giving the governess a chance to be a selfless caretaker for the rest of her life. But if that were Charlotte Brontë's message, she would have gone down in history as simply another creator of the Gothic novel—that poor-young-woman and rich-older-man standby that depends for its zing on sex plus a woman's inability to get rich on her own. Gothic romances provide for many women readers what sports and war stories do for many men: a fantasy of power.

In the real novel, however, Jane doesn't meet Mr Rochester until a quarter of the way through the story. By then, the reader is already hooked on seeing the world through the clear eyes of a very well-centred heroine. Jane Eyre is one of the first female versions of the classic hero's journey from adolescence to maturity—and an amazingly up-to-date one at that. From her first appearance as a ten-year-old orphan thrown on the mercies of a well-to-do aunt and cousins who humiliate her, to her graduation from a charity school where poor young women are turned into governesses for the wealthy, Jane shows herself to be one of those rare young girls who escape the fate society holds in store. Perhaps Jane's status as an orphan saved her by giving her such good reason to harden herself against the expectations of others, or perhaps her harsh circumstances placed her as far outside convention as the Brontës themselves were. In any case, she is rebellious from the beginning.

When Jane arrives at her aunt's house as a lonely little girl, for instance, she is advised to put up with anything and act grateful, but her child's sense of honesty won't let her. When 'the young master', her teenage cousin, hurls a book at her head to show that she is a beggar with no right to use the family library, she calls him all kinds of imaginative names. When her aunt locks her up as punishment, she gets sick from the sheer injustice of it. Strengthened and emboldened by the motherly affection of a servant, Jane confronts her cruel aunt-by-marriage with all the weapons in her small arsenal: 'I'm glad you are no relation of mine. I will never call you aunt again as long as I live. I will never come to see you when I am grown up; and if anyone asks me how I liked you, and how you treated me, I will say the very thought of you makes me sick, and that you treated me with miserable cruelty.'

Not only does she express anger, but she's not guilty about it: 'Ere I had finished this reply, my soul began to expand, to exult, with the strangest sense of freedom, of triumph, I ever felt. It seemed as if an invisible bond had burst and that I had struggled out into unhoped-for liberty.' It's little wonder that women readers taught to swallow angry words have loved this heroine who doesn't.

Branded a liar and sent to a Spartan school whose headmaster wants 'to mortify in these girls the lusts of the flesh', she has the good sense to form alliances with a kind teacher and a classmate who help her to survive—a sort of feminist underground within the school's patriarchy. Yet she knows they are not the ultimate authority either. Though still only ten, she has enough moral compass to disagree with this older classmate on the Christian wisdom of turning the other cheek. 'I must resist those who punish me unjustly,' she explains. 'It is as natural as that I should love those who show me affection, or submit to punishment when I feel it is deserved.' Indeed, this gift for seeing herself in perspective allows her to be the 'I' of her own story. It's almost impossible to imagine Heathcliff or Catherine as a narrator. At eighteen, having received an education and survived many hazards, Jane explains: 'I desired liberty...change, stimulus...at least a new servitude!' In this spirit of adventure she places an ad for a position as governess and becomes the teacher of a young French girl who is the ward (and illegitimate daughter) of the infamous Mr Rochester.

As we all know, she falls in love with him. According to Adrienne Rich: 'Jane, young, inexperienced, and hungry for experience, has to confront the central temptation of the female condition—the temptation of romantic love and surrender.'[20] But even with all the cards of worldly power stacked against her, Jane doesn't project longed-for qualities of her own onto this man: to a miraculous degree for Victorian England, she has refused to suppress them. Instead, she tries to understand him as an individual through long evenings of conversation in which, as intellectual equals despite their twenty-year age difference, they talk about everything from her paintings of internal landscapes to his affair with the woman who gave birth to her young student. When their first love scene does come about, it is after she saves his life, not vice versa. She wakes him from a smoke-drugged sleep (a fire set, as the reader will soon discover, by his mad first wife during a rare attempt at escape). He then confesses that he had known at first sight that 'you would do me good...delight...my very inmost heart'.

But, as we come to understand, this romantic focus on his own needs doesn't bode well. He later tries many deceptions: lying about his interest in another woman to make Jane jealous; trying to redesign her with clothes and jewellery; and finally, tricking her into confessing romantic feelings for him. He does succeed in becoming, as Jane says, 'my whole world; and more than the world; almost my hope of heaven', but by that time, both she and the reader have the uneasy sense that this romance is doomed. Though the existence of his first wife is revealed only on their wedding day, it isn't just propriety that makes Jane refuse his entreaties to flee to France and live with him. By the time he finally tells her the truth about this invalid wife kept in the attic—a wealthy West Indian he had married partly from greed and partly from lust—Jane is clear-sighted enough to understand that this romantic story he relates in a last-ditch bid for her sympathies, a tale of instant attraction and eventual revulsion, reveals a pattern that has doomed other women in his life and will doom her, too.[21]

'Hiring a mistress is the next worse thing to buying a slave,' Rochester had said in explaining his unhappy years in Europe while legally chained to a mad wife at home; 'both are often by nature, and always by position, inferior: and to live familiarly with inferiors is degrading. I now hate the recollection of the time I passed with Celine, Giacinta, and Clara.' Jane realizes that 'if I were so far to forget myself...as...to become the successor of these poor girls, he would one day regard me with the same feeling which now in his mind desecrated their memory'. Even his illegitimate daughter he refers to as 'a dancer's bastard'. Surrendering to romance, Jane realizes, might eventually reduce her, too, to a mad woman in the attic.

So, though she suffers enormous pain at leaving him, she flees this powerful, fascinating man with whom she has become so enmeshed—not as a Gothic heroine preserving her honour, but as a real woman saving her true self. With just enough money to take the first coach anywhere, she finds herself in a strange village and becomes ill from wandering in the cold rain. A young clergyman and his sisters rescue her. After she is well again and working as a teacher of farmers' children, she dreams of Rochester sometimes—but has no intention of returning. Better to be 'a village schoolmistress, free and honest,' she explains, than, 'fevered with delusive bliss one hour—suffocating with the bitterest tears of remorse and shame the next.'

There is one more temptation: the very modern one of giving her life to the cause of a high-minded husband. Asked by the young clergyman to marry him and go to India, she recognizes the coldness and egotism with which he assumes that her life should be secondary to his missionary work. 'If I were to marry you,' she tells him, 'you would kill me. You are killing me now.' He is shocked and calls her 'unfeminine'. Shouldn't a woman sacrifice herself to a husband's good cause? It's one of many questions that love would answer differently than romance.

But Jane shows her gratitude to this clergyman and his two sisters who saved her life. When an uncle dies and leaves her a tidy sum of money, she insists on sharing it equally with them. She also keeps enough money to be independent and refuses to sacrifice herself to her students. 'I want to enjoy my own faculties,' she explains, 'as well as to cultivate those of other people.' Thus she has work, people she loves, and even—that great rarity for a woman— financial independence, when, in a mystical experience, she hears the sound of Edward Rochester's voice calling her name across the miles. She is now ready to hear it.

With the exception of Mister in *The Color Purple*, perhaps no male character is more changed by events over the course of a novel than the one she now finds. His injury and blindness from a fatal fire set by his wife are the least of it. He has a new acceptance of much that is outside his control. Instead of anger at what has been taken away from him, he appreciates what is left, as if blindness had focused his view inward and allowed him to see himself for the first time. For her part, Jane tells him, 'I love you better now, when I can be really useful to you, than I did…when you disdained every part but that of the giver and protector.'

Their sensuousness and sensitivity together are very moving. Their long talks are as interesting as their earlier ones, but without the intellectual jousting. Their whimsy and tenderness together are a long way from the imbalance of a Gothic novel. Because they are two unique people who act loving towards each other, we believe Jane when she says, after one child and a decade of marriage at the end of the novel: 'To be together is for us to be at once as free as in solitude, as gay as in company.'

It's not easy to generalize about love. Like each person who feels its invisible filaments stretching to another person, it is unique in each instance. Unlike romance, whose plots are uniform enough to be conveyed by shorthand—'if-I-can't-have-you-no-one-will', 'transitional affair', 'middle-age crazy', 'the other woman', 'wartime romance', and so on—love has no standard storyline and no agenda except to deepen the joys and cushion the blows of very individual lives. As Robin Morgan sums up in *The Anatomy of Freedom*, 'Hate generalizes, love specifies.'[22] And romance generalizes, too. When we look for a missing part of ourselves in other people, we blot out their uniqueness. Since most of us have been deprived along gender lines, we generalize about the 'opposite sex' (or about any group that becomes 'the mysterious other'), thus rendering it a blank screen on which we project our hopes (in romance) or our fears (in hate). No wonder romance turns so easily to hate, and vice versa.

But characteristics of love hold as true for lesbian and gay couples, who may be love's pioneers in our own time, as for Charlotte Brontë's daring nineteenth-century lovers. As described by those who experience them, they are remarkably similar to the marks of high self-esteem: Each partner feels loved for an authentic self. Jane Eyre had to discover the independent part of herself through adventure, and Rochester found the dependent part of himself through tragedy. Romance, on the other hand, is about possessing and changing, and that's the way people discuss it. The man who falls in love with a strong and independent woman and then tries to tame her, for instance, is not loving but conquering— a common romantic plot ever since *The Taming of the Shrew*. The woman who is obsessed by the question 'How can I change him?' is not centred in her own life but trying to control his—a plot that's common when women marry their lives instead of leading them.

Each one knows she or he could get along without the other— but doesn't wish to. Free choice is essential to love. We can't say yes to anyone unless we can also say no. Catherine and Heathcliff could do neither. Jane could stay with Rochester only after she was sure she could survive on her own. To be locked in an intimacy one can't leave, for whatever reason, is to eventually feel resentment: what Camus described as 'an autointoxication—the evil secretion, in a sealed vessel, of prolonged impotence'.[23] Which is why, as Clare Boothe Luce once explained: 'With the equality of the sexes, there will be a lot more love in the world.'[24] There is plenty of room for playfulness, lightness and humour. When two realities bump up against each other in intimacy, romance views the contradictions with anger or disillusionment, but love acknowledges them with humour. Romance is inflexible because it tries to predict and control, while love is open-handed and can improvise. Perhaps that's why phrases like 'I married him because he made me laugh', 'We laugh a lot', and 'Joking about my day with her always makes it better' are so often heard when people try to describe the otherwise indescribable feeling of love. No wonder *Jane Eyre* has passages that make us smile, but *Wuthering Heights* does not.

Each partner feels empathy for the other. Between the 'masculine' extreme of focusing only on oneself (for instance, Heathcliff taking out his need for vengeance by marrying Catherine's sister-in-law) and the 'feminine' one of focusing only on other people (for instance, Catherine immobilized between Heathcliff and her husband), there is a midpoint of empathy and balance. Each partner maintains a strong internal 'centre', yet can also see life through the other's eyes. Charlotte Brontë embodies this image quite literally by having Jane 'see' for the blinded Rochester. She takes pleasure in reading to him, describing the countryside, the weather—and he, who had been unable to accept help even from his servants, accepts this service because he feels her pleasure in it. Because we can imagine Rochester feeling the same pleasure in being Jane's 'eyes' if their positions were reversed—a big change from all the romances that are far too 'gendered' to be reversible—we know Jane isn't just one more woman in a caretaking role. As Simone de Beauvoir wrote, 'Genuine love ought to be founded on the mutual recognition of two liberties; the lovers would then experience themselves both as self and the other.'[25]

Love is not about power. Romance is a means to the end of self-completion, but love is an end in itself. Or, as Margaret Anderson put it, 'In real love, you want the other person's good. In romantic love you want the other person.'[26] If we love someone, we want them to continue being the essence of themselves. If so, then we can't own, absorb, or change them. We can only help them to become what they already are. When we argue with someone we love, for instance, it's more about trying to make ourselves understood than trying to win. 'Perhaps that's what love is,' as essayist and biographer Phyllis Rose said, 'the momentary or prolonged refusal to think of another person in terms of power.'[27]

Of course, everything is a journey, and nothing is a destination. But it seems to be true that once we are past the early stages of absorbing parental love, some core of self-esteem is a vital preface to allowing ourselves to feel loved by others.

Take, as lawyers would say, a hypothetical case: Suppose the perfect lover was to suddenly appear. Without a core feeling of self-esteem, this perfection would soon be marred: What if he or she sees beneath my façade to who I really am? Jealousy would set in: Someone 'better' than I am will surely come along. So would possessiveness: If I lose this person, I will lose the only one who loves me—since I do not. With really low self-esteem, we might even bypass these steps and go straight to devaluing the lover: If he loves me, there must be something wrong with him. If she went to bed with me, she would go to bed with anyone. In the immortal words of Groucho Marx, 'I wouldn't want to belong to any club that would accept me as a member.' All this sounds like common sense—but unfortunately, it isn't common. There are many more people trying to meet the right person than to become the right person. The genius of *Jane Eyre* was in showing us that the wrongness or rightness of a lover depends partly on our readiness to appreciate what is unique and best in him or her. We may turn a wrong one into a right one—and vice versa—by how we feel about ourselves. But our world is no more ready to hear that message than Charlotte Brontë's was.

So here we are, locked in ideas of the romantic rescue, the magical 'other'. Yet, without looking inward, an individual woman may go on choosing angry men because they express the anger that she holds in. Or a man may go on marrying women he wouldn't hire because he can't imagine women as equals (think of the loneliness expressed by Rochester in his speech about mistresses). But even if we're lucky enough to have been raised in an exemplary way, women who express anger often get punished, and so do men who bond with women. We have to face the fact that striving for a whole self means going against—and thus helping to change— most of current culture. But however great the struggle, the rewards are even greater.

In spite of all our gender-role socialization, for instance, sex-typing scales show that females who are more 'androgynous'—that is, who incorporate more 'masculine' qualities along with their gender-appropriate ones—have considerably higher self-esteem than those who rate as exclusively 'feminine'. Perhaps this isn't a total surprise, since 'masculine' traits (for instance, independence and autonomy) are more valued in a male-dominant society than 'feminine' ones (for instance, interdependence and connectedness). But the reverse is also true. Males who incorporate more 'feminine' traits actually have slightly higher self-esteem than do those who rate as exclusively 'masculine'. This is true in spite of the fact that society creates more behavioural situations that reward 'gender-appropriate' traits, and also imposes more social penalties on men who deviate from gender norms than on women who do the same.[28] Even though imitation is the sincerest form of flattery—and it's far worse for men to become 'like women' than vice versa— wholeness still has the edge.

Studies of creativity make the same point: creative people have both higher-than-average self-esteem and higher-than-average degrees of androgyny. The ability to impose one's own view of reality, as the artist does, requires a degree of self-confidence. Furthermore, creativity is most likely to come from intrinsic interest, not external reward; from a desire to express the true self.[29] It's not surprising that our cultural images of creativity tend toward the androgynous, from the erotic androgyny of the double-sexed god Eros to the Hindu Kama and other gods of love and creation, from the intellectual androgyny of Virginia Woolf and the Bloomsbury group to priests in skirts giving symbolic birth with baptismal/birth fluid, and long-haired male artists.[30]

But for most men and most women, gender differences are only too distinct, and nowhere are the consequences of their differentness more painfully felt than in relations with each other. While women are encouraged to communicate, nurture and otherwise develop those qualities that have special importance in maintaining loving relationships, men are rarely allowed to put as much energy into their intimate relationships as into their work, or to develop those 'feminine' skills that would make those relationships rewarding. One has only to look in a bookstore to see the consequences. I picked up four current books that profess to be for the sensitive 'new man', for instance, but not one listed 'love' or 'romance' in the index. Though there is a new emphasis on men connecting emotionally with their fathers, there is no parallel emphasis on men connecting intellectually with their mothers. Among the more plentiful books for the 'new woman', however, there were a dozen that put 'love' or 'romance' right up in the title; many on mother–daughter problems; and several with chapters on the importance of the father–daughter connection. *Women Who Love Too Much* and other such books are helpful—but why is there nothing called *Men Who Love Too Little*? Until men are as focused on love, connectedness and relationship as women are, the problems in those mutual areas can't be solved.

If a long-term solution is in sight, it comes from raising children. Men who raise them do change. In one study, single fathers and employed married mothers had almost identical levels of 'feminine' traits, in spite of all their preceding years of socialization.[31] Charlotte Brontë's transformed Rochester has been ridiculed by critics as a 'woman's man', someone symbolically castrated by blindness who thus becomes more sensitive and connected to others. But perhaps he is a harbinger of a future man who will be made whole not by a tragedy, but by the daily needs and joys of nurturing children. Though Rochester was an idealization in Charlotte Brontë's day, he might turn out to be, to reverse her comment about Jane Austen's novels, 'more true than real'. After all, patience, flexibility, empathy and interdependence—all these things are present in every male child. They only need to be required and rewarded instead of ignored and punished.

What if men not only raised children but were raised to raise children—so that even men who are not fathers, like women who are not mothers, still develop these traits that allow them to better connect to other people? As Dorothy Dinnerstein explains in such historic depth in *The Mermaid and the Minotaur*, the imbalance that so pains both sexes could diminish, and so could violence, both public and private.[32] We might realize, as Rilke wrote in *Letters to a Young Poet*, that 'the sexes are more related than we think, and the great renewal of the world will perhaps consist in this, that man and maid, freed from all false feeling and aversion, will seek each other not as opposites, but as brother and sister, as neighbours, and will come together as human beings.'[33]

Whatever is best for our collective future, we will only discover it by looking with clear eyes at what made love possible in our individual pasts. Here is a story of mine—in the hope of eliciting yours.

When we first met in the late 1960s, he was a quiet presence in a noisy group arguing about the merits of a political campaign. I remember thinking that he looked like a large friendly tree, inclining slightly toward us as he listened intently, with an occasional response when the wind of our talk rustled in his branches.

Later, as our group of political organizers and reporters toured the Southern inner city where this man had been born and to which he had returned as a doctor, I could feel the suspicion in a storefront clinic: Was I the only person of the wrong colour for this neighbourhood, just one more reporter come to record poverty and do nothing and leave? After a while, he said quietly in an apparent non sequitur, 'She can't help what colour she is, you know.' The conversation went right on like water flowing over a rock, but the suspicion dissolved.

As our tired group went to dinner at the end of the day, I noted again that, unique among us, he seemed to feel no need to talk, to entertain, to show off what he knew. Some of the local activists began to relax into reminiscing about the great musicians who had been born in this neighbourhood, perhaps eaten at these very tables, and both this man and I began remembering favourite lyrics. I realized that we were moved by the same things—and I could feel him sensing this, too. We continued our group conversation, but now, we were really talking to each other.

For the rest of that summer, he came for weekends to my city, I went to his, or we met in between. We walked the hot streets that everyone else was trying to get out of, went to movies, enjoyed free concerts, and ate every possible kind of ethnic food. It felt as if we had always known each other, yet also as if we were just exploring and exploding into a new part of ourselves. Sometimes we stayed in all weekend, talking, making love, listening to the new music tapes we brought each other, watching old movies, and ordering in food so we never had to go out. Sometimes, we explored new places to dance, buy old books, or shop for clothes. Always there were just the two of us. Somehow, we felt complete on our own. Once when an older white man in a movie line struck up a conversation with us, he punched my friend in the stomach and asked about 'pro ball' (assuming any tall black man must be an athlete), then made a sexual comment to me (assuming any white woman with a black man must be fair game). Later, we talked and laughed about the linkage between those stereotypes. Being together made it possible to laugh.

In spite of our different lives, we discovered just how much we shared: from mothers who got tears in their eyes when they talked about Roosevelt to feeling like outsiders and optimists at the same time. I could see he hadn't known a woman before who was in movement work, too—his wife had left him for a better prospect when he gave up his prosperous medical practice to set up free clinics—and this made him surprised and appreciative when I could help with speeches or strategizing. For my part, I hadn't known a man before who was so comfortable with what were usually female experiences. I was touched when he heard what I said and its emotional subtext, delighted that he enjoyed shopping for groceries or sprucing up a room, and amazed to discover that he noticed the little peripheral things that many men miss.

After meeting his parents, I could see where these companionable gifts had come from. As the oldest child looking after younger ones, he had learned to iron clothes, braid hair, cook very well, and always temper his strength with gentleness. In his parents, I could see the source of his inner strength. They were two deep-rooted trees, too. They had taught him to feel neither higher nor lower than anyone—but as good as anyone; to feel sorry for those who thought some people were born better or worse than others; and to know that he was worthy of the best. The suit they bought him for his grade-school graduation and could ill afford, for instance, was literally the best in the store. It was an object lesson he never forgot: even if you could afford almost nothing, you still deserved the best. After he met my mother and understood my childhood, I think he also sensed why I had come to be 'the man of the family' very young. Though we just enjoyed each other without examining why at the time, I can see now that I was more of a companion for him because of the 'masculine' in me, and he made me feel at ease and understood because of the 'feminine' in him.

We went on in this way for several years. Then our friendship went through a gradual process of change. I travelled too much; he had too little respite from his work. He was frighteningly ill for a while and, as I realized later, taking care of him pressed such a painful and familiar nerve in me after the years of caretaking for my mother that I responded to him in the same way: I was right there and responsible, but turned off emotionally—a familiar form of automatic pilot. And then there was a more lasting phenomenon: we worried about such similar things that we each began to need someone with perspective to get us out of deep grooves in our minds.

After a year or so of painful times of which the above is only a summary, we entered into a new era of being each other's chosen family. We both have other partners, which is a private part of our lives, but on all the other basics, we talk. There are many moves I wouldn't make, from political decisions to major life changes, without his advice—and many that he wouldn't undertake without mine. I realize as I write this that in these last twenty years, there hasn't been a week in which we haven't checked in, asked for an opinion, calmed our mutual paranoia that something has happened to the other, shared a joke, commiserated about some injustice, brought the other a present from some far-off place, celebrated a birthday, recommended a book, helped with a speech or an article, taught each other a new dance step, or shared a cup of tea.

I know he is right there with unconditional love and loyalty—and he knows I am, too. Neither of us can imagine growing old without the other. With health and luck, we'll never have to.

Perhaps what characterizes romance is its separateness from other deep feelings—for a friend or a child, for the ocean or a sheltering tree. What marks love is: It's all the same.

We have far better chances for love than in the Brontës's day—yet our consciousness of them lags far behind.

For instance: We still think of love as 'happily ever after'. That was a myth even in the nineteenth century when, as Margaret Mead pointed out, marriage worked better because people only lived to be fifty. (Charlotte Brontë herself died at thirty-nine of toxaemia during her first pregnancy.) Though an average lifespan is now thirty years longer in many countries of the world, we haven't really accepted the idea of loving different people at different times, in different ways. It's possible to raise children with a loved partner and then move amicably on to a new stage of life, to love someone and yet live apart, to forge new relationships at every phase of life, even at the very end—in short, to enjoy many different kinds of love, in a way that doesn't hurt but only enriches. For instance: Many more women now have the freedom that comes with self-support, not just a few with the unlikely inheritance of Jane Eyre; yet many still assume a man must be older, taller, earn more, weigh more, be the 'right' race, class and religion, better educated, and so on. In other words, we are still looking for forms of security, strength and social approval that we no longer need—and thus missing love.

For instance: Many women and men who considered themselves heterosexual have found themselves deeply in love with someone of the same sex, and many who considered themselves exclusively gay or lesbian have discovered the reverse. It seems that sexuality is not a label but a continuum. Even Heathcliff's cry, 'I cannot live without my life!' was given new meaning by the late writer and peace activist Barbara Deming, who used it to express her right to live openly as a lesbian. Black women in Boston then used it to protest their lack of safety in the streets. If we follow the feeling of love, for ourselves and others, it leads us to many new meanings.

For instance: We are more free to explore sensuality and sexuality as part of the pleasurable language of love. 'Pleasure—which includes erotic joy but is not limited to it,' as Marilyn French wrote, 'is the opposite of power, because it is the one quality that cannot be coerced'.[34] Pleasure is an expression of the true self.

We need nothing less than a re-mything of love. I think this poem by Alice Walker—my favourite love poem—is a good beginning:

> I have learned not to worry about love;
> but to honour its coming
> with all my heart.
> To examine the dark mysteries
> of the blood
> with headless heed and
> swirl,
> to know the rush of feelings
> swift and flowing
> as water.
> The source appears to be
> some inexhaustible
> spring within our twin and triple
> selves;
> the new face I turn up
> to you
> no one else on earth
> has ever
> seen.[35]

—1992

# EROTICA VERSUS PORNOGRAPHY

India has become the third largest user of Internet pornography in the world in the last ten years.[1] In fact, police investigations reveal that the six men who perpetrated the rape on the bus in Delhi on 16 December 2012 and the two men in the Delhi slum who raped the five-year-old as well as the men who raped the photo-journalist at the Shakti Mills compound in Mumbai on 22 August 2012, had all viewed online pornography before going out in search of their victims. The same culture that produced the *Kamasutra* is now embracing pornography, and has become unable to make a difference between mutual pleasure and the pleasure based on domination.

In the essays, 'Erotica Versus Pornography' and 'The Real Lovelace', Steinem explores the difference between erotica and pornography, the saturation of pornography in the media, its impact on women and men, as both the consumer and the consumed. The struggles of the US feminist movement in uprooting pornography and the exposure by the real Linda Lovelace to the use and abuse of women in producing pornography can be helpful lessons for Indian feminists.

—Ruchira Gupta

Look at images of or imagine people making love, really making love. Those images may be very diverse, but there is likely to be a mutual pleasure and touch and warmth, an empathy for each other's bodies and nerve-endings, a shared sensuality and a spontaneous sense of two people who are there because they want to be.

Now look at or imagine images of sex in which there is force, violence or symbols of unequal power. They may be very blatant: whips and chains of bondage, even torture and murder presented as sexually titillating, the clear evidence of wounds and bruises, or an adult's power being used sexually over a child. They may be more subtle: the use of class, race, authority or body poses to convey conqueror and victim; unequal nudity, that leaves one person's body exposed and vulnerable while the other is armoured with clothes; or a woman by herself, exposed for an unseen but powerful viewer whom she clearly is trying to please. (It's interesting that even when only the woman is seen, we often know whether she is there for her own pleasure or being displayed for someone else's.) But blatant or subtle, there is no equal power or mutuality. In fact, much of the tension and drama comes from the clear idea that one person is dominating another.

These two sorts of images are as different as love is from rape, as dignity is from humiliation, as partnership is from slavery, as pleasure is from pain. Yet they are confused and lumped together as 'pornography' or 'obscenity', 'erotica' or 'explicit sex', because sex and violence are so dangerously intertwined and confused. After all, it takes violence or the threat of it to maintain the dominance of any group of human beings over another. Between men and women, the threat must be the strongest wherever they come together intimately and are most in danger of recognizing each other's humanity.

This confusion of sex with violence is most obvious in any form of sadomasochism. The inability to empathize with the 'opposite sex' has become so great that a torturer or even murderer may actually believe pain or loss of life to be the natural fate of the victim; and the victim may have been so deprived of self-respect or positive human contact that she expects pain or loss of freedom as the price of any intimacy or attention at all. Nonetheless, it's unlikely that even a masochist expects death, yet 'snuff' movies and much current pornographic literature insist that a slow death from sexual torture is the final orgasm and the ultimate pleasure. Of course, it's a form of 'suicide' reserved for women. Though men, in fact, are far more likely to kill themselves, male suicide is almost never presented as sexually pleasurable.

Sex is also confused with violence and aggression in all forms of popular culture, as well as in respectable theories of psychology and sexual behaviour. The idea that aggression is a 'normal' part of male sexuality, and that female passivity or need for male aggression is a 'normal' part of female sexuality, are part of the male-dominant culture we live in, the books we learn from and the air we breathe.

Even the words we are given to express our feelings are suffused with the same assumptions. Sexual phrases are the most common synonyms for conquering and humiliation (being had, being screwed, getting fucked); the sexually aggressive or even expressive woman may be a slut or even a nymphomaniac, but the sexually aggressive man may be normal or even admired. Accepted scientific descriptions of sex may perpetuate the same roles, for instance, a woman is penetrated by a man though she might also be said to have enveloped him.

Obviously, untangling sex from aggression—from violence or the threat of it—is going to take a very long time. And the process is going to be greatly resisted as a challenge to the very heart of male dominance and male centrality.

But we do have a wisdom to guide us: the common wisdom of our bodies. Pain is a warning of damage and danger. If it is not mixed with the intimacy we are given as children, we are unlikely to confuse pain with pleasure. As we discover our free will and strength, we are also likely to discover our own initiative and pleasure in sex. As men can no longer dominate and have to find an identity that doesn't depend on superiority, they also discover that cooperation is more interesting than submission, that empathy with their sex partner increases their own pleasure, and that anxieties about their ability to 'perform' tend to disappear along with stereotyped ideas about masculinity.

But women will be the main fighters in this new sexual revolution. It is our freedom, our safety, our lives and our pleasure that are mostly at stake.

In this wave of feminism, we began by trying to separate sex and violence in those areas where the physical danger was and is the most immediate; challenging rape as the one crime that was considered biologically irresistible for the criminal and perhaps invited by the victim; refusing to allow male-female beatings to be classified as 'domestic violence' and ignored by the law; and exposing forced prostitution and sexual slavery as national and international crimes. With the exception of male violence against wives or partners, those challenges were made somewhat easier by men who wanted to punish other men for taking their female property. Women still rarely have the power to protect each other.

Looking at all these instances of anti-woman warfare led us directly to the propaganda that teaches and legitimizes them— pornography. For the same reasons that we had begun to differentiate rape from sex, we realized that we must find some way of separating pornographic depictions of sex as an anti-woman weapon from those images of freely chosen, mutual sexuality.

Fortunately, there is also wisdom in the origin of words. Pornography comes from the Greek root *porné* (harlot, prostitute, or female captive) and *graphos* (writing about or description of). Thus, it means a description of either the purchase of sex, which implies an imbalance of power in itself, or sexual slavery.

This definition includes, and should include, all such degradation, regardless of whether it is females who are the slaves and males who are the captors or the rare examples that are vice versa. There is also homosexual pornography in which a man plays the 'feminine' role of victim, just as there is homosexual erotica in which two men give each other pleasure.

There is even role-reversal pornography, with a woman whipping or punishing a man, though it's significant that this genre seems to be created by men for their own pleasure, not by or for women, and allows men to pretend to be victims—but without real danger. There is lesbian pornography, with a woman assuming the 'masculine' role of victimizing another woman, as well as lesbian erotica. That women rarely choose the role of victimizer is due not to biological superiority, but to a culture that is far less likely to addict women to violence and dominance. But whatever the gender of the participants, all pornography is an imitation of the male-female, conqueror-victim paradigm, and almost all of it actually portrays or implies enslaved woman and masterful male.

Even the 1970 Presidential Commission on Obscenity and

Pornography, whose report has been accused of suppressing or ignoring evidence of the causal link between pornography and violence against women, defined the subject of their study as pictorial or verbal descriptions of sexual behaviour that was characterized by 'the degrading and demeaning portrayal of the role and status of the human female'.

In short, pornography is not about sex. It's about an imbalance of power that allows and requires sex to be used as a form of aggression.

Erotica is a word that can help us to differentiate sex from violence, and therefore rescue sexual pleasure. It comes from the Greek root *eros* (sexual desire or passionate love, named for Eros, the son of Aphrodite), and so contains the idea of love and mutuality, positive choice and the yearning for a particular person. Unlike pornography's reference to a harlot or prostitute, erotica leaves entirely open the question of gender. (In fact, we may owe its connotation of shared power to the Greek belief that a man's love for another man was more worthy than love for a woman, but at least bias isn't present in the word.)

Though both erotica and pornography usually refer to verbal or pictorial representations of sexual behaviour, they are as different as a room with doors open from one with doors locked. The first might be a home, but the second could only be a prison.

The problem is that there is so little erotica. Women have rarely felt free, powerful and safe enough to pursue erotic pleasure in our own lives, much less to create it in the worlds of film, magazines, art, books, television and popular culture—areas we rarely control. Very few male authors and filmmakers have been able to escape society's message of what a man should do, much less to imagine their way into the identity of a woman. Even depictions of sex between men or between women often fall into the dominant-passive paradigm. Some women are now trying to portray equal and erotic sex—whether with men or with other women—but it is still not a part of popular culture.

And the problem is that there is so much pornography. This underground stream of anti-woman propaganda has existed in all male-dominant societies, but mass communication, profiteering corporations and a backlash against female equality have now turned it into an inescapable flood in our streets and theatres and even our homes. Perhaps that's useful in the long run. Women can no longer pretend pornography does not exist. We must either face our own humiliation and torture every day on magazine covers and television screens, or fight back.

There is hardly a news-stand without women's bodies in chains and bondage, in full labial display for the conquering male viewer, bruised or on our knees, screaming in real or pretended pain, pretending to enjoy what is hurting and killing us. The same images are in mainstream movie theatres and respectable hotel rooms via closed-circuit TV for the travelling businessman.

They are brought into our own homes not only in magazines, but also in video cassettes and on cable TV channels. Even video games offer such features as a smiling, rope-bound woman and a male figure with an erection, the game's object being to rape the woman as many times as possible. (Like much of pornography, that game is fascist on racial grounds as well as sexual ones. The smiling woman is a Native American maiden, the rapist is General Custer, and the game is called 'Custer's Revenge'.)

Though 'snuff' movies, in which real women are eviscerated and finally killed, have been driven underground (in part because the graves of many murdered women were discovered around the shack of just one filmmaker in California), movies that simulate these torture-murders of women are still going strong. (Snuff is the porn term for killing a woman for sexual pleasure. We are not even allowed the seriousness of a word like murder.) So are the 'kiddie porn' or 'chicken porn' movies and magazines that show adult men undressing, fondling and sexually abusing children; often with the titillating theme that 'fathers' are raping 'daughters'. Some 'chicken porn' magazines offer explicit tips on how to use a child sexually without leaving physical evidence of rape. The premise is that children's testimony is even less likely to be believed than that of adult women—and as we see in the few cases of the sexual abuse of children that reach the courts, this is true.

Add this pornography industry up, from magazines like *Playboy* and *Hustler*, to movie classics like *Love Gestapo Style*, *Deep Throat*, or

*Angels in Pain*, and the total sales come to a staggering ten billion dollars a year—more than all the sales of the conventional film and record industry combined. And that doesn't count the fact that many 'conventional' film and music images are also pornographic, from gynocidal record jackets, like the famous 'I'm Black and Blue from the Rolling Stones—and I Love It!' (which showed a semi-nude black woman bound to a chair) to the hundreds of teenage sex-and-horror movies in which young women die sadistic deaths, and rape is presented not as a crime but as sexual excitement. There are also an increasing number of mainstream films and TV shows that tailor pornography to pass minimal standards, plus the sales of the supposedly 'literary' forms of pornography, from *The Story of O* to the works of the Marquis de Sade.

If Nazi propaganda that justified the torture and killing of Jews were the theme of half of our most popular movies and magazines, would we not be outraged? If Ku Klux Klan propaganda that preached and glamorized the enslavement of blacks were the subject of much-praised 'classic' novels, would we not protest? We know that such racist propaganda precedes and justifies the racist acts of pogroms and lynchings. We know that watching a violent film makes test subjects more likely to condone violence, to be willing to perpetrate it themselves and to believe the victim must deserve such treatment. Why is the propaganda of sexual aggression against women of all races the one form of group hatred in which the 'conventional wisdom' sees no danger? Why is pornography the only media violence that is supposed to be a 'safety valve' to satisfy aggressiveness somewhere short of acting it out?

The first reason is the confusion of all non-procreative sex with pornography. Any description of sexual behaviour, or even nudity, may be called pornographic or obscene (a word whose Latin derivative means dirty or containing filth) by those who insist that the only moral purpose of sex is procreating within marriage, or even that any portrayal of sexuality or nudity is against the will of God.

In fact, human beings seem to be the only animals that experience the same sex drive and pleasure when we can and cannot conceive. Other animals experience periods of heat or oestrus in which sexual activity is concentrated. Humans do not. Just as we developed uniquely human capacities for language, planning, memory and invention along our evolutionary path, we also developed sexuality as a form of expression, a way of communicating that is separable from reproduction. For human beings, sexuality can also be a way of bonding, giving and receiving pleasure, bridging differences, discovering sameness and communicating emotion.

We developed this and other human gifts through our ability to change our environment, adapt to it physically, change again, re-adapt, and so in the very long run to affect our own evolution. But, as an emotional result of this spiralling path away from other animals, we seem to alternate between periods of exploring our unique abilities and feelings of loneliness in the unknown that we ourselves have created, a fear that sometimes sends us back to the comfort of the animal world by encouraging us to look for a sameness that is not there.

For instance, the separation of 'play' from 'work' is a feature of the human world. So is the difference between art and nature, or an intellectual accomplishment and a physical one. As a result, we celebrate play, art and invention as pleasurable and important leaps into the unknown; yet any temporary trouble can send us back to a nostalgia for our primate past, and a conviction that the basics of survival, nature and physical labour are somehow more worthwhile or even more moral.

In the same way, we have explored our sexuality as separable from conception: a pleasurable, empathetic, important bridge to others of our species. We have even invented contraception, a skill that has probably existed in some form since our ancestors figured out the process of conception and birth, in order to extend and protect this uniquely human gift for sexuality as a means of expression. Yet we also have times of atavistic suspicion that sex is not complete, or even legal or intended by God, if it does not or could not end in conception.

No wonder the very different concepts of 'erotica' and 'pornography' can be so confused. Both assume that sex can be separated from conception; that human sexuality has additional uses and goals. This is the major reason why, even in our current culture, both may be condemned as equally obscene and immoral. Such gross condemnation of all sexuality that isn't harnessed to childbirth (and to patriarchal marriage so that children are properly 'owned') has been increased by the current backlash against women's independence.

Out of fear that the whole patriarchal structure will be upset if we as women really have the autonomous power to decide our sexual and reproductive futures (that is, if we can control our own bodies, and thus the means of reproduction), anti-equality groups are not only denouncing sex education and family planning as 'pornographic', but have tried to use obscenity laws to stop the sending of all contraceptive information through the mail. Any sex or nudity outside the context of patriarchal marriage and childbirth is their target. In fact, Phyllis Schlafly once denounced the entire women's movement as 'obscene', and the Moral Majority, the Christian Coalition and other such groups are trying to re-impose virginity, abstinence and repression.

Not surprisingly, this religious backlash has a secular, intellectual counterpart that relies heavily on applying the 'natural' behaviour of the animal world to humans. This is questionable in itself, but such Lionel Tiger-ish studies make their political purpose even clearer by the animals they choose and the habits they emphasize.[2] For example, some male primates carry and generally 'mother' their infants, male lions care for their young, female elephants lead the clan and male penguins literally do everything except give birth, from hatching the eggs to sacrificing their own membranes to feed the new arrivals.

Perhaps that's why many male supremacists prefer to discuss chimps and baboons (studied in atypical conditions of captivity) whose behaviour is suitably male-dominant. The message is that human females should accept their animal 'destiny' of being sexually dependent, and devote themselves to bearing and rearing their young.

Defending against such repression leads to the temptation of merely reversing the terms and declaring that all non-procreative sex is good. In fact, however, this human activity can be as constructive or destructive, moral or immoral, as any other. Sex as communication can send messages as different as mutual pleasure and dominance, life and death, 'erotica' and 'pornography'.

The second kind of problem comes not from those who oppose women's equality in non-sexual areas, whether on grounds of God or nature, but from men (and some women, too) who present themselves as friends of civil liberties and progress. Their objections may take the form of a concern about privacy, on the grounds that a challenge to pornography invades private sexual behaviour and the philosophy of 'whatever turns you on'. It may be a concern about class bias, on the premise that pornography is just 'working men's erotica'. Sometimes, it's the simple argument that the objectors themselves like pornography, and therefore, it must be okay. Most often, however, this resistance attaches itself to or hides behind an expressed concern about censorship, freedom of the press and the First Amendment.

In each case, such liberal objections should be more easily countered than the right-wing ones because they are less based on reality. It's true that women's independence and autonomy would upset the whole patriarchal apple cart: the right wing should be worried. It's not true, however, that pornography is a private concern. If it were just a matter of men making male-supremacist literature in their own basements to assuage their own sexual hang-ups, there would be sorrow and avoidance among women, but not the anger, outrage and fear produced by being confronted with the preaching of sexual fascism on our news stands, movie screens, television sets and public streets.

It is a multi-billion-dollar industry, which involves the making of public policy, if only to decide whether, as is now the case, crimes committed in the manufacture and sale of pornography will continue to go largely unprosecuted. Zoning regulations on the public display of pornography are not enforced, the sexual slavery and exploitation of children used in pornography go unpunished, the forcible use of teenage runaways is ignored by police, and even the torture and murder of prostitutes for men's sexual titillation is obscured by some mitigating notion that the women asked for it.

In all other areas of privacy, the limitation is infringement on the rights and lives and safety of others. That must become true for pornography. Right now, it is exempt, almost 'below the law'.

As for class bias, it's simply not accurate to say that pornography is erotica with less education. From the origins of the words, as well as the way they are commonly used, it's clear there is a difference of content, not just artistic or economic form. Pornography is about dominance and often pain. Erotica is about mutuality and always pleasure. Any man able to empathize with women can easily tell the difference by looking at a photograph or film and putting himself in the woman's skin. Perhaps the most revealing thing is that this argument is generally made on behalf of the working class by pro-pornography liberals who are middle or upper class themselves.

Of course, the notion that enjoying pornography makes it okay is a popular male idea. From Alfred Kinsey forward, research has confirmed that the purchasers of pornography are almost all males, and that the majority of men are aroused by it, while the majority of women find it angering, humiliating and not a turn-on at all.[3] This was true even though women were shown sexually explicit material that may have included erotica, since Kinsey and others did not make that distinction.

If such rare examples of equal sex were entirely deleted, pornography could probably serve as sex-aversion therapy for most women; yet many men and some psychologists continue to call women prudish, anti-sex, or generally uptight if they are not turned on by their own domination. The same men would be less likely to argue that anti-Semitic and racist literature was okay because it gave them pleasure. The problem is that the degradation of women of all races is still thought to be normal. A male-dominant system teaches men that dominance over women is normal—and that's just what pornography does.

Nonetheless, there are a few well-meaning women who are both turned on by pornography and angered that other women are not. Some of their anger is misunderstanding: objections to pornography are not condemnations of women who have been raised to believe sex and domination are synonymous, for we have all internalized some degree of sexism and are struggling to dig it out. Other women's anger results from an underestimation of themselves:

being turned on by a rape fantasy is not the same as wanting to be raped. As Robin Morgan has pointed out, the distinguishing feature of a fantasy is that the fantasizer herself is in control. (Both men and women have 'ravishment' fantasies in which we are passive while others act out our unspoken wishes—but they are still our wishes.) And some anger, especially when it comes from women who consider themselves feminists, is a refusal to differentiate between what may be true for them now, and what may be desirable in the future. For example, a woman may be attracted only to men who are taller, heavier and older than she, but still understand that such superficial restrictions on the men she loves and enjoys going to bed with won't exist in a more free and less stereotyped future; or more seriously, she may be drawn to cruel and distant men because she is still trying to get her cruel and distant father to love her, but understands that a future of mutuality is possible and preferable.

Similarly, some lesbians may follow the masculine–feminine patterns that were our only model for intimate relationships, heterosexual or not, and even choose them freely and equally, yet still see these old patterns clearly and work towards a future without them. It isn't that women attracted to pornography cannot also be feminists, but that pornography itself must be recognized for its impact on women's safety and equality.

Finally, there is the First Amendment argument against feminist anti-pornography campaigns: the most respectable and publicized opposition, but also the one with the least basis in fact. Feminist groups are not arguing for censorship of pornography through prior restraint, just as we are not arguing that Nazi literature or racist propaganda of the Ku Klux Klan cannot be published. For one thing, any definition of pornography by a male-dominant society (or of racist literature by a racist society) might well be used to punish the powerless even more.

Freely chosen gay or lesbian expression might be deemed more 'pornographic' than snuff movies, school sex education courses more 'obscene' than bondage, just as statements against European Americans might be more punished than those against African Americans. Furthermore, censorship in itself, even with the proper definitions, might only drive pornography into more underground activity and, were it to follow the pattern of drug traffic, into even more profitability.

Most important, the First Amendment is part of a statement of individual rights against government intervention that feminism seeks to expand, not contract: for instance, a woman's right to decide whether and when to have children. When we protest against pornography and educate others about it, as I am doing now, we are strengthening the First Amendment by exercising it.

The only legal steps suggested by feminists thus far have been the prosecution of those pornography makers who are accused of such crimes as murder, assault and kidnapping; prosecution of those many who use children under the age of consent; enforcement of existing zoning and other codes that are breached because of payoffs to law-enforcement officials and the enormous rents paid to pornography's landlords; the use of public-nuisance statutes to require that pornography not be displayed in public places where its sight cannot reasonably be avoided; and civil rights ordinances, like that proposed in Minneapolis, that allow civil suits for damages against the makers of any pornography (or other hate literature) that can be shown to the satisfaction of a jury to have contributed to a crime.[4]

None of these measures keeps material from being published: 'prior restraint', in the terms of censorship law. Most just require that those responsible for pornography no longer be immune from prosecution for crimes committed during its production and distribution.

Perhaps the reason for this 'First Amendment' controversy is less substance than smokescreen. Just as earlier feminist campaigns against rape were condemned by some civil libertarians as efforts that would end by putting only men of colour or poor men in jail, or in perpetuating the death penalty then on the books in some states as a punishment for rape, anti-pornography campaigns are now similarly opposed. When rape victims began to come forward, however, the public learned that white psychiatrists, educators and other professionals were just as likely to be rapists as were poor men or men of colour. Furthermore, changing the patriarchal definition of rape to degrees of sexual assault made the law more realistic and thus more likely to be administered, eliminated the death penalty for rape, and protected males against sexual assault, too.

Though there are no statistics on the purchasers of pornography, those who serve this clientele—clerks, movie-house owners, video cassette dealers, mail-order houses and the like—usually remark on their respectability, their professional standing, their suits, briefcases, white skins and middle-class zip codes. For instance, the last screening of a snuff movie showing a real murder was traced to the monthly pornographic film showings of a senior partner in a respected New York law firm, an event regularly held by him for a group of friends, including other lawyers and judges. One who was present reported that many were 'embarrassed' and 'didn't know what to say'. But not one man was willing to object, much less to report this evidence of murder to the police.

Though much concern about censorship is sincere—the result of false reports that feminist anti-pornography campaigns were really calling for censorship and prior restraint, or of confusion with right-wing groups who both misdefine pornography and want to censor it—much of it seems to be a cover for the preservation of the pornographic status quo by a left/right coalition that is dependent on this huge industry, whether psychologically or financially.

In fact, the arguments against taking on pornography seem suspiciously like the virgin–whore divisions that have been women's only choices in the past. The right wing says all that is not virginal or motherly is pornographic, and thus they campaign against sexuality and nudity in general. The left wing says all sex is good as long as it's male-defined, and thus they campaign to protect it. Women who feel endangered by seeing ourselves as the victims, and men who feel demeaned by seeing themselves as victimizers, have a long struggle ahead.

In fact, pornography in some form will continue as long as boys are raised to believe they must control or conquer women as a proof of their 'masculinity', and as long as society rewards men who believe that their success or even functioning—in sex, as in other areas of life—depends on women's subservience.

But at least now we have words to describe our outrage, and to separate sex from aggression. We have the courage to demonstrate publicly against pornography, to throw its magazines and films out of our houses, to boycott its purveyors, even to take friends and family members who support it as seriously as we would if they were supporting and enjoying Nazi literature or the teachings of the Klan.

But until we finally end the male dominance that has equated sexuality with violence and aggression, there will be more pornography in our lives and less erotica. There will be little murders in our beds—and very little love.

—1977

# THE REAL LINDA LOVELACE

As the star of the first full-length pornographic film, *Deep Throat*, Linda Lovelace (nee Boreman) became a household name in the 1970s. But there was reportedly a dark story behind her fame. She was often abused by her mother growing up, and her first husband forced her into porn. Once the industry's biggest star, Lovelace later stood up against porn, testifying about its dangers before Congress.

In 1980, Linda Boreman stated that her ex-husband Chuck Traynor had violently coerced her into making *Deep Throat* and other pornographic features. Boreman made her charges public for the press corps at a conference, together with lawyer Catherine MacKinnon, and with members of Women against Pornography and feminist writer Andrea Dworkin offering statements in support. After the press conference, Dworkin, MacKinnon, Gloria Steinem and Boreman began discussing the possibility of using federal civil rights law to seek damages from Traynor and the makers of *Deep Throat*. Linda Boreman was interested, but backed off after Steinem discovered that the statute of limitations for a possible suit had passed.

MacKinnon and Dworkin, however, continued to discuss civil rights litigation as a possible approach to combating pornography. MacKinnon opposed traditional arguments against pornography based on the idea of morality or sexual innocence, as well as the use of traditional criminal obscenity law to suppress pornography. Instead of condemning pornography for violating 'community standards' of sexual decency or modesty, they characterized pornography as a form of sex discrimination, and sought to give women the right to seek damages under civil rights law. 'Pornography, in the feminist view is a form of forced sex, a practice of sexual politics, an institution of gender inequality.'[1]

Pornography in turn promotes the idea of men's sexuality being dominant over women and combines dominance and submission into the natural construct of men and women in relation to each other.

In 1983, the Minneapolis city government hired MacKinnon and Dworkin to draft an anti-pornography civil rights ordinance as an amendment to the Minneapolis city civil rights ordinance. The amendment defined pornography as a civil rights violation against women, and allowed women who claimed harm from pornography to sue the producers and distributors for damages in civil court. The law was passed twice by the Minneapolis city council but vetoed by the mayor. Another version of the ordinance was passed in Indianapolis, Indiana, in 1984.

This ordinance was ruled unconstitutional by the Seventh Circuit Court of Appeals. MacKinnon continued to support the civil rights approach in her writing and activism, and supported anti-pornography feminists who organized later campaigns in Cambridge, Massachusetts, in 1985 and 1988 to pass versions of the ordinance by voter initiative. MacKinnon represented Boreman from 1980 until Boreman's death in 2002.

—Ruchira Gupta

Remember *Deep Throat?* It was the porn movie that made porn movies chic: the first stag film to reach beyond the bounds of X-rated theatres and into much bigger audiences. Though it was created in 1972 as a cheap feature that took only forty thousand dollars and a few days to make, it ended the decade with an estimated gross income of six hundred million dollars from paying customers for the film itself, plus its sub-industry of sequels, cassettes, T-shirts, bumper stickers and sexual aids. In fact, so much of the media rewarded it with amused approval that *Deep Throat* entered our language and our consciousness, whether we ever saw the film or not. From the serious Watergate journalists of the *Washington Post* who immortalized *Deep Throat* by bestowing that title on their top-secret news source, to the sleazy pornocrats of *Screw* magazine—a range that may be, on a scale of male-supremacists, the distance from A to B—strange media bedfellows turned this cheap feature into a universal dirty joke and an international profit centre.

At the heart of this dirty and profitable joke was Linda Lovelace (née Linda Boreman), whose innocent face and unjaded manner was credited with much of the film's success. She offered moviegoers the titillating thought that even the girl next door might love to be the object of porn-style sex.

Using Linda had been the idea of Gerry Damiano, the director-writer of *Deep Throat*. 'The most amazing thing about Linda, the truly amazing thing,' she remembers him saying enthusiastically to Lou Peraino, who bankrolled the movie, 'is that she still looks sweet and innocent.' Nonetheless, Peraino (who was later arrested by the FBI as a figure in alleged organized-crime activities in the illicit film industry) complained that Linda wasn't the 'blond with big boobs' that he had in mind for his first porn flick. He continued to complain, even after she had been ordered to service him sexually.

In fact, watching Linda perform in public as a prostitute had given Damiano the idea for *Deep Throat* in the first place. He had been at a party where men lined up to be the beneficiaries of the sexual sword-swallower trick that Linda had been taught by her husband and keeper, Chuck Traynor. By relaxing her throat muscles, she had learned to receive the full-length plunge of a penis without choking; a desperate survival technique for her, but a constant source of amusement and novelty for clients. Thus creatively inspired, Damiano had thought up a movie gimmick, one that was second only to Freud's complete elimination of the clitoris as the proper source of female pleasure when he invented the vaginal orgasm. Damiano decided to tell the story of a woman whose clitoris was in her throat, and who was constantly eager for oral sex with men.

Though his physiological fiction about one woman was far less ambitious than Freud's fiction about all women, this porn movie had a whammo audio-visual impact; a teaching device that Freudian theory had lacked.

Literally millions of women seem to have been taken to *Deep Throat* by their boyfriends or husbands (not to mention prostitutes who were taken by their pimps) so that each one might learn what a woman could do to please a man if she really wanted to. This instructive value seems to have been a major reason for the movie's popularity, and its reach beyond the usual universe of male-only viewers.

Of course, if the female viewer were really a spoilsport, she might identify with the woman on screen—sense her humiliation, danger and pain—but the smiling, happy face of Linda Lovelace could serve to cut off empathy, too. She's there because she wants to be. Who's forcing her? See how she's smiling? See how a real woman enjoys this?

Eight years later, Linda told the humiliating and painful answer in *Ordeal*, her autobiography.[2] She described years as a sexual prisoner during which she was tortured and kept isolated from all normal human contact.

Nonetheless, it's important to understand how difficult it would have been at the time (and probably still is, in the case of other victims) to know the truth.

At the height of *Deep Throat*'s popularity, for instance, Nora Ephron wrote an essay about going to see it. She was determined not to react like those 'crazy feminists carrying on, criticizing non-political films in political terms'.

Nonetheless, she sat terrified through a scene in which a hollow glass dildo is inserted in Linda Lovelace's vagina and then filled with Coca-Cola, which is drunk through a surgical straw. ('All I could think about,' she confessed, 'was what would happen if the glass broke.') Feeling humiliated and angry, she was told by her male friends that she was 'overreacting', that the Coca-Cola scene was 'hilarious'. She used her licence as a writer to get a telephone interview with Linda Lovelace. 'I totally enjoyed myself making the movie,' she was told by Linda. 'I don't have any inhibitions about sex. I just hope that everybody who goes to see the film...loses some of their inhibitions.'

So Nora wrote an article that assumed Linda to be a happy and willing porn queen who was enjoying '$250 a week...and a piece of the profits'. She wrote off her own reaction as that of a 'puritanical feminist who lost her sense of humour at a skin flick'.

What she did not know (how could any interviewer know?) was that Linda would later list these and other answers among those dictated by Chuck Traynor for just such journalistic occasions. He punished her for showing any unacceptable emotion (when, for instance, she cried while being gang-banged by five men in a motel room, thus causing one customer to refuse to pay). In fact, she had been beaten and raped so severely and regularly that she suffered rectal damage, plus permanent injury to the blood vessels in her legs.

What Nora did not know was that Linda would also write of her three escape attempts and three forcible returns to a life of sexual servitude: first by the betrayal of another prostitute; then by her own mother who was charmed by Chuck Traynor's protestations of remorse and innocence into telling him where her daughter was hiding; and finally by Linda's fear for the lives of two friends who had sheltered her after hearing that she had been made to do a sex film with a dog, and outside whose home Traynor had parked a van that contained, Linda believed, his collection of hand grenades and a machine gun.

Even now, these and other facts about Traynor must be read with the word 'alleged' in front of them.

Because of Linda's long period of fear and hiding after she escaped, the time limitations of the law, and the fact that Traynor forced her to marry him, legal charges are difficult to bring. Linda's book documents her account of more than two years of fear, sadism and forced prostitution. Traynor has been quoted as calling these charges 'so ridiculous I can't take them seriously'. He has also been quoted as saying, 'When I first dated her she was so shy, it shocked her to be seen nude by a man…I created Linda Lovelace.'

Linda's account of being 'created' includes guns put to her head, turning tricks while being watched through a peephole to make sure she couldn't escape, and having water forced up her rectum with a garden hose if she refused to offer such amusements as exposing herself in restaurants or to passing drivers on the highway.

*Ordeal* is a very difficult book to read. It must have been far more difficult to write. But Linda says she wanted to purge forever the idea that she had become 'Linda Lovelace' of her own free will.

Was profit a motive for this book? Certainly, she badly needs money for herself, her three-year-old son, her imminently expected second baby and her husband, a childhood friend named Larry Marchiano, whose work as a TV cable installer has been jeopardized by his co-workers' discovery of Linda's past. For a while, they were living partially on welfare. But Linda points out that she has refused offers of more than three million dollars to do another porn movie like *Deep Throat*. (For that filming, Linda was paid twelve hundred dollars; a sum that, like her fees for turning tricks as a prostitute, she says she never saw.) 'I wouldn't do any of that again,' she says, 'even if I could get fifty million dollars.'

A different motive for writing *Ordeal* is clear from Linda's response to a postcard written by a young woman who had been coerced into prostitution, a woman who said she got the courage to escape after seeing Linda on television. 'Women have to be given the courage to try to escape, and to know that you can get your self-respect back,' she says. 'It meant the whole world to me to get that postcard.'

Ironically, her own hope of escape came from the surprising success of *Deep Throat*. She had become a valuable property. She had to be brought into contact with outsiders occasionally, and with a world that she says had been denied to her, even in the form of radio or newspapers. Now, she says soberly, 'I thank God today that they weren't making snuff movies back then…'

She says she escaped by feigning trustworthiness for brief periods, a little longer each time until after about six months, she was left unguarded during rehearsals for a stage version of *Linda Lovelace*. Even then, she spent weeks hiding out in hotels alone, convinced she might be beaten or killed for this fourth try at escape, but feeling stronger this time for having only her own life to worry about. It took a long period of hiding, with help and disguises supplied by a sympathetic secretary from Traynor's newly successful Linda Lovelace Enterprises (but no help from the police, who said they could do nothing to protect her 'until the man with the gun is in the room with you'), before the terror finally dwindled into a nagging fear. Traynor continued to issue calls and entreaties for her return. He filed a lawsuit against her for breach of contract. But he had also found another woman to star in his porn films— Marilyn Chambers, the model who appeared in a comparatively non-violent porn movie called *Behind the Green Door*.

And then, suddenly, she got word through a lawyer that Traynor was willing to sign divorce papers. The threats and entreaties to return just stopped.

Free of hiding and disguises at last, she tried to turn her created identity into real acting by filming *Linda Lovelace for President*, a comedy that was supposed to have no explicit sex, but she discovered that producers who offered her roles always expected nudity in return. She went to a Cannes Film Festival, but was depressed by her very acceptance among celebrities she respected. 'I had been in a disgusting film with disgusting people... What were they doing watching a movie like that in the first place?'

Once she started giving her own answers to questions and trying to explain her years of coercion, she discovered that reporters were much more reluctant to rush into print. Her story was depressing, not glamorous or titillating. Because she had been passed around like a sexual trading coin, sometimes to men who were famous, there was also fear of lawsuits.

Only in 1978, when she was interviewed by Mike McGrady, a respected newspaper reporter on Long Island where she had moved with her new husband, did her story begin the long process of reaching the public. McGrady believed her. In order to convince a publisher, he also put her through an eleven-hour lie-detector test with the former chief polygraphist of the New York district attorney's office, a test that included great detail and brutal cross-questioning. But even with those results and McGrady himself as a collaborator, several major book publishers turned down the manuscript. It was finally believed and accepted by Lyle Stuart, a maverick in the world of publishing who often takes on sensational or controversial subjects.

One wonders: Would a male political prisoner or hostage telling a similar story have been so disbelieved? *Ordeal* attacks the myth of female masochism that insists women enjoy sexual domination and pain, but prostitution and pornography are big businesses built on that myth. When challenged about her inability to escape earlier, Linda wrote: 'I can understand why some people have such trouble accepting the truth. When I was younger, when I heard about a woman being raped, my secret feeling was that could never happen to me. I would never permit it to happen. Now I realize that can be about as meaningful as saying I won't permit an avalanche.'

There are other, nameless victims of sexual servitude: the young blondes from the Minnesota Pipeline, runaways from the Scandinavian farming towns of Minnesota, who are given drugs and 'seasoned' by pimps and set up in Times Square; the welfare mothers who are pressured to get off welfare and into prostitution; the 'exotic' dancers imported from poorer countries for porn films and topless bars; the torture victims whose murders were filmed in Latin America for snuff movies made to be imported here, or others whose bodies were found buried around a California filmmaker's shack; the body of a prostitute found headless and handless in a Times Square hotel, a lesson to others who would disobey their pimps. Perhaps some of their number will be the next voiceless, much-blamed women to speak out and begin placing the blame where it belongs. Perhaps Linda's example will give them hope that if they return, some of society will accept them. Right now, however, they are just as disbelieved as rape victims and battered women were a few years ago.

To publicize her book, Linda is sitting quiet and soft-spoken on TV's *Phil Donahue Show.* Under her slacks she wears surgical stockings to shield the veins that were damaged by the beatings in which she curled up, foetus-like, to protect her stomach and breasts from kicks and blows: this she explains under Donahue's questioning. Probably, she will need surgery after her baby is born. The silicone injected into her breasts by a doctor (who, like many other professionals to whom she was taken, was paid by Linda's sexual services) has shifted painfully, and surgery may be necessary there, too.

Yet Donahue, usually a sensitive interviewer, is asking psychological questions about her background: How did she get along with her parents? What did they tell her about sex? Didn't her fate have something to do with the fact that she had been pregnant when she was nineteen, and had given birth to a baby that Linda's mother put up for adoption?

Some of the women in the audience take up this line of questioning, too. They had been poor. They had strict and authoritarian parents, yet they didn't end up as part of the pornographic underground. The air is thick with self-congratulation. Donahue talks on about the tragedy of teenage pregnancy, and what parents can do to keep their children from a Linda-like fate.

Because Traynor had a marriage ceremony performed somewhere along the way (Linda says this was to make sure she couldn't testify against him on his drug charges), she has to nod when he is referred to as 'your husband'. On her own, however, she refers to him as 'Mr Traynor'.

Linda listens patiently to doubts and objections, but she never gives up trying to make the audience understand. If another woman had met a sadistic man who 'got off on pain', as Linda has described in her book, she might have ended up exactly the same way. No, she never loved him, he was the object of her hatred and terror. Yes, he was very nice, very gentlemanly when they first met. They had no sexual relationship at all. He had just offered an apartment as a refuge from her strict childlike regime at home. And then he did a 180-degree turn. She became, she says quietly, a prisoner. A prisoner of immediate violence and the fear of much more.

She describes being so isolated and controlled that she was not allowed to speak in public or to go to the bathroom without Traynor's permission. There was no choice. It could happen to anyone. She says this simply, over and over again, and to many women in the audience the point finally comes through. But to some, it never does. Donahue continues to ask questions about her childhood, her background. What attracted her to this fate? How can we raise our daughters to avoid it? If you accept the truth of Linda's story, his questions are enraging, like saying, 'What in your background led you to a concentration camp?'

No one asks how we can stop raising men who fit Linda's terrified description of Chuck Traynor. Or what attracted the millions of people who went to *Deep Throat*. Or what to do about the millions of 'normal' men who assume that some sexualized violence and aggression are quite okay.

A woman in the audience asks if this isn't an issue for feminism. Linda says that yes, she has heard there are anti-pornography groups, she is getting in touch with Susan Brownmiller who wrote

*Against Our Will.*[6] That definitive book on rape has led Brownmiller to attack other pornographic violence against women.

But it's clear that, for Linda, this is a new hope and a new connection.

For women who want to support Linda now [1980] and to save others being used sexually against their will, this may be the greatest sadness. At no time during those months of suffering and dreams of escape, not even during the years of silence that followed, was Linda aware of any signal from the world around her that strong women as a group or feminists or something called the women's movement might be there to help her.

Surely a victim of anti-Semitism would know that the Jewish community was there to help, or a victim of racism would look to the civil rights movement. But feminist groups are not yet strong enough to be a presence in the world of pornography, prostitution and gynocide; or for that matter, in the world of welfare and the working poor that Linda then joined.

Even now, most of her help and support come from sympathetic men: from McGrady who believed her life story, from her husband who loses jobs in defence of her honour, from the male God of her obedient Catholic girlhood to whom she prayed as a sexual prisoner and now prays in her life as homemaker and mother.

Even her feelings of betrayal are attached to her father, not her mother. During her long lie-detector test, the only time she cried and completely broke down was over an innocuous mention of his name. 'I was watching that movie *Hardcore*,' she explained, 'where George C. Scott searches and searches for his daughter. Why didn't my father come looking for me? He saw *Deep Throat*. He should've known… He should've done something. Anything!'

After all, who among us had mothers with the power to rescue us, to do something? We don't even expect it. In mythology, Demeter rescued her daughter who had been abducted and raped by the King of the Underworld. She was a strong and raging mother who turned the earth to winter in anger at her daughter's fate. Could a powerful mother now rescue her daughter from the underworld of pornography? Not even Hollywood can fantasize that plot.

But Linda has begun to uncover her own rage, if only when talking about her fears for other women as pornography becomes more violent. 'Next,' she says quietly, as if to herself, 'they're going to be selling women's skins by the side of the road.'

And women have at least begun to bond together to rescue each other as sisters. There are centres for battered women, with publicized phone numbers for the victims but private shelters where they cannot be followed. It's a system that might work for victims of prostitution and pornography as well, if it existed, and if women knew it was there.

In the meantime, Linda takes time out from cleaning her tiny house on Long Island ('I clean it twice a day,' she says proudly) to do interviews, to send out her message of hope to other women who may be living in sexual servitude right now, and to lecture against pornography with other women, who are now her friends. She keeps answering questions, most of them from interviewers who are far less sympathetic than Donahue.

How could she write such a book when her son will some day read it? 'I've already explained to him,' she says firmly, 'that some people hurt Mommy—a long time ago.' How can her husband stand to have a wife with such a sexual past? ('It wasn't sexual. I never experienced any sexual pleasure, not one orgasm, nothing. I learned how to fake pleasure so I wouldn't get punished for doing a bad job.') And the most popular doubt of all: If she really wanted to, couldn't she have escaped sooner?

Linda explains as best she can. As I watch her, I come to believe the question should be different: Where did she find the courage to escape at all?

Inside the patience with which she answers these questions— the result of childhood training to be a 'good girl' that helps make victims of many of us—there is some core of strength and stubbornness that is itself the answer. She will make people understand. She will not give up.

In the microcosm of this one woman, there is a familiar miracle: the way in which women survive—and fight back.

And a fight there must be.

*Deep Throat* plays continuously in a New York theatre and probably

in many other cities of the world. Bruises are visible on Linda's legs
in the film itself, supporting her testimony that she was a prisoner
while she made it. Do viewers see the bruises—or only her smile?
No invasion of privacy or legal means has been found to stop this
film, partly because the statute of limitations has run, and partly
because her story of imprisonment runs counter to many sexual
myths. If I had not interviewed others who could confirm parts of
her story, I might also have believed this could not happen. As it is,
money continues to be made from images of her humiliation.

*Deep Throat* has popularized a whole new genre of pornography.
Added to all the familiar varieties of rape, there is now an ambition
to rape the throat. Porn novels treat this theme endlessly. Some
emergency-room doctors believe that victims of suffocation are on
the increase.

As for Chuck Traynor himself, he is still the husband and
manager of Marilyn Chambers.

Larry Fields, a columnist for the *Philadelphia Daily News*,
remembered interviewing them both for his column when Marilyn
was performing a song-and-dance act in a local nightclub. Traynor
bragged that he had taught Linda Lovelace everything she knew,
but that 'Marilyn's got what Linda never had—talent'.

While Traynor was answering questions on Marilyn's behalf, she
asked him for permission to go to the bathroom. Permission was
refused. 'Not right now,' Fields remembers him saying to her. And
when she objected that she was about to appear onstage: 'Just sit
there and shut up.'

When Fields also objected, Traynor was adamant. 'I don't tell
you how to write your column,' he said angrily. 'Don't tell me how
to treat my broads.'

### Postscript (1995)

After many health problems because of the physical punishment
she endured, and harassment because of her recognizability, Linda,
her husband and two teenage children did live a quiet life far away
from New York till she passed away. She suffered flashbacks when
kidnappings, murders and domestic violence assaulted her in the
media, she also travelled out of state to speak about her experience,

and testify in court cases on the realities of prostitution and pornography. Using her life to help others is the final stage of healing. As for those who created *Deep Throat*, there is still no legal way of eliciting damages or ending its distribution.

## Postscript (2013)

A Hollywood movie on the reality behind the hype of her life was released in 2013; it was called *Lovelace.*

—1980

# I WAS A PLAYBOY BUNNY

In November 2012, PB Lifestyle, a franchisee of the California-based Playboy Club Company, announced plans for a launch of the Playboy Club in Goa, to be followed by 120 other clubs, hotels and cafés around the country. Playboy founder, Hugh Hefner, made the final decision on the design of the costumes that the Bunnies would wear, with long drapes of chiffon to the bottom half, while the upper half—the satin bustier—would remain tight and revealing. So far, the plan has been delayed for two reasons: a) a politician from Goa went on hunger strike and threatened to set himself on fire if a licence was granted to the club and b) the company had falsely applied for permission to operate as a beach shack. It's possible, however, that the club simply needs to reapply as a city club rather than a beach shack.

The local press reported that six hired Bunnies—all foreign women—had arrived in India in 2012 to undergo 'a rigorous four-week service training program conducted by the US-based parent company' to prepare for the leporine role.[1]

Steinem documents in this article what we are up against and what life in a Playboy Club is like for a Bunny and how US Feminist had to organize to close down the clubs in the US.

—Ruchira Gupta

I undertook a reporting assignment armed with a large diary and this ad:

GIRLS:

Do Playboy Club Bunnies Really
Have Glamorous Jobs,
Meet Celebrities, And
Make Top Money?

Yes, it's true! Attractive young girls can now earn $200–$300 a week at the fabulous New York Playboy Club, enjoy the glamorous and exciting aura of show business, and have the opportunity to travel to other Playboy Clubs throughout the world. Whether serving drinks, snapping pictures, or greeting guests at the door, the Playboy Club is the stage—the Bunnies are the stars.

The charm and beauty of our Bunnies has been extolled in *Time*, *Newsweek*, and *Pageant*, and Ed Sullivan has called The Playboy Club 'the greatest new show biz gimmick.' And the Playboy Club is now the busiest spot in New York.

If you are pretty and personable, between 21 and 24, married or single, you probably qualify. No experience necessary.

Apply in person at SPECIAL INTERVIEWS being held Saturday and Sunday, January 26–27, 10 a.m.–3 p.m.
Please bring a swimsuit or leotards.

THE PLAYBOY CLUB
5 East 59th Street
THURSDAY, 24 JANUARY 1963

I've decided to call myself Marie Catherine Ochs. It is, may my ancestors forgive me, a family name. I have some claim to it, and I'm well versed in its European origins. Besides, it sounds much too square to be phony.

*Friday, 25th*

I've spent the entire afternoon making up a background for Marie. She shares my apartment, my phone and my measurements. Though younger than me by four years (I am beyond the Bunny age limit), Marie celebrates the same birthday and went to the same high school and college. But she wasn't a slave to academics—not Marie. After one year she left me plodding along the path to a BA and boarded a tourist flight to Europe. She had no money, but short periods as a waitress in London, a hostess-dancer in Paris and a secretary in Geneva were enough to sustain her between beachcombing and other escapades. Last year, she came back to New York and worked briefly as a secretary. Three mutual friends have agreed to give her strong personal recommendations. To know her is to love her.

Tomorrow is the day. Marie makes her first trip out of this notebook and into the world. I'm off to buy her a leotard.

*Saturday, 26th*

Today I put on the most theatrical clothes I could find, packed my leotard in a hatbox, and walked to the Playboy Club. It is impossible to miss. The discreet six-storey office building and art gallery that once stood there has been completely gutted and transformed into a shiny rectangle of plate glass. The orange-carpeted interior is clearly visible, with a modern floating stairway spiralling upwards at dead centre. The total effect is cheerful—and startling.

I crossed over to the club where a middle-aged man in a private guard's uniform grinned and beckoned: 'Here Bunny, Bunny, Bunny!' He jerked his thumb towards the glass door on the left. 'Interviews downstairs in the Playmate Bar.'

The inside of the club was so dramatically lit that it took a few seconds to realize it was closed and empty. I walked down a short flight of stairs and was greeted by Miss Shay, a thin, thirtyish woman who sat at a desk in the darkened bar. 'Bunny?' she asked briskly. 'Sit over there, fill out this form, and take off your coat.' I could see that two of the tables were already occupied by girls hunched over pencils, and I looked at them curiously. I had come in the middle of the interview period, hoping to see as many applicants as I could, but there were only three. 'Take off your coat,' said Miss Shay again. She looked at me appraisingly while I did so. One of the girls got up and crossed to the desk, her high-heeled plastic sandals slapping smartly against her heels. 'Look,' she said, 'you want these measurements with or without a bra?'

'With,' said Miss Shay.

'But I'm bigger without,' said the girl.

'All right,' said Miss Shay wearily, 'without.' Two more girls came down the steps looking fresh and innocent of cosmetics. 'Bunny?' said Miss Shay.

'Not really,' said one, but the other took a card. Their long hair and loafers looked collegiate.

The application form was short: address, phone, measurements, age and last three employers. I finished it and began to stall for time by looking at an accompanying brochure entitled BE A PLAYBOY CLUB BUNNY! Most of it was devoted to photographs: a group picture showing Bunnies 'chosen from all over the United States' surrounding 'Playboy Club President and Playboy Editor-Publisher Hugh M. Hefner'; a close-up of a Bunny serving Tony Curtis, 'a Playboy Club devotee [who] will soon star in Hugh M. Hefner's film titled, appropriately enough, *Playboy*'; two Bunnies smiling with Hugh M. Hefner on 'Playboy's nationally syndicated television show'; Bunnies handing out copies of *Playboy* in a veterans' hospital as 'just one of the many worthwhile community projects in which Bunnies participate'; a blonde Bunny standing before a matronly woman, the 'Bunny Mother' who offered 'friendly personal counselling'; and, on the last page, a bikini-clad girl crouching on a yacht flying a Bunny flag. 'When you become a Bunny,' said the text, 'your world will be fun-filled, pleasant, and always exciting.' It cited an average salary of two hundred dollars a week.

Another girl came down the steps. She wore glasses with blue rims and a coat that looked as if she had outgrown it. I watched her as she nervously asked Miss Shay if the club hired eighteen-year-olds. 'Sure,' said Miss Shay, 'but they can't work the midnight shift.' She gave the girl an application card, glanced down at her plump legs, and did not ask her to take off her coat. Two more girls came in, one in bright pink stretch pants and the other in purple. 'Man, this place is a gas,' said Pink.

'You think this is wild, you should see Hefner's house in Chicago,' said Purple. Miss Shay looked at them with approval.

'I don't have a phone,' said Blue Glasses sadly. 'Is it all right if I give you my uncle's phone? He lives in Brooklyn, too.'

'You do that,' said Miss Shay. She called me over, pointed to a spot three feet in front of her desk, and told me to stand up straight. I stood.

'I want to be a Bunny so much,' said Blue Glasses. 'I read about it in a magazine at school.'

Miss Shay asked me if I were really twenty-four. 'That's awfully old,' she warned. I said I thought I might just get in under the wire. She nodded.

'My uncle isn't home all day,' the girl said, 'but I'll go to his house and stay by the phone.'

'You do that, dear,' said Miss Shay and, turning to me, she added, 'I've taken the liberty of making an appointment for you on Wednesday at six-thirty. You will come to the service entrance, go to the sixth floor, and ask for Miss Burgess, the Bunny Mother.' I agreed, but then she added, 'Are you sure you haven't applied before? Someone named Marie Ochs came in yesterday.' I was startled: Could Marie have escaped from my notebook? I had a thirty-second fantasy based on *Pygmalion*. Or was there another Marie Ochs? Possible, but not likely. I decided to brave it out. 'How strange,' I murmured, 'there must be some mistake.' Miss Shay shrugged and suggested I bring 'bathing suit or leotard' on Wednesday.

'Could I call you?' said Blue Glasses.

'Don't do that, dear,' said Miss Shay. 'We'll call you.'

I left the club worrying about the life expectancy of Marie Ochs. Would they find out? Or did they know already? When I got halfway up the block I saw the two college girls. They were leaning against a building, their arms wrapped around themselves in a spasm of giggles, and suddenly I felt better about everything.

Everything, perhaps, except the thought of Blue Glasses sitting by her uncle's phone in Brooklyn.

*Wednesday, 30th*

I arrived at the club promptly at six-thirty, and business appeared to be booming. Customers were lined up in the snow to get in, and several passers-by were standing outside with their faces pressed to the glass. The elevator boy, a Valentino-handsome Puerto Rican, cheerfully jammed me in his car with two uniformed black porters, five middle-aged male customers, two costumed Bunnies and a stout matron in a mink coat. We stopped at the sixth floor. 'Is this where I get out?' said the matron.

'Sure, darling,' drawled the elevator boy, 'if you want to be a Bunny.' Laughter.

I looked around me. Dim lights and soft carpets had given way to unpainted cement block and hanging light bulbs. There was a door marked UNNIES; I could see the outlines where the B had been. A sign, handwritten on a piece of torn cardboard, was taped underneath: 'KNOCK!! Come on, guys. Please cooperate?!!' I walked through the door and into a bright, crowded hallway.

Two girls brushed past me. One was wearing nothing but bikini-style panties; the other had on long black tights of fine mesh and lavender satin heels. They both rushed to a small wardrobe room on my right, yelled out their names, collected costumes and rushed back. I asked the wardrobe mistress for Miss Burgess. 'Honey, we just gave her a going-away present.' Four more girls bounced up to ask for costumes, collars, cuffs and tails. They had on tights and high heels, but nothing from the waist up. One stopped to study a bulletin-board list titled 'Bunny of the Week'.

I retreated to the other end of the tiny hall. It opened into a large dressing room filled with metal lockers and long rows of dressing tables. Personal notes were taped to the mirrors ('Anybody want to work B Level Saturday night?' and 'I'm having a swingin' party Wednesday at Washington Square Village, all Bunnies welcome.') Cosmetics were strewn along the counters and three girls sat in a row applying false eyelashes with the concentration of yogis. It looked like a cartoon of a chorus girls' dressing room.

A girl with very red hair, very white skin and a black satin Bunny costume turned her back to me and waited. I understood that I was supposed to zip her up, a task that took several minutes of pulling and tugging. She was a big girl and looked a little tough, but her voice when she thanked me was tiny and babylike. Judy Holliday could not have done better. I asked her about Miss Burgess. 'Yeah, she's in that office,' said Baby Voice, gesturing towards a wooden door with a glass peephole in it, 'but Sheralee's the new Bunny Mother.' Through the glass, I could see two girls, a blonde and a brunette. Both appeared to be in their early twenties and nothing like the matronly woman pictured in the brochure. Baby Voice tugged and pulled some more. 'This isn't my costume,' she explained, 'that's why it's hard to get the crotch up.' She walked away, snapping her fingers and humming softly.

The brunette came out of the office and introduced herself to me as Bunny Mother Sheralee. I told her I had mistaken her for a Bunny. 'I worked as a Bunny when the club opened last month,' she said, 'but now I've replaced Miss Burgess.' She nodded towards the blonde who was trying on a three-piece beige suit that I took to be her going-away present. 'You'll have to wait a while, honey,' said Sheralee. I sat down.

By 7:00 I had watched three girls tease their hair into cotton-candy shapes and four more stuff their bosoms with Kleenex. By 7:15 I had talked to two other prospective Bunnies, one a dancer, the other a part-time model from Texas. At 7:30, I witnessed the major crisis of a Bunny who had sent her costume to the cleaners with her engagement ring pinned inside. At 7:40, Miss Shay came up to the office and said, 'There's no one left but Marie.' By 8:00, I was sure she was waiting for the manager of the club to come tell me that my real identity had been discovered. By 8:15, when I was finally called in, I was nervous beyond all proportion.

I waited while Sheralee looked over my application. 'You don't look twenty-four,' she said. Well, that's that, I thought. 'You look much younger.' I smiled in disbelief. She took several Polaroid pictures of me. 'For the record,' she explained. I offered her the personal history I had so painstakingly fabricated and typed, but she gave it back with hardly a glance. 'We don't like our girls to have any background,' she said firmly. 'We just want you to fit the Bunny image.' She directed me to the costume room.

I asked if I should put on my leotard.

'Don't bother with that,' said Sheralee. 'We just want to see that Bunny image.'

The wardrobe mistress told me to take off my clothes and began to search for an old Bunny costume in my size. A girl rushed in with her costume in her hand, calling for the wardrobe mistress as a wounded soldier might yell, 'Medic!' 'I've broken my zipper,' she wailed, 'I sneezed!'

'That's the third time this week,' said the wardrobe mistress sternly. 'It's a regular epidemic.' The girl apologized, found another costume, and left.

I asked if a sneeze could really break a costume.

'Sure,' she said. 'Girls with colds usually have to be replaced.'

She gave me a bright blue satin costume. It was so tight that the zipper caught my skin as she fastened the back. She told me to inhale as she zipped again, this time without mishap, and stood back to look at me critically. The bottom was cut up so high that it left my hip bones exposed as well as a good five inches of untanned derriere. The boning in the waist would have made Scarlett O'Hara blanch, and the entire construction tended to push all available flesh up to the bosom. I was sure it would be perilous to bend over. 'Not too bad,' said the wardrobe mistress, and began to stuff an entire plastic dry-cleaning bag into the top of my costume. A blue satin band with matching Bunny ears attached was fitted around my head like an enlarged bicycle clip, and a grapefruit-sized hemisphere of white fluff was attached to hooks at the costume's rear-most point. 'Okay, baby,' she said, 'put on your high heels and go show Sheralee.' I looked in the mirror. The Bunny image looked back.

'Oh, you look sweet,' said Sheralee. 'Stand against the wall and smile pretty for the birdie.' She took several more Polaroid shots.

The baby-voiced redhead came in to say she still hadn't found a costume to fit. A tiny blonde in lavender satin took off her tail and perched on the desk. 'Look,' she said, 'I don't mind the demerits— okay, I got five demerits—but don't I get points for working over time?'

Sheralee looked harassed and turned to Miss Burgess. 'The new kids think the girls from Chicago get special treatment, and the old kids won't train the new ones.'

'I'll train the little buggers,' said Baby Voice. 'Just get me a costume.'

I got dressed and waited. And listened:

'He gave me thirty bucks, and I only got him cigarettes.'

'Bend over, honey, and get yourself into it.'

'I don't know, he makes Milk of Magnesia or something.'

'You know people commit suicide with those plastic bags?'

'Then this schmuck orders a Lace Curtain. Who ever heard of a Lace Curtain?'

'I told him our tails were asbestos, so he tried to burn it to find out.'

'Last week I netted thirty bucks in tips. Big deal.'

Sheralee called me back into the office. 'So you want to be a Bunny,' she said.

'Oh yes, very much,' I said.

'Well…' she paused significantly, 'we want you to be!' I was startled. No more interviews? No investigation? 'Come in tomorrow at three. We'll fit your costume and have you sign everything.' I smiled and felt foolishly elated.

Down the stairs and up Fifth Avenue. Hippety-hop, I'm a Bunny!

*Thursday 31st*

I now have two Bunny costumes—one orange satin and one electric blue. The colour choice and the quality of satin are about the same as those in athletic supply catalogues. Costume bodies, pre-cut to body and bra-cup size, are fitted while you wait. I waited, standing on the cement floor in bare feet and bikini pants. The wardrobe mistress gave me a small bathroom rug to stand on. 'Can't have brand-new Bunnies catching cold,' she said. I asked if she could follow the line of my bikini pants in fitting the bottom; the costume I had tried the day before was cut up higher than any I had seen in photographs. She chuckled. 'Listen, baby, you think that was high, you should see some.' The whole costume was darted and seamed until it was two inches smaller than any of my measurements everywhere except the bust. 'You got to have room in there to stuff,' she said. 'Just about everybody stuffs. And you keep your tips in there. The "vault" they call it.'

A girl with jet-black hair, chalky make-up and a green costume stopped at the door. 'My tail droops,' she said, pushing it into position with one finger. 'Those damn customers always yank it.'

The wardrobe mistress handed her a safety pin. 'You better get a cleaner tail too, baby. You get demerits running around with a scruffy old tail like that.' More girls began calling for their costumes, checking them out in a notebook chained to the counter. I learned that costumes were not allowed out of the building and that each girl paid $2.50 a day to cover the cost of her costume's upkeep and cleaning. Bunnies also paid five dollars a pair for their thin black nylon tights and could be given demerits if they wore tights with runs in them. The wardrobe mistress gave me swatches from my two costumes and told me to have shoes dyed to match. I asked if the club allowed us any money for shoes. 'You crazy or something, baby?' she said. 'This place don't allow you no money for nothing. Make sure you get three-inch heels. You get demerits, you wear 'em any lower.'

I dressed and went to the Bunny Mother's room. Sheralee was at the desk. With her long hair pinned back she looked about eighteen. She gave me a large, shocking pink form marked 'Bunny Application' and a brown plastic briefcase with a miniature nude girl and the Playboy Club printed on it in orange. 'This is your Bunny bible,' she said seriously, 'and I want you to promise me you'll study it all weekend.'

The application form was four-pages long. I had already made up most of the answers for my biography, but some questions were new. Was I dating any Playboy Club key-holders, and what were their names? None. Did I plan to date a particular key-holder? No. Did I have a police record? No. The space for Social Security number I left blank.

Up one flight in the main office, I delivered the form to Miss Shay. The cement-floored room was chequered with desks but, as personnel director, Miss Shay rated a corner position. She scanned the form and began taking more Polaroid pictures of me. 'Be sure and bring your Social Security card tomorrow,' she said. I wondered what to do about the fact that Marie Ochs had none. A stout man in a blue suit, black shirt and white tie approached and gestured towards a chubby girl standing behind him. 'Mr Roma told me to bring her over, and I'd sure appreciate anything you can do for her,' he said, and winked.

'In cases of extreme personal recommendation,' said Miss Shay coolly, 'we do schedule a girl's interview right away.' She signalled to Sheralee, who took the girl downstairs. The stout man looked relieved.

A red-haired woman and two men came over, but Miss Shay asked them to wait. The younger man tapped the redhead's chin with his fist and grinned. 'You ain't got a thing to worry about, baby.' She gave him a look of utter scorn and lit a cigarette.

I signed an income tax form, a meal ticket, a receipt for the meal ticket, an application form, an insurance form and a release of all photographs for any purpose—publicity, editorial, or otherwise—deemed fit by Playboy Clubs International. A harried looking young man in shirtsleeves came to tell Miss Shay that two men working in the basement were going to quit. They had expected to work six days for seventy-five dollars and were working only five days for sixty dollars. They were upset about it because they had families to support. 'I can't make changes,' she said crisply. 'I can only implement Mr Roma's decisions.'

Miss Shay stapled a set of Polaroid pictures to my employment form and gave me my schedule. 'Tomorrow, you'll have make-up guidance at Larry Mathews's, this weekend is Bunny-bible study, and Monday I've made an appointment for you to see our doctor for a physical exam.' She leaned forward confidentially. 'A complete physical,' she said. 'Monday afternoon is the Bunny Mother lecture and Bunny Father lecture. Tuesday you'll have Bunny school, and Wednesday you'll train on the floor.' I asked if I could go to my own doctor. 'No,' she said, 'you must go to our doctor for a special physical. All Bunnies have to.'

Miss Shay gave me one last form to sign, a request that Marie Ochs's birth record be sent to the Playboy Club. I signed it, hoping that the state of Michigan would take a while to discover that Marie did not exist. 'In the meantime, I'll need your birth certificate,' she said. 'We can't let you work without it.' I agreed to send a special-delivery letter home for it.

Of course I wouldn't be allowed to serve liquor or work late hours without proof of age. Why didn't I think of that?

Well, Marie's future may be short, but she can still try to make it through Bunny school.

*Friday 1st*

I was fitted for false eyelashes today at Larry Matthews's, a twenty-four-hour-a-day beauty salon in a West Side hotel. As a make-up expert feathered the eyelashes with a manicure scissors, she pointed out a girl who had just been fired from the club 'because she wouldn't go out with a Number One key-holder'. I said I thought we were forbidden to go out with customers. 'You can go out with them if they've got Number One keys,' the make-up girl explained. 'They're for club management and reporters and big shots like that.' I explained that being fired for not going seemed like a very different thing. 'Well,' she said thoughtfully, 'I guess it was the way she said it. She told him to go screw himself.'

I paid the bill; $8.14 for the eyelashes and a cake of rouge, even after the 25 per cent Bunny discount. I had refused to invest in darker lipstick even though 'girls get fired for looking pale'. I wondered how much the Bunny beauty concession was worth to Mr Matthews. Had beauty salons sent in sealed bids for this lucrative business?

I am home now, and I have measured the lashes. Maybe I don't have to worry so much about being recognized in the club. They are three quarters of an inch long at their shortest point.

*Sunday 3rd*

I've spent an informative Sunday with the Bunny bible, or the Playboy Club Bunny Manual, as it is officially called. From introduction ('You are holding the top job in the country for a young girl.') to appendix ('Sidecar: Rim glass with lime and frost with sugar.')—it is a model of clarity.

Some dozen supplements accompany the bible. Altogether, they give a vivid picture of a Bunny's function. For instance:

...You...are the only direct contact most of the readers will ever have with Playboy personnel...We depend on our Bunnies to express the personality of the magazine.

...Bunnies will be expected to contribute a fair share of personal appearances as part of their regular duties for the Club.

...Bunnies are reminded that there are many pleasing means they can employ to stimulate the club's liquor volume, thereby increasing their earnings significantly... The key to selling more drinks is Customer Contact...they will respond particularly to your efforts to be friendly... You should make it seem that [the customer's] opinions are very important...

The Incentive System is a method devised to reward those table Bunnies who put forth an extra effort... The Bunny whose [drink] average per person is highest will be the winner... Prize money...will likewise be determined by over-all drink income.

There is a problem in being 'friendly' and 'pampering' the customer while refusing to go out with him or even give him your last name. The manual makes it abundantly clear that Bunnies must never go out with anyone they meet in the club—customer or employee—and adds that a detective agency called Willmark Service Systems, Inc., has been employed to make sure that they don't. ('Of course, you can never tell when you are being checked out by a Willmark Service representative.') The explanation written for the Bunnies is simple: 'Men are very excited about being in the company of Elizabeth Taylor, but they know they can't paw or proposition her. The moment they felt they could become familiar with her, she would not have the aura of glamour that now surrounds her. The same must be true of our Bunnies.' In an accompanying letter from Hugh Hefner to Willmark, the explanation is still simpler: 'Our licenses are laid on the line any time any of our employees in any way engages, aids, or abets traffic in prostitution...' Willmark is therefore instructed to 'Use your most attractive and personable male representatives to proposition the Bunnies, and even offer...as high as $200 on this, "right now", for a promise of meeting you outside the Club later.' Willmark representatives are told to ask a barman or other male employee 'if any of the girls are available on a cash basis for a "friendly evening".... Tell him you will pay the girls well or will pay him for the girls.' If the employee does act 'as a procurer', Willmark is to notify the Club immediately. 'We naturally do not tolerate any merchandising of the Bunnies,' writes Mr Hefner, 'and are most anxious to know if any such thing is occurring.'

If the idea of being merchandised isn't enough to unnerve a prospective Bunny, there are other directives that may. Willmark representatives are to check girls for heels that are too low, runs in their hose, jewellery, underwear that shows, crooked or unmatched ears, dirty costumes, absence of name tags and 'tails in good order'. Further: 'When show is on, check to see if the Bunnies are reacting to the performers. When a comic is on, they are supposed to laugh.' Big Brother Willmark is watching you.

In fact, Bunnies must always appear gay and cheerful ('Think about something happy or funny...your most important commodity is personality.') in spite of all their worries, including the demerit system. Messy hair, bad nails and bad make-up cost five demerits each. So does calling the room director by his first name, failing to keep a make-up appointment, or eating food in the Bunny Room. Chewing gum or eating while on duty is ten demerits for the first offence, twenty for the second and dismissal for the third. A three-time loser for 'failure to report for work without replacement' is not only dismissed, but blacklisted from all other Playboy Clubs. Showing up late for work or after a break costs a demerit a minute, failure to follow a room director's instructions costs fifteen. 'The dollar value of demerits,' notes the Bunny bible, 'shall be determined by the general manager of each Club.'

Once the system is mastered, there are still instructions for specific jobs. Door Bunnies greet customers and check their keys. Camera Bunnies must operate Polaroids. Cigarette Bunnies explain why a pack of cigarettes can't be bought without a Playboy lighter, Hat-check Bunnies learn the checking system, Gift-shop Bunnies sell Playboy products, Mobile-gift-shop Bunnies carry Playboy products around in baskets, and Table Bunnies memorize thirteen pages of drinks.

There's more to Bunnyhood than stuffing bosoms.

Note: Section 523 says: 'Employees may enter and enjoy the facilities of the Club as bona fide guests of 1 [Number One] key-holders.' Are these the big shots my make-up expert had in mind?

*Morning, Monday 4th*

At 11:00 a.m. I went to see the Playboy doctor at his office in a nearby hotel. ('Failure to keep doctor's appointment, twenty demerits.') The nurse gave me a medical-history form to fill out.

'Do you know this includes an internal physical? I've been trying to get Miss Shay to warn the girls.' I said I knew, but that I didn't understand why it was required. 'It's for your own good,' she said, and led me into a narrow examining room containing a medicine chest, a scale and a gynaecological table. I put on a hospital robe and waited. It seemed I had spent a good deal of time lately either taking off clothes, waiting, or both.

The nurse came back with the doctor, a stout, sixtyish man with the pink and white skin of a baby. 'So you're going to be a Bunny,' he said heartily. 'Just came back from Miami myself. Beautiful club down there. Beautiful Bunnies.' I started to ask him if he had the coast-to-coast franchise, but he interrupted to ask how I liked Bunnyhood.

'Well, it's livelier than being a secretary,' I said, and he told me to sit on the edge of the table. As he pounded my back and listened to me breathe, the thought crossed my mind that every Bunny in the New York Club had rested on the same spot. 'This is the part all the girls hate,' said the doctor, and took blood from my arm for a Wassermann test. I told him that testing for venereal disease seemed a little ominous. 'Don't be silly,' he said, 'all the employees have to do it. You'll know everyone in the club is clean.' I said that their being clean didn't really affect me and that I objected to being put through these tests. Silence. He asked me to stand to 'see if your legs are straight'. 'Okay,' I said, 'I have to have a Wassermann. But what about an internal examination? Is that required of waitresses in New York State?'

'What do you care?' he said. 'It's free, and it's for everybody's good.'

'How?' I asked.

'Look,' he said impatiently, 'we usually find that girls who object to it strenuously have some reason...' He paused significantly. I paused, too. I could either go through with it or I could march out in protest. But in protest of what?

Back in the reception room, the nurse gave me a note to show Miss Shay that, according to preliminary tests at least, I had passed. As I put on my coat, she phoned a laboratory to pick up 'a blood sample and a smear'. I asked why those tests, but no urine sample?

Wasn't that the most common laboratory test of all? 'It's for your own protection,' she said firmly, 'and anyway, the Club pays.'

Down in the lobby, I stopped in a telephone booth to call the Department of Health. I asked if a Wassermann test was required of waitresses in New York City? 'No.' Then what kind of physical examination was required? 'None at all,' they said.

*Afternoon, Monday*

The Bunny Mother lecture turned out to be a casual and much interrupted talk with Sheralee in her small windowless office. There were seven other trainees, two of them already in costume. There was also a delicate blonde, the part-time model from Texas whom I had already met, a very big girl with very long hair who said she was a magician's assistant, a square-looking girl in a plaid suit and a pretty brunette who never took off her coat.

For the most part, Sheralee's talk repeated the Bunny bible, but some points were new.

1. Because of the minimum wage in New York City, we must get a salary of fifty dollars for a forty-hour week. We get tips, but the club takes 50 per cent of the first thirty dollars' worth of those that are charged, 25 per cent of amounts up to sixty dollars and 5 per cent after that. 'That means half of everything,' whispered a girl in costume. 'Who gets more than thirty dollars a day?'

2. We may keep all tips that are given to us in cash, but if we indicate any preference for cash tips, we will be fired.

3. 'We don't even want you kids to know what "drink average" means,' said Sheralee, and explained that it meant the number of drinks per customer. 'But if you give good service, you're bound to get more re-orders, and you get merits for good service. A hundred merits equals twenty-five dollars.'

4. If we meet boyfriends or husbands after work, we must do it at least two blocks from the Club. Customers must never see us meeting other men.

5. We should never leave money in our lockers. Two girls have just been fired for stealing.

6. Because of 'special problems in New York', we can't be charged money for demerits, so instead, we may buy them back

with merits. 'If a hundred merits are worth twenty-five dollars,' I asked, 'isn't it the same thing?' Sheralee said it wasn't.

7. Number One key-holders are given special treatment, that is, we bring them telephone, pad and pen immediately. Playboy International then 'absorbs' the amount of their bill. Number One keys go to the executives of all the clubs, important members of the press and a few other VIPs. We may also give them our names, accompany them in the Club and go out with them. The magician's assistant asked if we had to go out with them.

Sheralee said, 'Of course not.'

'But,' the girl said, 'one of the room directors got mad at me for not telling my last name to a Number One key-holder. I explained that I was married, but he said I should give my last name anyway.'

Sheralee said she was sure the room director didn't mean it. 'You never have to do anything you don't want,' she said comfortingly.

8. The apartment of Vic Lownes is used for Playboy's promotional parties in New York, just as Hugh Hefner's house is used in Chicago. ('Mr Lownes used to run the clubs,' Sheralee explained, 'but now he's associated mostly with the magazine.') When we go to such parties, we are not allowed to bring men. 'Not even husbands?' the magician's assistant asked. 'Absolutely no men,' said Sheralee. 'But of course, you don't have to go if you don't want to.'

We all went down to the VIP Room for the Bunny Father lecture, but not before a Bunny stopped at the door of Sheralee's office and called 'Gloria!' I froze. After what seemed an eternity, the Bunny sitting next to me answered. I have learned to answer to Marie. Now I must learn to stop answering to Gloria.

There was no Bunny Father, but two slide shows with taped narration and jazz background were presented as his lecture. One was on Bunnies in general and offered nothing new except that when customers tried to 'get familiar', we were to say, 'Sir, you are not allowed to touch the Bunnies.' The second half of the Bunny Father lecture was called 'Cocktail Bunny'. It showed how to set up trays, fill out bills and place drinks on tables. The narration didn't synchronize with the slides, the room was cold and I emerged with a splitting headache.

Sheralee said that Miss Shay wanted to see me. My heart sank.

The main office was the same fluorescent-lit chaos as before, but Miss Shay was an island of calm. I would need an identification card, she said, to get in and out of the building. I gave her the note from the doctor and my real Social Security number. I explained that I had lost the card. She looked doubtful but took the number.

I wanted to ask about this morning's medical puzzle, but decided against it for the moment. By calling attention to myself, I might only jog her memory about the missing birth certificate. I told her that my file was complete except for a chest X-ray, and I left. It's hard to believe that the efficient Miss Shay won't catch up with me soon, but I'll stay until discovered.

*Afternoon, Tuesday 5th*

At noon today I waited in line for a free chest X-ray at the Department of Health, muttering under my breath: 'Flamingo gets cherry, orange and lime circle. Mist gets lemon twist, cordials go in London docks.' These bits of wisdom from my drink script and all the other documents in that brown plastic briefcase were to be the subject of a written Bunny quiz at three o'clock.

I reported to Sheralee and she greeted me with a rush. 'Oh, sweetie, I'm absolutely desperate!' She needed an 'over-twenty-one girl', she said, to work the hat-check concession from seven-thirty that evening to four in the morning. Would I help her out? Of course I would, I said, if she thought I could handle it. 'Oh, sure, sweetie,' said Sheralee, 'it's terrifically simple.' My matching shoes weren't ready yet, but never mind, I could wear black, she said. All I had to do was to be there in make-up by seven. I was surprised and elated. I would have at least one night 'on the floor'. I would, that is, if I could successfully avoid Miss Shay.

The quiz turned out to be a list of sixty-one short-answer questions. Our class of eight scribbled seriously while Sheralee read the questions aloud. I could see the Texas model looking perplexed, her mouth slightly open, and the Bunny named Gloria was chewing on her knuckle. I decided it wouldn't pay to be too smart, and wrote down six wrong answers. We scored one another's papers and read out the results. I was top of the class with nine wrong, the magician's assistant had ten, and everyone else missed fourteen or more. Texas missed nearly thirty. When the Club says a Bunny is chosen for '1) Beauty, 2) Personality, and 3) Ability,' the order must be significant.

We went to the penthouse, a large fourth-floor room with a back-lit plastic panel depicting rooftops. Sheralee seated us at a row of deserted tables and began to quiz us on drinks. 'What is Fleischmann's?'

'Gin.'

'What is Vat Sixty-Nine?'

'I haven't studied these,' said Texas.

'Scotch,' said the pretty brunette.

'What's Courvoisier?'

'I know, I memorized that. It's…cognac!' said Gloria.

'What's Piper Heidsieck?' The delicate blonde didn't know. 'Haven't you ever had champagne?' asked Sheralee. The blonde said no, she'd never seen it. 'It looks just like ginger ale,' said Sheralee, 'only it costs lots and lots of money.' After several rounds of quizzing, everyone except Texas had been able to answer a few. She hung her hennaed head and Sheralee lectured her severely.

A very tall, very pale black girl came over and introduced herself as our training Bunny. She was as thin and fragile as a high-fashion model, and very pretty. 'She's one of the oldest Bunnies here. Everybody just loves her,' said Gloria. 'The men call coloured girls chocolate Bunnies,' said another girl and giggled.

We spent a hurried hour learning the Bunny stance (a model's pose with one hip jutted out) and the Bunny dip (a back-leaning way of placing drinks on low tables without falling out of our costumes). We learned the ritual serving sentences: 'Good evening, sir, I am your Bunny, Marie. May I see the member's key, please? Are you the key-holder or is this a borrowed key? Thank you. Now I'll be happy to take your order.' No deviation allowed. I wondered if the uniformity ever bored the customers. 'Is there anything else I can get you, Mr Jones?' 'Thank you, Mr Jones, come back and see us again.' I was being programmed.

At home, I retreat behind greasepaint and false eyelashes. The club's office will be closed when I get there: no Miss Shay to forbid me to work. At least my career will include one night of 'Customer Contact'.

*Evening, Tuesday 5th*

The Bunny Room was chaotic. I was pushed and tugged and zipped into my electric-blue costume by the wardrobe mistress, but this time she allowed me to stuff my own bosom, and I was able to get away with only half a dry-cleaner's bag. I added the tiny collar with clip-on bow tie and the starched cuffs with Playboy cuff-links. My nameplate was centred in a ribbon rosette like those won in horse shows, and pinned just above my bare right hipbone. A major policy change, I was told, had just shifted name-tags from left hip to right. The wardrobe mistress also gave me a Bunny jacket because it was a below-zero night, and I was to stand by the front door. The jacket turned out to be a brief shrug of imitation white fur that covered the shoulders but left the bosom carefully bare.

I went in to be inspected by Bunny Mother Sheralee. 'You look sweet,' she said, and advised that I keep any money I had with me in my costume. 'Two more girls have had things stolen from their lockers,' she said, and added that I should be sure and tell the lobby director the exact amount of money I had with me. 'Otherwise they may think you stole tips.' Table Bunnies, she explained, were allowed to keep any tips they might receive in cash (though the club did take up to 50 per cent of all their charge tips), but Hat-check Bunnies could keep no tips at all. Instead, they were paid a flat twelve dollars for eight hours. I told her that twelve dollars a day seemed a good deal less than the salary of two to three hundred dollars mentioned in the advertisement. 'Well, you won't work hat-check all the time, sweetie,' she said. 'When you start working as a Table Bunny, you'll see how it all averages out.'

I took a last look at myself in the mirror. A creature with three-quarter-inch eyelashes, blue satin ears and an overflowing bosom looked back. I asked Sheralee if we had to stuff ourselves so much. 'Of course you do,' she said. 'Practically all the girls just stuff and stuff. That's the way Bunnies are supposed to look.'

The elevator opened on the mezzanine and I made my professional debut in the Playboy Club. It was crowded, noisy and very dark. A group of men with organizational name-tags on their lapels stood nearby. 'Here's my Bunny honey now,' said one, and flung his arm around my shoulders as if we were fellow halfbacks leaving the field.

'Please, sir,' I said, and uttered the ritual sentence we had learned from the Bunny Father lecture: 'You are not allowed to touch the Bunnies.' His companions laughed and laughed. 'Boy oh boy, guess she told you!' said one, and tweaked my tail as I walked away.

The programmed phrases of the Bunny bible echoing in my mind, I climbed down the carpeted spiral stairs between the mezzanine ('Living Room, Piano Bar, buffet dinner now being served') and the lobby ('Check your coats, immediate seating in the Playmate Bar'), separated from the street by only a two-storey sheet of glass. The alternative was a broad staircase at the back of the lobby but that, too, could be seen from the street. All of us, customers and Bunnies alike, were a living window display. I reported to the lobby director. 'Hello, Bunny Marie,' he said. 'How's things?' I told him that I had fifteen dollars in my costume. 'I'll remember,' he said. I had a quick and humiliating vision of all the Hat-check Bunnies lined up for bosom inspection.

There was a four-deep crowd of impatient men surrounding the Hat-check Room. The head Hat-check Bunny, a little blonde who had been imported from Chicago to 'straighten out the system', told me to take their tickets and call the numbers out to two 'hang boys' behind the counter. 'I'll give you my number if you give me yours,' said a balding man, and turned to the crowd for appreciation.

After an hour of helping men on with coats, scarves and hats, the cocktail rush had subsided enough for the Chicago Bunny to show me how to pin numbers on coat lapels with straight pins or tuck them in hatbands. She gave me more ritual sentences. 'Thank you, sir, here is your ticket.' 'The Information Bunny is downstairs to your right.' 'Sorry, we're unable to take ladies' coats.' (Only if the club was uncrowded, and the coats were not fur, was the Hat-check Room available to women.) She emphasized that I was to put all tips in a slotted box attached to the wall, smile gratefully and not tell the customers that the tips went to the Club. She moved to the other half of the check-room ('The blue tickets are next door, sir.') and sent a tall, heavyset Swiss Bunny to take her place.

The two of us took care of a small stream of customers and talked a little. I settled down to my ever-present worry that someone I knew was going to come in, recognize me, and say 'Gloria!' If the rumour were true that one newspaper reporter and one news-magazine reporter had tried to become Bunnies and failed, the management must be alert to the possibility. I had seen more than enough Sydney Greenstreet movies to worry about the Club's reaction. If someone I knew did come in, I would just keep repeating: 'There must be some mistake,' and hope for the best.

Dinner traffic began, and soon there was a crowd of twenty men waiting. We worked quickly, but coats going in and out at the same time made for confusion. One customer was blundering about behind the counter in search of a lost hat, and two more were complaining loudly that they had been waiting ten minutes. 'The reason there's a line outside the Playboy Club,' said one, 'is because they're waiting for their coats.' A man in a blue silk suit reached out to pull my tail. I dodged and held a coat for a balding man with a row of ballpoint pens in his suit pocket. He put it on, but backwards, so that his arms were around me. The hang-boy yelled at him in a thick Spanish accent, 'Leave her alone,' and he told the hang-boy to shut up. Three women in mink stoles stood waiting for their husbands. I could see them staring, not with envy, but coldly, as if measuring themselves against the Swiss Bunny and me. High up on the opposite wall, a camera stared down at all of us and transmitted the scene to screens embedded in walls all over the club, including one screen over the sidewalk: 'the closed-circuit television camera that flashes your arrival throughout the Club', explained publicity folders. I was overcome by a nightmare sensation of walking naked through crowds and the only way back to my own clothes was the glass-encased stairway. As men pressed forward with coats outstretched, I turned to the hang-boy for more tickets. 'Don't worry,' he said kindly, 'you get used to it.'

Business let up again. I asked the Swiss Bunny if she liked the work. 'Not really,' she shrugged. 'I was an airline hostess for a while, but once you've seen Hong Kong, you've seen it.' A man asked for his coat. I turned around and found myself face-to-face with two people whom I knew well, a television executive and his wife. I looked down as I took his ticket and kept my back turned while the boy found the coat, but I had to face him again to deliver it. My television friend looked directly at me, gave me fifty cents, and walked away. Neither he nor his wife had recognized me. It was depressing to be a non-person in a Bunny suit, but it was also a victory. To celebrate, I helped a slight, shy-looking man put on his long blue-and-white scarf, asked him if he and the scarf were from Yale. He looked startled, as if he had been recognized at a masquerade.

There were no clocks anywhere in the club. I asked the hang boy what time it was. 'One o'clock,' he said. I had been working for more than five hours with no break. My fingers were perforated and sore from pushing pins through cardboard, my arms ached from holding heavy coats, I was thoroughly chilled from the icy wind that blew in the door each time a customer opened it and, atop my three-inch black satin heels, my feet were killing me. I walked over to ask the Chicago Bunny if I could take a break.

'Yes,' she said, 'a half-hour to eat, but no more.'

Down the hall from the Bunny Room was the employees' lounge where our meal tickets entitled us to one free meal a day. I pulled a metal folding chair up to a long bare table, took my shoes off gingerly and sat down next to two black men in grey work uniforms. They looked sympathetic as I massaged my swollen feet. One was young and quite handsome, the other middle-aged and greying at the temples. Like all employees at the club, they seemed chosen, at least partly, for their appearance. The older one advised me about rolling bottles under my feet to relax them and getting arch supports for my shoes. I asked what they did. 'We're garbage men,' said the younger. 'It don't sound so good, but it's easier than your job.'

They told me I should eat something and gestured to the beef stew on their paper plates. 'Friday we get fish,' one said, 'but every other day is the same stew.'

'The same, except it gets worse,' said the other, and laughed. The older one told me he felt sorry for the Bunnies, even though some of them enjoyed 'showing off their looks'. He advised me to be careful of my feet and not to try to work double shifts.

Back downstairs, I tried to categorize the customers as I checked their coats. With the exception of a few teenage couples, the majority seemed to be middle-aged businessmen. Less than half had women with them, and the rest came in large all-male bunches that seemed entirely subsidized by expense accounts. I saw only four of the type pictured in club advertisements—the young, lean, nattily dressed Urban Man—and they were with slender, fashionable girls who looked rather appalled by our stuffed costumes and bright make-up. The least confident wives of the businessmen didn't measure themselves against us, but seemed to assume their husbands would be attracted to us and stood aside, looking timid and embarrassed. There were a few customers, a very few, either men or women (I counted ten), who looked at us not as objects but smiled and nodded as if we might be human beings.

The Swiss Bunny took a break, and a hang boy began to give me a gentle lecture. I was foolish, he said, to put all the money in the box. The tips were cash. If we didn't take some, the man who counted it might. I told him I was afraid they would look in my costume and I didn't want to get fired. 'They only check you girls once in a while,' he said. 'Anyway, I'll make you a deal. You give me money. I meet you outside. We split it.' My feet ached, my fingers were sticky from dozens of sweaty hatbands and my skin was gouged and sore from the bones of the costume. Even the half-hour dinner break had been on my own time, so the club was getting a full eight hours of work. I felt resentful enough to take him up on it. Still, it would hardly do to get fired for stealing. I told him that I was a new Bunny and too nervous to try it. 'You'll get over that,' he said. 'One Saturday night last week, this check room took in a thousand dollars in tips. And you know how much we get paid. You think about that.'

It was almost 4:00 a.m. Quitting time.

The lobby director came over to tell us that the customer count for the night was about two thousand. I said that sounded good. 'No,' he said. 'Good is four thousand.'

I went back to the Bunny Room, turned in my costume, and sat motionless, too tired to move. The stays had made vertical indentations around my rib cage and the zipper had left a welt over my spine. I complained about the costume's tightness to the Bunny who was sitting next to me, also motionless. 'Yeah,' she said, 'a lot of girls say their legs get numb from the knee up. I think it presses on a nerve or something.'

The street was deserted, but a taxi waited outside by the employees' exit. The driver held a dollar bill out the window. 'I got four more of these,' he said. 'Is that enough?' I kept on walking. 'What's a matter?' he said, irritated. 'You work in there, don't you?'

The streets were brightly lit and sparkling with frost. As I walked the last block to my apartment, I passed a grey English car with the motor running. A woman was sitting in the driver's seat, smoking a cigarette and watching the street. Her hair was bright blonde and her coat bright red. She looked at me and smiled. I smiled back. She looked available—and she was. Of the two of us, she seemed the more honest.

*Wednesday 6th*

I got up just in time to rush back to the club for my Table-Bunny training at two o'clock, and arrived feeling that I had never left. As I changed into my costume, one of the Bunnies was reading aloud from a weekly tabloid called *Leo Skull's Show Guide*. 'Listen to this,' she said. 'It says, "Although a thousand girls were interviewed for the club and 125 are working there now, the Playboy Club's fantastic business, the lines and crowds of customers thronging there daily, have made it necessary to add another fifty Bunnies."' I had heard Sheralee say that only 103 Bunnies were on schedule. I asked the girl who was reading if we really needed fifty more. Probably, she said, because the club had opened with 140 Bunnies—and nearly fifty of them had quit.

Another girl disagreed. 'I heard that twenty were fired and forty more quit—but I think it's more, because we've only got about a hundred now, and a lot of them are new Bunnies.' I said I was going to ask Miss Shay, just out of curiosity, how many Bunnies quit. 'Don't bother, sweetie. Nobody around here ever tells us anything.'

I picked up the paper and read on: 'The girls, in this reporter's opinion, are the most beautiful ladies ever seen together under one roof. Most of them have superior education as well, and fine breeding. They are trained to give the optimum in restaurant service... Their earnings are three to ten times as much as they could earn in any similar position. Average earnings are two hundred to three hundred dollars, and "Bunnies" meet the most attractive people.' The article ended with the Club's address and how to apply. 'Two hundred dollars to three hundred a what?' said the dissident Bunny. 'I got a 108 dollars this week, and the girl with the biggest cheque got a 145.' I asked if she was waiting on tables. She said she was.

'The next time Leo Shull comes in here,' said the dissident, 'I'm going to ask him where he gets his figures.'

'Watch out,' said the Newspaper Bunny. 'He's a Number One key-holder.'

Sheralee called me into her office. She was still desperate for 'over-twenty-one girls' who could work until four in the morning. Would I take the hat-check concession again? I deliberated. It was another chance to work before Miss Shay remembered that I had never turned in the requested birth certificate. On the other hand, I would be training as a Table Bunny until six o'clock and going right back to a full day's work at seven-thirty. My feet were still so swollen that I could barely get my regulation three-inch heels on, and I had gauze wrapped around my middle where the costume had dug in and rubbed my skin raw. I decided to take a chance on not being found out for a little longer, so I explained my tiredness to Sheralee. Couldn't she find someone else? 'I'll try,' she said, and looked annoyed. 'But if I can't, I'm still counting on you.'

I took the lift to the mezzanine again and crossed to the spiral stairs. To be in costume walking down that staircase seemed even more surrealistic in broad daylight with dozens of lunchtime shoppers staring in. One of the room directors was waiting for me at the bottom. 'Go back up and come down again,' he said, gesturing toward the crowds in the street. 'Give the boys a treat.'

Disobeying a room director was an automatic fifteen demerits, according to the Bunny bible. I searched for an excuse. 'Look,' I said, 'I'm late to meet a Number One key-holder.'

'Go ahead, kid,' he said, smiling approvingly. 'Get a move on.'

I walked down the stairs at the back of the lobby to the Playmate

Bar where I was to report for training. It had been dark and deserted when I came there for my first interview. Now it was alive with a lunchtime crowd, and the wall behind the bar glowed with blown-up colour transparencies of semi-nude Playmates from the centrefold of *Playboy*.

I went to the service area at the end of the bar to set up a tray with a bar cloth, Playboy lighter and all the other items prescribed in Bunny school. My training Bunny gave me checks (coupons) from her pad and told me to follow her as she made the rounds of her station. At each table she said, 'This is Bunny Marie and she is a Bunny in training.' Two men told me I would be okay if I did everything they said, and the first thing to do was get rid of my sourpuss training Bunny. 'Don't pay any attention to those jerks,' she said. 'They've been guzzling all afternoon and just think they're smart.' I asked if they could be from Willmark and just being difficult to test her. 'Don't be silly,' she said. 'You can always spot a Willmark man. He never has more than two drinks.'

Two of her tables were empty, and she told me to wait on anyone who sat there. My first two customers carried plastic briefcases and wore veterans' buttons in their lapels. Approaching them as confidently as I could, I embarked on the serving ritual. 'Good afternoon, sir, I am your Bunny, Marie,' I said, and put a napkin in front of each man ('this procedure informs the room director which guests have been served'), taking care to look directly at him as I did so ('eye-contact each of your guests immediately'). 'May I see the member's key please?' One of the customers gave me his Playboy key together with a room key from the Hotel Astor. I gave it back and started to fill out the coupon.

'Well,' he said, slapping the table with delight, 'you can't blame a man for trying.'

'Nope,' said his friend, 'you can't tell us your address, but nothing's to stop you from remembering ours.'

I filled glasses with ice, called in their order at the bar for two Old Fashioneds, and asked how I was supposed to put in the proper 'garbage'—Bunny-ese for drink garnishes. 'With your hands, how else?' said the bartender. I picked up two orange slices and dredged around in a large trough full of juice until I found two cherries.

With the drinks balanced on my tray, I approached the two veterans. 'Are you married?' asked the table-slapper. I said no. 'Well, it wouldn't matter anyway, because I'm married, too!' Pointing my right hip into the table, I bent my knees, inclined myself backwards in the required Bunny dip, and placed the glasses squarely on the napkins. I felt like an idiot.

'You're doing just fine,' my training Bunny whispered sweetly, and yelled, 'One J&B, one CC and two martinis straight up,' at the bartender.

I waited on three more parties, all men. Two said, 'If you're my Bunny, can I take you home?' One asked if my picture was above the bar.

My veterans left me a dollar tip. I thanked them and told them they were my first customers. The table-slapper punched his friend in the arm and doubled over with laughter. 'This girl,' he said, still laughing, 'this girl's a virgin Bunny!' He wiped tears from his eyes.

At six o'clock, I turned my checks (coupons) back in to the Training Bunny. All tips charged on them went to her, presumably her reward for training me. I told her the veterans had left a dollar. 'You can keep it,' she said magnanimously. I tucked it into the 'vault', as I had seen the other Bunnies do, and went upstairs to change.

I was unfurling the plastic dry-cleaner's bag from my bosom when Miss Shay entered the Bunny Room. I had never seen her there before. Had my lack of credentials caught up with me? She might not have been aware of my emergency hat-check duty, but she probably did know about tomorrow's assignment of serving drinks from eight o'clock to midnight. Miss Shay stopped next to me. 'Keep up the good work,' she said, confidentially. 'I hear you're a very good Bunny.'

I decided to risk asking about 'the other Marie Ochs' she mentioned at my first interview. 'What other Marie Ochs?' she said, and disappeared into the Bunny Mother's office.

I am at home, and Sheralee has just phoned to say that she found another Hat-check Bunny for tonight. My luck is holding.

*Thursday 7th*

I went to the Bunny Room an hour early tonight to see what I could learn about my sister Bunnies. Newspapers described them as college girls, actresses, artists and even linguists. I asked the Bunny dressing next to me about the linguists. She said yes, that there were quite a few foreign girls working the VIP Room. (As I had read in the Bunny bible, 'That stands for Very Important Playboy, of course.') In fact, they had to speak English with a foreign accent in order to work that room specializing in dinner and midnight supper. Did Bunnies make a lot of money there? 'Not really,' she said. 'It only seats fifty, and it's for dinner, so the turnover is slow. You're better off serving drinks and getting the jerks in and out fast.' I asked about the college girls. 'Oh, sure,' she said, 'I think there are three or four who go to classes during the week and work on weekends.' How could they always get the weekends, which were the big tip nights? 'Listen, friend,' she said, 'there are some people around here who get to pick whatever shift they want, and the rest of us get stuck with a week of lunches or that lousy hat-check bit. Mostly, it's the old girls from Chicago or somebody who's got an "in" with the management.' I asked if that couldn't just be seniority. 'Sure,' she said, searching for a place to put the Bunny ears on her upswept hairdo, 'only there isn't supposed to be a seniority system. "You're all treated alike"—that's what they tell us.' I asked what she had done before becoming a Bunny. 'Nothing much, a little modelling once in a while.' And what did she hope working as a Bunny would lead to? 'I thought maybe I could save enough money to get some test shots and a composite and I could be a real model,' she said. 'But after three months of this, I want to get married. Guys I wouldn't look at before, now I think they aren't so bad.'

I moved to the other side of the dressing table where four girls were eating doughnuts and drinking chocolate milk ('...eating in the Bunny Room, five demerits...'), and introduced myself as a new Bunny. First-name introductions were made all around. They seemed glad for the diversion and offered me a doughnut. I asked about the college girls again. 'Yeah, there are some,' said one. 'I met a girl the other day, she was taking a course in photography.' I asked what they had done before and what they wanted to do.

Three said they wanted very much to be models—not high-fashion, but in advertising or the garment industry. The fourth said she was married, had a baby and was just picking up money as a Bunny because she wasn't trained to do anything. They asked about me, and I repeated what I had put on my application as a likely, but not startling, background for a Bunny: that I had worked as a waitress (true, though it was at college), that I had danced in nightclubs and once hoped to be a professional dancer (also true, though I had to do some switching of dates to make myself younger) and that I had most recently worked as a secretary (untrue, but it was the only thing I could make up references for).

'Say, you've done a lot,' said the girl who was hoping to crash the garment industry. 'If you can type, what the hell do you want to be a Bunny for?'

I told them that everything I'd heard about the club sounded great. I read to them from the latest 'Playboy Club News': 'Bunnies don't give up wages for glamour. A Bunny can easily earn twice the amount in a week that a good secretary averages... An exciting extra is the anticipation of being discovered. Many Bunnies have moved on into the entertainment field and now can be seen in movies, nightclub acts, or as models...' There was a small silence.

'Well, sure,' said one, 'if they say that, it must have happened to some girls.' Another said that one of the Chicago Bunnies had been on the cover of *Playboy* about a year ago and there was supposed to be a Bunny on a cover again soon.

'Yeah,' said a third, 'but I hear that's just because they're short of Bunnies and they're trying to get more.'

It was nearly eight o'clock, time to put on my bright orange costume (more comfortable, I hoped, than the electric blue) and serve drinks in the Living Room.

Again, I had a Training Bunny whose checks (coupons) I used, but this time I also had a whole station, because one Table Bunny was missing. 'Wouldn't you know it,' said my Training Bunny. 'A girl gets in a car accident and it has to be from my shift.'

My tables were in the 'Cartoon Corner', that is, a corner of the Living Room whose walls were hung with mounted cartoons from *Playboy*. Because it was the depth of the building from the bar, with four steps to climb in between, it was considered a difficult station. The Bunny tray technique involved carrying our small round trays balanced high on the palm of the left hand as we looked straight ahead and did the stylish, faintly wiggly Bunny walk. It seemed simple enough, but after an hour of carrying trays loaded with ice cubes, full bottles of mixes and a half-dozen drinks, my left arm began to shake and the blood seemed permanently drained from my fingers.

Furthermore, I still hadn't been paid. I complained to my Training Bunny, but she said I had no grounds for it. The girls hired before the December opening of the Club had trained for three weeks with no pay at all.

I did learn a lot. I served twenty-two customers, spilled two drinks (one on me and one on a customer) and got propositioned twice. I also learned from the musicians at the Piano Bar that there is a song called 'Playboy's Theme'. These are some of its lyrics:

> If your boy's a Playboy,
> Loosen your control.
> If his eye meanders,
> Sweet goose your gander's,
> Just one more ornery critter,
> Who goes for the glitter.
> So if you've been over-heatin' your oven
> Just remember that the boy is a Playboy,
> And the gal that makes a fireside lovin' man of the boy,
> Gets him to stay.
> Never talks to him but sweetly,
> When he plays it indiscreetly,
> Never takes the play completely
> Away.

One of the diverse duties of the Willmark men is to make sure this theme is played at the beginning and end of every musical show every evening—like 'God Save the Queen'.

*Friday 8th*

I have finished my first night as a full-fledged professional Table Bunny, and I am almost totally absorbed with my feet. They ache like bad teeth. They are so swollen that I can't even get sneakers on. My foremost fear is that my arches may be falling. Nonetheless, random impressions of this endless evening do come back.

*Item*: I had all the tables in Cartoon Corner, twice as many as last night, from 7.30 p.m. to 4.00 a.m. with no break. With loaded trays balanced on one hand, I made sixteen round trips to the bar each hour until I lost count. I also had three iced drinks spilled down my back by customers who bumped into me or my tray and two green olives to eat all evening. Why didn't I just give up, lie down, kick, refuse, quit? I wish I knew.

*Item*: The bartender in the Living Room is an artist. Fast, graceful, exact and calm, he kept the room going almost single-handedly. 'Last week, including overtime and bonus,' he said, 'I made 180 dollars—and I'm the highest-paid bartender in the house.' I asked him why he didn't quit. 'I'm going to,' he said.

*Item*: Employees eat on the run from communal plates of food swiped from the customers' buffet. We're one big family.

*Item*: $29.85 in cash tips—all in one dollar bills and silver—makes for increased prosperity but a very uncomfortable costume. And I lost five pounds last night.

*Saturday 9th*

My arches did not fall. I put on my rain boots (the only shoes big and loose enough to bear) and went to a chiropodist ('I do all the Copa girls.'), who said there was nothing wrong with my feet except long hours, high heels and muscle strain. 'In a job like that,' he said cheerfully, 'your feet are bound to get a few sizes bigger.'

I worked the Living Room again tonight, but at a station right next to the bar. By wearing borrowed shoes three sizes too large, wrapping my ribs in gauze inside the costume and coaxing busboys to help me carry heavy trays, I managed to get through the night. I was rewarded with the following information:

1. A Bunny who has been a Playmate—that is, who has posed for the foldout picture in *Playboy*—gets five dollars a day more salary than other Bunnies. She is also obliged to approach customers with, 'I'm your Playmate Sue,' instead of, 'I'm your Bunny Sue,' and autograph her centrefold if requested.

2. In a letter written to mollify New Yorkers who had bought keys to a supposedly private club, which is now open to the public, Hugh Hefner said that non-members 'must secure a temporary pass good for one visit only and they must pay cash in advance before they are served'. Perhaps contrary to Mr Hefner's instructions, Bunnies are told to collect after each round on cash sales, but there are few who do even that. Most allow cash customers to run up bar bills just as if they were key-holders. If anything, Bunnies prefer serving a non-member, because they are assured of a cash tip instead of splitting a charge tip with the house.

3. Bunnies and busboys have a love-hate relationship. A good busboy can make a Bunny wealthier by keeping her tables cleared for new customers. A bad busboy can whisk away cash tips before she sees them and insist that the customer 'stiffed' her. As a result, a Bunny may spend all her working hours cajoling and vamping a boy whom she wouldn't dream of spending time with outside the club. It's a hothouse relationship, but a close one. Like some women and their hairdressers, they tell each other everything.

4. Many Bunnies regard plastic dry-cleaner's bags as dangerous for bosom stuffing because they make you perspire, thereby causing a weight loss where you least want it. Kleenex and absorbent cotton are preferred.

5. The-Way-to-Get-Something-to-Eat, though a Table Bunny, is to snitch it from the customers' buffet (on pain of instant dismissal, according to a recent memo) and hide it in the supply room. You can then grab a bite whenever you pass by. Almost no one goes to the employees' room to eat stew.

*Sunday 10th*

I got home at four in the morning and had to be back at the club and in costume by eleven for publicity photos. I was furious at first (twenty-five demerits if I didn't show up), but once awake and outside, I was glad. It was the first time in nearly three days that I'd seen full daylight.

The Playboy photographer was posing girls on the broad, curving staircase at the back of the lobby. Each of us was put through a cheesecake series: sitting on the steps with legs outstretched, standing with our hands posed on the railing ('bend over from the waist, dear, over a little more') and walking down the stairs with tray held high.

I asked what the photographs would be used for. 'I don't know,' he said, 'I just got rush orders from Chicago.' As a matter of routine, new Bunnies were asked to sign a release of all photographs. I asked if our pictures would turn up in some Playboy Club promotion, or in *Playboy* itself. No one knew.

A voice called to me from the darkness of the Playmate Bar. It was Miss Shay, sitting at the desk where I had first seen her, waiting for prospective Bunnies to come in for interviews. The photographer had asked if we could turn on taped music. 'Marie will play,' she said. 'Marie plays the piano very well, don't you dear?' No, I said, I didn't play at all. 'I'm sure you told me so when I interviewed you,' she said firmly.

The oversight of my credentials, the other Marie Ochs, and now my piano-playing. I thought of the several times I had heard the seemingly efficient Miss Shay call busboys by a first name that was the wrong one. For the first time, I was sure that unless someone recognized me, I could work at the Playboy Club for as long as I liked.

Out in the bright sunlight again, I wondered just how long I did want to stay. If Marie wasn't going to be discovered, Marie would have to end her own career.

Still, I had lived through those weekend nights that were the worst of it. According to this week's Bunny schedule, I would be serving lunch for four hours each day and no more. It wasn't an envied assignment because the tips were bad, but it would give me more time to talk to Bunnies.

I decided Marie could live till Friday.

*Monday 11th*

A story in today's *Metropolitan Daily* was the talk of the Bunny Room. Two ex-Bunnies are suing the club for back tips and 'misrepresentation' of the amount of money a Bunny could earn. One has told reporters she received anonymous death threats immediately after filing the suit.

'I knew Phyllis Sands,' said one girl, 'but not this Betsy McMillan who got the threats.' She studied their pictures. 'They made sure to give out good publicity shots.' Did she think the alleged threats were made up just for publicity? 'Who knows?' she shrugged. 'Maybe she wasn't told the club would take half her tips, and maybe her salary was a lot lower than she had expected. On the other hand, maybe she just had her boyfriend call up and threaten her so she'd get her name in the paper. Who knows?'

I went downstairs to the Playroom and began setting up tables for lunch. Of the six other Bunnies working there, I had met three: A Chinese Bunny, a Bunny who announced that she didn't have to stuff her bosom and the big, baby-voiced redhead whom I'd met the first day in the Bunny Room. The room director assigned us our stations and we sat down on the apron of the stage to wait for customers. The unstuffed Bunny talked about how much better tips were in Chicago. 'They're dumber there,' she said. 'I mean it's easier to make them think you'll go out with them and then they tip you more.'

'It's lousy at the Miami club, too,' said Baby Voice. 'One time we all got together and said we'd quit if they didn't pay us more, but they said to go right ahead, they'd just hire more girls.'

I said, 'Maybe the girls had been out-bluffed.'

A little dark-haired Bunny said, 'Sure, it would cost the club a hell of a lot if we all quit together. What would they do?'

'Bring in girls from the other clubs,' said Baby Voice. 'You can't win.' There was a piano at centre stage. She went over to it and pretended to play a jazz arrangement that was being piped into the room. 'Laaaa-tee-ta-tee-tum,' sang Baby Voice.

A Bunny with long brown hair got up and went through the motions of a very professional striptease. 'They asked me to be a Playmate once,' she said, 'but I couldn't do it now. I'm too thin.' The little dark-haired Bunny told her it didn't matter because they always used a fake composite body anyway, and that she personally knew a girl who did the breasts. I said I doubted it, there's only so much you can do with an airbrush. 'Anyway, they must use different girls,' said the stripping Bunny, 'because the breasts are in different shapes.'

'They co-omme in different shapes,' sang Baby Voice, and got up to do her own striptease. She took off her bow tie, collar and cuffs and tossed them off the stage, accompanying each with an expert bump.

'Okay, girls,' said the room director in a voice like ice. 'Cut it.' Three middle-aged customers, the first of the lunchtime onslaught, were squinting into the spot-lit gloom from the doorway.

'Wouldn't you know it,' said Baby Voice, disgusted. 'Here come the suckers.'

Serving lunch for four hours wasn't quite enough to open up all my old foot wounds, but the piled-up plates of roast beef (which is all we serve, our room director is called 'The Roast Beef King') make a tray even heavier than a full load of drinks. The customers are all men. The heavy sprinkling of dates and wives in the evening crowd disappears at lunch. One told me over and over again that he was vice president of an insurance company and that he would pay me to serve at a private party in his hotel. Another got up from his fourth martini to breathe heavily down my neck. When I pulled away, he was sincerely angry. 'What do you think I come here for,' he said, 'roast beef?'

At three o'clock, when the final table had been cleared, I went back to the Bunny Room. The wardrobe mistress stopped me. 'Baby,' she said, 'that costume is way too big on you.' It was true that I had lost ten pounds in the few days since the costume had been fitted and it was also true that, for the first time, it was no more uncomfortable than a tight girdle. She marked the waist with pins where the tucks should be taken and told me to take it off. 'I'll have it fitting you right when you come tomorrow,' she said. 'Needs two inches off on each side.'

I took the 'Playboy Club News' out of my locker and read aloud: 'The Playboy Club world is filled with good entertainment, beautiful girls, fun-loving playboys...like a continuous house party. Cheerful Bunnies feel as though they are among the invited guests...'

My co-workers from the Playroom giggled. 'Some party,' said Baby Voice. 'You're not even supposed to go out with the customers.' I asked if any of the Willmark representatives had tried to trap her. 'Nooooo,' she said thoughtfully, 'but one did offer another Bunny two hundred dollars just for promising she'd meet him after work—and she took it,' said Baby Voice contemptuously. 'She should have known. Nobody but a schmuck or a Willmark man would offer you the money before.'

*Tuesday 12th*

Two of my classmates from Bunny school, Gloria and the magician's assistant, joined us in the Playroom today. I found myself explaining how to serve roast beef and convince customers that it was rare, medium, or well-done, though it was, in fact, all the same.

It was Lincoln's birthday and business was slow. I listened to the unstuffed Bunny explain that she liked older men because they gave you money. 'I went out with this old guy I met in the Club and fixed up two other Bunnies with his friends. You know, he gave me a hundred dollars just because he liked me?'

The unstuffed Bunny also explained that one of the Playboy executives had given her seven hundred dollars for a dress. 'I had five hundred dollars,' she said, 'and I bought a dress for twelve hundred and he took me to a party in it.' A dark-haired Bunny said yes, she knew the same guy in Chicago. 'Doesn't everybody?' said the unstuffed Bunny. 'If you counted all the Bunnies who went out with that guy, you...'

The dark-haired Bunny looked pensive. 'We had this crazy thing going for three weeks,' she said. 'It was wild. I guess I should have known that nothing would come of it...'

'All the girls think something will come of it,' said the unstuffed Bunny comfortingly, 'but it never does.' They talked about this executive's huge apartment, great wealth and romantic impulses. He sounded like an artist of overkill.

Unstuffed got up to serve a customer and the dark-haired Bunny looked after her with disdain. 'I don't believe he ever gave her seven hundred dollars for a dress,' she said firmly. 'Nobody ever gets money out of him.'

*Wednesday 13th*

I've completed my unofficial list of Bunny bosom-stuffers:
1. Kleenex

2. plastic dry-cleaner's bags
3. absorbent cotton
4. cut-up Bunny tails
5. foam rubber
6. lamb's wool
7. Kotex halves
8. silk scarves
9. gym socks

I've also learned that we can not only go out with Number One key-holders but anyone they introduce us to. Also, anyone we meet at Vic Lownes' parties. There is, however, only so far I'm willing to go with research.

*Friday 15th*

The Playroom was crowded with men drinking heavily at lunch because it was Friday. I carried plates of roast beef and the Friday-only alternate, trout. Bunny Gloria was standing with a tray loaded with cups, waiting for the coffee urn to be filled. 'You know what we are?' she said indignantly. 'We're waitresses!' I said maybe we ought to join a union.

'Unions just take your money,' said Baby Voice, 'and won't let you work double shifts.'

The magician's assistant was serving a table next to mine and agreeing earnestly that our costumes were 'so intelligently made, so flattering to a girl's body'. She tried so hard to do things 'like a gracious hostess', as the Bunny bible instructed, that she wasn't an efficient waitress. In programming us with, as one Bunny put it, 'all that glamour shit', the club sometimes defeated itself.

It was my last day of lunches and I was glad. Somehow, the usual tail-pullings and propositions and pinching and ogling seemed all the more depressing when, outside this windowless room of perpetual night, the sun was shining.

I found Sheralee in her office and told her the story I had chosen because it left the door open, should I need more information: that my mother was ill and I had to go home for a while. She was dismayed. 'But we're so short of Bunnies now!' she said, and asked when I could come back. I told her I didn't know but I would call. She gave me my first week's pay cheque: $35.90 net for two nights in the Living Room. I asked about my first night at the hat-check stand. 'You don't get paid for training,' said Sheralee. I protested that it wasn't training. 'I'll talk to the bookkeeper,' she said doubtfully.

*Thursday 21st*

Nearly a week has passed. I called Sheralee to say I had just come back to pick up my clothes and that I would have to quit permanently. She pleaded with me to work the Playmate Bar just one more night. Somehow, (might I learn something new?) I found myself saying yes.

*Friday 22nd*

But it was just the same:

Room Director: 'That's your station, four fours and three deuces.'

Customer: 'If you're my Bunny, can I take you home with me?'

Bartender: 'They keep changing the size of the shots—up and down, up and down. It's enough to drive you crazy.'

Bunny: 'I worked that LoLo Cola private party, and they gave me a six-pack. Big deal.'

Customer: 'I'm in the New Yorker Hotel, room 625. Can you remember that?'

Man: 'If little girls were blades of grass, what would little boys be?'

Bunny: 'Ummm...lawn mowers?'

Man: 'No. Grasshoppers!'

Sign in supply room: THIS IS YOUR HOME. PLEASE DON'T THROW COFFEE GRINDS IN SINK.

Busboy: 'The money's coming out of your costume, sweetie.'

Bunny: 'He's a real gentleman. He treats you just the same whether you've slept with him or not.'

It was four in the morning when I went to the Bunny Room and took off my costume. A pretty blonde was putting chairs together to sleep on. She had promised to take another girl's lunch shift after her regular eight hours in the Playmate Bar, and there wasn't time to go home in between. I asked why she did it.

'Well,' she said, 'the money's not too bad. Last week I made two hundred dollars.'

At last I had found a girl who made at least the low end of the promised salary—but only by working round the clock.

In Sheralee's office, pinned to the bulletin board, was a list of cities next in line for Playboy clubs (Pittsburgh, Boston, Dallas and Washington D.C.) and a yellow printed sheet titled: WHAT IS A BUNNY?

'A Bunny,' began the text, 'like the Playboy Playmate, is...beautiful, desirable... We'll do everything in our power to make you—the Bunny—the most envied girl in America, working in the most exciting and glamorous setting in the world.'

I turned in my costume for the last time. 'So long, honey,' said the blonde. 'See you in the funnies.'

## Postscript (1999)

Among the short-term results of this article were:

1. A long letter from Hugh Hefner saying that 'your beef about the physical given the girls before they start work at the club prompted my eliminating it'. (He defended it as 'a good idea', but noted that my article was not the first time it had been 'misunderstood and turned into something questionable'.) He also included the first seven instalments of his own Playboy Philosophy. For most of the three-page letter, however, he insisted he didn't mind the article at all.

2. A one-million-dollar libel suit against me, as well as against a small (now defunct) New York newspaper that had printed a report on my article and allegations that the manager of the New York Playboy Club had clear Mafia connections. Though those allegations were not in any quote from me, I seem to have been included in the libel suit as a harassment gesture. I spent many unpleasant hours in depositions, and being threatened with punitive damages. Eventually, the newspaper settled out of court without reference to me. I was told by other reporters that such harassing actions, with or without actionable grounds, were a frequent way of discouraging or punishing journalists.

3. Serving as a witness for the New York State Liquor Authority to identify printed instructions given to me as a Bunny so they

could be entered in evidence in a case against the Playboy Club for maintaining a public liquor licence while advertising as a private club. This was related to the fact that the Playboy Club had paid to get its liquor licence, then turned state's evidence against the same officials. The State Liquor Authority fought back with the public/private suit in which they asked me to testify. Lawyers told me that other Bunnies they had approached had been afraid to testify, even on the simple question of identifying instruction sheets in which we were told to emphasize the private, exclusive nature of the club. Having seen many movies about courtroom proceedings in which justice prevailed, I agreed. After a Playboy Club lawyer had spent cross-examination time trying to demonstrate that I was a liar and a female of low moral character, I began to understand why the other Bunnies had refused. In the end, the Playboy Club kept their public liquor licence.

4. Several weeks of obscene and threatening phone calls from a man with great internal knowledge of the Playboy Club.

5. Loss of serious journalistic assignments because I had now become a Bunny—and it didn't matter why.

Among the long-term results of this article are:

1. Feet permanently enlarged by a half size by the very high heels and long hours of walking with heavy trays.

2. Satisfaction two decades later when the Playboy Club's payments for a New York State liquor licence were cited as one of the reasons for New Jersey's decision that Playboy Enterprises was unfit to operate a gambling casino in Atlantic City until its relationship with Hugh Hefner, its founder and principal owner, was severed.

3. Continual printing by *Playboy* magazine of my employee photograph as a Bunny amid ever more pornographic photos of other Bunnies. The 1983 version of the photo insisted in a caption that my article 'boosted Bunny recruiting'. The 1984 version was a photo taken at a dinner while I was reaching upwards and my evening gown had slipped, exposing part of one breast. It was a benefit for the Ms. Foundation for Women, and also my fiftieth birthday. No other publication used this photo. But *Playboy* never forgets.

4. Thirty years of occasional phone calls from past and present Bunnies with revelations about their working conditions and the sexual demands on them. In the first few years, my callers were amazed that I had used my own name on the article. One said she had been threatened with 'acid thrown in my face' when she complained about the sexual use of the Bunnies. Another quoted the same alleged threat as a response to trying to help Bunnies unionize. All said they were amazed to find my name listed in the phone book. Eventually, I had to switch to an unlisted phone.

5. In 1984, a dramatized version of this article starring Kirstie Alley, then an unknown, in my role as reporter, was made for television. It had a terrible title, *A Bunny's Tale*, but was a good film, largely because director Karen Arthur got the women together to not only rehearse but to get to know each other—something virtually unheard of in television. A former Bunny from the Chicago Playboy Mansion also volunteered to be technical director. She had seen young women destroyed by drugs, and wanted to help us show the backstage realities of these women's lives. Though she said she received threatening phone calls, she stayed on the set; an exact replica of the New York Playboy Club constructed from the architect's drawings. Hugh Hefner was said to have tried to use his other television properties to pressure ABC out of doing this production, but it was shown, continued to be aired for four years on ABC, and is still re-run on Lifetime. Last year, the young woman in my neighbourhood coffee shop said it had meant a lot to her, that her boyfriend also watched and finally understood what she went through as a waitress. That meant a lot to me.

6. Realizing that all women are Bunnies. After feminism arrived in my life, I stopped regretting that I had written this article. Thanks to the television version, I also began to take pleasure in the connections it made with women who might not have picked up a feminist book or magazine, but who responded to the rare sight of realistic working conditions and a group of women who supported each other.

—1963

# WORDS AND CHANGE: WHO WERE YOU BEFORE THIS WAVE OF FEMINISM BEGAN?

In this essay Steinem reminds us of the gains made in our lives because of feminism—how it has impacted on our consciousness, to such an extent that even our language has changed. Crimes such as domestic violence were simply considered life before feminism.

—Ruchira Gupta

Think for a minute. Who were you before this wave of feminism began?

Trying to remember our way back into past realities, past rooms, past beliefs is a first step towards measuring the depth of change. Sharing those measures—in the same way we have learned to share problems and solutions—is probably the most bias-proof way of eliciting our own history. After all, if people of diverse experience and age and background begin to see patterns of similarity emerge from changes in our lives and even in the words we use, then we are probably on the track of an accurate historical pattern. If we write down those changes as we have experienced them, then history may cease to be limited mainly to the documented acts of national leaders, or to the interpretations of scholars proving a particular theory. We can begin to create a women's history, and a people's, that is accurate and accessible.

New words and phrases are one organic measure of change. They capture transformations of perception and sometimes of reality itself.

Now, we have terms like sexual harassment and battered women. A few years ago, they were just called life.

Now, we are becoming the men we wanted to marry. Once, women were trained to marry a doctor, not be one.

Now, placing 'womens' in front of words like centre or newspaper, network or rock band, indicates a positive choice. Before feminism, it was a put-down.

Now, we've made the revolutionary discovery that children have two parents. Once, even the kindly Dr Spock held mothers solely responsible for children.

In 1972, a NASA official's view of women's function in space was 'sexual diversion' [on] 'long-duration flights such as Mars'. Now, women are simply 'astronauts'.

Until recently, an older woman on campus was an oddity. Now, so many women have returned for a college education once denied them that the median age of the female undergraduate is twenty-seven years old. Colleges are community resources, with a new definition of 'students'.

Until the 1970s, most colleges had never heard of Women's Studies. Now, there are tens of thousands of such courses on more than a thousand campuses.

A few years ago, moving up the economic ladder for women meant becoming a doctor not a nurse, a boss not a secretary: a token not a movement. Now, nurses are striking, secretaries are organizing, there is an uprising in the pink-collar ghetto, and jobs are no longer valued just because men do them.

Art used to be definable as what men created. Crafts were made by women and natives. Only recently have we discovered they are the same, thus bringing craft techniques into art, and art into everyday life.

Now, anti-equality politicians in both parties worry about the women's vote or the gender gap. Until the 1980s, political experts said there was no such thing.

In the 1970s, policemen were protesting against the very idea of working with women. Now, females serve in every major city and the policeman has become the police officer.

In the 1960s, Americans talked about white women who

controlled the economy or black women who were matriarchs, thus sugar-coating powerlessness with the myth of power. Only two decades later, more than 70 per cent of men and women agree that sex discrimination exists—and that it's wrong.

Until the 1970s, women had to choose between Miss or Mrs, creatures who would use contraception to avoid childbirth totally, behave sinfully, and thus weaken the patriarchal family and civilization itself.

In the seventies, however, feminism transformed the terms of discussion by popularizing reproductive freedom as a phrase and as a basic human right. This umbrella term includes safe contraception and abortion, as well as freedom from coerced sterilization (of women or of men) and decent health care during pregnancy and birth. In other words, reproductive freedom stated the right of the individual to decide to have or not to have a child. Though obviously a right that is more important to women, it also protects men. Furthermore, it allowed the building of new trust and coalitions between white women and women of colour, in this country and elsewhere, who had rightly suspected that the power implied by population control would be directed at some groups more than others.

To the surprise of liberal population experts, the choice of reproductive freedom has been exercised eagerly by women wherever it was even marginally allowed. Population journals began to feature mystified articles about the declining rate of population growth, even in many areas of the world where the rate of illiteracy among women is still tragically high. A 1979 United Nations women's conference of East and West Europe concluded that women were not only limiting their pregnancies for their own health reasons, but were, statistically speaking, on something of a 'baby strike', perhaps because of double-role problems; that is, the burden of working both outside and inside the home. Some countries recommended the remedy of encouraging men to share child-rearing and relieve women's burdens, but other more authoritarian governments simply tried to ensure compulsory child-bearing by suppressing contraception and abortion. Since some US government experts were speaking of our 'unsatisfactorily low birth rate' quite openly by 1979—and some right-wing anti-abortion leaders were openly fearful that cultural differences in birth rates would make the US 'a non-white country'—the question for the future is clear: Will reproductive freedom make childbirth and child-rearing a valuable, rewarded function that is supported and aided by the community (as feminists advocate)? Or simply functions that are forced on women, especially racially 'desirable' women (as the anti-equality right wing advocates)?

Obviously, reproductive freedom is simply a way of stating what feminism has been advancing for thousands of years. Witches and gypsies were freedom fighters for women because they taught contraception and abortion. It was mainly this knowledge that made them anathema to the patriarchs of the past. In the worldwide wave of feminism of the nineteenth and early twentieth centuries, advocating 'birth control' or 'fertility control', even for married women, was enough to jail many feminist crusaders.

But the modern contribution is to elevate reproductive freedom to a universal human right, at least as basic as freedom of speech or assembly. Regardless of marital status, the racist need to limit or increase certain populations, or nationalistic goals of having more or fewer soldiers and workers, individual women have the right to decide the use of their own bodies. Men who want children must at least find women willing to bear them; that seems little enough to ask. And governments that want increased rates of population growth must resort to such humane measures as reducing infant mortality rates, improving health care during pregnancy, sharing the work of child-rearing through childcare and equal parenthood, and lengthening people's lives.

Obviously, this reproductive veto power on the part of women is exactly what male supremacists fear most. That's why their authoritarian impulse is so clearly against any sexuality not directed toward childbirth within the patriarchal family (that is, against extramarital sex, homosexuality and lesbianism, as well as contraception and abortion). This understanding helped feminists to see why the adversaries of such apparently contradictory concerns as contraception and homosexuality are almost always the same. It also helped us to stand together on the side of any consecrating, freely chosen sexuality as a rightful form of human expression.

In recent years, words like lover (whether referring to someone of the same or different gender), sexual preference, and gay rights have begun to be commonly used. Homophobia was invented to describe the irrational fear of sexual expression between people of the same gender, a fear so common in the past that it needed no name. There was also a challenge of such rote phrases as man-hating lesbian. As American writer and feminist Rita Mae Brown pointed out, it's not lesbians who hate men, but women who depend on men and are thus more likely to be hurt and angry.[1]

In the 1960s, any sex outside marriage was called the Sexual Revolution, a non-feminist phrase that simply meant women's increased availability on men's terms. By the end of the seventies, feminism had brought an understanding that liberation meant the power to make a choice; that sexuality, for women or men, should be neither forbidden nor forced. With that in mind, words like virgin, celibacy, autonomy, faithfulness and commitment took on a positive meaning. Such blameful words as frigid and nymphomaniac were being replaced by non-judgemental ones like *pre*-orgasmic and sexually active. Indeed, nymphomaniac, a medically non-existent term, had often been used to condemn any woman who enjoyed sex or made sexual demands.

It still may take some explaining, but many more women are keeping their birth names (and not calling them maiden names, with all the sexual double standard that implies). A handful of women have even exchanged their patriarchal names for matriarchal ones ('Mary *Ruthchild*'), or followed the black movement tradition of replacing former owners' names with place names or letters (for instance, 'Judy Chicago' or 'Laura X'). Many tried to solve the dilemma of naming with the reformist step of just adding their husband's name ('Mary Smith Fanes'), but that remained an unequal mark of marriage unless their husbands took both names, too.

Hardly anyone has yet succeeded in interrupting the patriarchal flow of naming children: they are still given their father's name only, or their mother's name as the dispensable one in the middle. It remains for the future to legalize an egalitarian choice, as some European countries have done, by giving children both parents' names, thus indicating their real parentage (and eliminating the need for such constant explanations like 'This is my daughter by my first marriage' or 'This is my son by my second'). They could choose their own adult name, whether a parental or totally new one, when they are old enough to get a social security card or register to vote. After all, each of us should be able to name ourselves. The power of naming goes very deep.

As an adjective, pro-choice began to replace pro-abortion, the latter being a media-created term that implied advocacy of abortion, as opposed to support for it as a legal choice. To include the word abortion as an honourable one, there were other phrases like safe and legal abortion. And a decade that had begun with the necessity of proving the Freudian-dictated vaginal orgasm to be neurologically non-existent, plus explaining the clitoral orgasm to be literally true, finally ended up more equally with just orgasm (no adjectives necessary) being more talked about and experienced.

The feminist spirit has reclaimed some words with defiance and humour. Witch, bitch, dyke and other formerly pejorative epithets started to turn up in the brave names of small feminist groups. A few women artists dubbed their new female imagery 'cunt art' in celebration of the discovery that not all sexual symbols were phallic. Humour encouraged the invention of jockocracy to describe a certain male obsession with athletics and victory; also loserism as a rueful recognition of women's cultural discomfort with anything as 'unfeminine' as success. Supermom and Superwoman were words that relieved us all by identifying the Perfect Wife and Mother, plus the Perfect Career Woman, as humanly impossible goals.

Women's Lib or Women's Libber were trivializing terms that feminists argued against. (Would we say 'Algerian Lib'? 'Black Libber'?) Their use has diminished, but not disappeared.

The nature of work has been a major area of new understanding, beginning with the word itself. Before feminism, work was largely defined as what men did or would do. Thus, a working woman was someone who laboured outside the home for money, masculine-style. Though still alarmingly common, the term is being protested, especially by homemakers, who work harder than any other class of workers, and are still called people who 'don't work'. Feminists tend to speak of work inside the home or outside the home, of salaried or unsalaried workers. Attributing a financial value to work in the home would go a long way towards making marriage an equal partnership and ending the semantic slavery inherent in the phrase 'women who don't work'. It would also begin to untangle the double role problem of millions of women who work both inside and outside the home. Defining human maintenance and home care as a job in itself, clarifies that men can and should do it as well as women.

Equal pay for equal work, the concept with which we entered the sixties, fell short of helping women in the mostly female, non-unionized jobs of the pink-collar ghetto—another new term. Blue-collar workers, who are overwhelmingly male, usually earn far more than workers in mostly female jobs. What did equal pay do for the nurse, for instance, who was getting the same low salary as the woman working next to her? Equal pay for comparable work has become the new goal, and comparability studies have been done on the many jobs done largely by men that require less education and fewer skills but still get more pay than jobs done largely by women.

Many ideas have been transformed by adding one crucial adjective—women's bank, women's music, women's studies, women's caucus. It implied a lot of new content: childcare, flexible work hours, new standards of creditworthiness, new symbolism, new lyrics. Such groups also experimented with new structures. Whether out of a conscious belief that hierarchy was rooted in patriarchy or an unconscious discomfort with authority, women's groups often changed vertical organization into a more lateral one. Collective, communal, supportive, constituency and skill-sharing were more likely to be heard than organizational chart, credentials, or chain of command. Though such new forms were often condemned as impractical, their ability to make individuals more productive—combined with the current productivity crisis of traditional, hierarchical forms in industry—have caused some management consultants to look at them as possible models.

In short, truth-telling and the creation of alternate institutions have begun to delineate and give value to a women's culture, a set of perspectives that differs from the more traditional, masculine ones, not because of biology but because of the depth of gender conditioning. We need to learn, but so do men. Together, we can create a culture that combines the most useful and creative features of each.

Power is being redefined. Women often explain with care that we gain power to control our lives, but not to dominate others.

Language has also been used to shift some of the burden back to where it belongs. Alimony is sometimes referred to as back salary or reparations. If even the US Labour Department counts the replacement value of one homemaker's work at a minimum of eighteen thousand dollars a year, why shouldn't a wife be entitled to some back salary? Similarly, many feminists stopped pleading with corporations and professional groups for contributions and started to ask for reparations for past damages done to women. Women's Studies, Black Studies, Native American Studies and the like were often referred to as remedial studies in order to put the blame where it belonged and to show that such courses must one day be integrated into the basic curriculum for everyone, into human history. The self-description of the authoritarian, anti-equality backlash as pro-family caused many feminists to take great care about using the plural families, in order to show that there are many different family forms. The patriarchal nuclear one acceptable to the right wing (father as breadwinner, woman at home with children) excludes about 85 per cent of all American households. Understanding what the right wing means by 'family' helps to understand why, in their view, all guarantees of individual rights to women and children *are* anti-family, from the Equal Rights Amendment to laws against child abuse.

Of course, one importance of words is their power to exclude. Man, mankind and the family of man have made women feel left out, usually with good reason. People, humanity and humankind are more inclusive. So are rewrites like 'Peace on Earth, Good Will to People'. Feminists tried to educate by asking men to imagine receiving a Spinster of Arts or Mistress of Science degree, and then working hard for a sistership. Wouldn't they feel a little left out?

Racial minorities, both women and men, have sometimes been

defined in the negative as non-white (would we speak of white people as non-black?), and in any case, those who are counted as minorities in this country are actually the majority in the world. In order to be more accurate and cross-cultural, feminists often adopted the description of people of colour. For a while, Fourth World was also used as a way of describing the commonality of *all* women in the patriarchal world, regardless of race, but that term was taken over as a label for the poorest, non-industrialized countries that did not get included as developing or Third World. To continue this reference, women are now sometimes self-described as the Fifth World—the half of the population that tends to be used as cheap labour and to have the least control over capital or technology, wherever we are.

In order to reach each other across barriers, feminists have tried to be sensitive to our own linguistically divisive habits: for instance, the racist habit of using images of darkness or blackness as negative (the dark side of human nature, a black heart, blackmail) and whiteness as positive (a white lie, white magic, fair-haired boy). If one group requires an adjective (an Asian–American poet), so do all (a European–American teacher).

Similarly, qualified was a word only deemed necessary when describing 'out' groups, as if white men were qualifiedly their birth. They remained the adult, the professional (worker, doctor, poet), while the rest of us still needed a kind of qualifier that often disqualified (woman worker, black doctor, lady poet).

The difficult efforts to make language more accurate often include the invention of such alternatives as chairperson or spokesperson. Clearly, only a single-sex organization can have a position of chairman or chairwoman. An integrated organization needs to have a position that can be occupied by any of its members—thus, chairperson or better yet, just chair. Given the imbalance of power, however, these gender-free words are sometimes used to neuter women and leave men as the status quo. Thus, a woman might be a spokesperson, but a man remained a spokesman, Females might become people, but men remained men.

Women sometimes collaborated with their own exclusion by

trying to skip to gender-free words too soon. Humanism was a special temptation (as in, 'Don't be threatened, feminists are really just talking about humanism'). Androgyny also raised the hope that female and male cultures could be perfectly blended but because the female side of the equation has yet to be affirmed, androgyny usually tilted towards the male. As a concept, it also raised anxiety levels by conjuring up a unisex or de-sexed vision, the very opposite of the individuality and freedom that feminism has in mind.

Whether in life or language, integration without equal power means going right back to our usual slots in the hierarchy. Once that is learned, we will be less likely to let fear of conflict force us into a pretended unity with 'mankind', or even into a false unity as 'womankind'. This lesson helps to clarify the need for consciousness-raising through specific language. 'Judges will be elected on their merits', for instance, is a perfectly okay sentence. The only problem is that we're all accustomed to visualizing male judges, and a gender-free sentence may do nothing to jog our consciousness. For a while, we may need sentences like 'a judge will be elected on her or his merits' to force us to recognize that women judges do exist, just as we may need to enumerate by race in order to make diversity visible.

Another symbolic confusion was the invention of male chauvinist pig, a hybrid produced by trying to combine feminism with leftist rhetoric, which was often anti-feminist in itself: in this case, a willingness to reduce adversaries to something less than human as a first step toward justifying violence against them. (Years of being chicks, dogs and cows may have led to some understandable desire to turn the tables, but it also taught us what dehumanization feels like.) Police had been pigs in the sixties—as in 'Off the Pigs!'–so all prejudiced men became the same for a while; a period that has mercifully passed.

In fact, male chauvinist itself is a problem. Since chauvinist referred to a super-patriot, all we were saying was that this was a man obsessed with loyalty to his country. Instead, many feminist writers began to use male-supremacists as a more accurate description of the problem at hand. Some male-supremacists took advantage of the earlier error by wearing ties and pins proclaiming: 'I am a male chauvinist pig.' This was an indication, of course, of the lack of seriousness with which sexism is treated. Few of those men would so cheerfully proclaim: 'I am an anti-Semite' or 'I am a racist'. 'Battered women' is a phrase that named major, long-hidden violence. It helped us to face the fact that, statistically speaking, the most dangerous place for a woman is in her own home, not on the streets. Sexual harassment on the job also exposed a form of intimidation that about a third of all women workers suffer. Naming it allowed women to come forward and legal remedies to be created. By identifying pornography(literally, 'writing about female slavery') as the preaching of woman hatred, and thus quite different from erotica, with its connotation of love and mutuality, there was also the beginning of an understanding that pornography is a major way in which violence and dominance are taught and legitimized; that it is as socially harmful as Nazi literature is to Jews or Klan literature is to blacks.

Even female sexual slavery (once known by the nineteenth-century racist term 'white slavery' because it was the only form of slavery to which whites were also subjected) has been exposed by this wave of feminism. We now know it flourishes in many cities where prostitution and pornography are big business and facts of international life.

In response to such realizations of injustice, it's no wonder that radicalism began to lose some of its equation with excess or unreasonableness. By exposing the injustice of the sexual caste system and its role as a root of other 'natural' injustices based on race and class, radical feminism laid the groundwork for a common cause among diverse women. And by challenging this masculine-feminine, dominant-passive structure as the chief cause and justification of violence, it also proved that radicalism can not only take non-violent forms, but is the only way to challenge the origins of violence itself.

These new feminist connections among women are very tenuous, but worldwide. Feminism was international and anti-national during its last massive advance in the nineteenth and early twentieth centuries. (If we call that 'the first wave', it's only because we live in such a young country—the feminist revolution has been a contagious and progressive recurrence in history for thousands of years.) The last wave won for many women of the world a legal identity as human beings, not the possessions of others. Now we seek to complete that step for all women, and to gain legal equality, too. But there will be many more waves of feminism before male-supremacist cultures give way.

In this wave, words and consciousness have forged ahead, so reality can follow. Measuring the distance between the new and the old evokes the unique part of history that lives in each of us.

A dozen years later, there are many readers who can no longer answer the question: 'Who were you before this wave of feminism began?' They were simply born into some degree of feminist consciousness, and their higher expectations, their lack of the female cultural problem known as terminal gratitude, are necessary for the long path ahead.

For instance: Yes, many more women are becoming the men they wanted to marry, but too few men are becoming the women they wanted to marry. That leaves most women with two jobs, one outside the home and one in it, a problem that poor women always had, but that is now shared by middle-class women—which means that together, we ought to be able to solve it. At a deeper level, many of us have raised our daughters more like our sons, but too few have raised our sons more like our daughters. Until men are socialized to raise children and care for the home as much as women are, this double burden will continue to restrict women, deprive children of nurturing fathers and perpetuate gender roles.

In many areas, there is now more recognition of ways that polarized, *either/or* choices—modelled on dividing human nature into 'feminine' and 'masculine'—are disappearing or uniting into *and*—a non-hierarchical, full-circle paradigm. In science, the new physics and chaos theory have blown apart our old linear, mechanistic and hierarchical assumptions. They have helped us think about linking, not ranking. Feminist scientists offer us field dependency: the understanding that nothing can be studied out of its context. In sexuality, the assumption that a person must be either heterosexual or homosexual has begun to loosen up enough to honour both the ancient tradition of bisexuality and the new one of individuals who themselves are transgender and cross what once seemed an immutable line. Many groups within the lesbian and gay movement now add these two words to their descriptions. People in couples are also more likely to speak of each other as partner or life partner, a relationship that goes beyond the limited connotation of lover. Homophobic has been joined by heterosexist, a way of describing a person or entity that places heterosexuality at the centre, or assumes that all other sexualities are peripheral or non-existent. At the same time, sexual preferences frequently replaced by the term 'sexual identity', a way of including both those who feel they were born with a particular sexuality and those who feel they chose it.

Even heterosexuality is changing its language, with married couples preferring to say partner, too, rather than the culturally loaded terms of husband and wife. Others are trying to change the passive-dominant terms of sexuality by suggesting a word like 'envelopment' to replace penetration or at least abandoning the old slang that implied sex was about conquering.

We're also looking at the way language has allowed the victim to be identified, but not the victimizer. In addition to talking about how many women have been raped, for instance we've begun to talk about how many men rape. In addition to talking about why women don't or can't leave a violent situation, we're beginning to question why men are violent. The term 'domestic violence' itself has begun to seem trivializing and inadequate, as if it were a lesser kind of violence. Since violence in the home is actually the training ground and origin of most other violence, whether it is criminal behaviour or many assumptions of foreign policy, original violence is one suggested alternative. In these dozen years, hate crimes have finally begun to include crimes against women as well as those directed at people of a particular race, religion, ethnicity, or sexuality; all the categories that have been taken more seriously in the past because they also include men. Terrorism is now also applied to the bombing of abortion clinics, not just to acts that are perceived as political by a masculine definition.

Feminist academics have brought into feminism an imitative

AS IF WOMEN MATTER | 209

but perhaps necessary group of words. Deconstruction is the act of divorcing something from its original context and meaning. Phrases like 'the production of women's agency' are substituted for empowerment; 'problematize' instead of simply talking about problems and what creates them; and even 'feminist praxis' 'when feminist practice would do just as well. Academic and other generalized language often obfuscates, distances and removes insight and information from readers who need them most, but perhaps this is all necessary to get taken seriously and tenured in an academic world.

On the other hand, 'politically correct', a term that originated as a self-deprecating and humorous way to describe movement efforts to be inclusive, has become very serious as groups that prefer exclusion have turned it into an accusation.

If there was any doubt about the importance of language, it has, been put to rest by an anti-equality right wing that is insisting again on using 'unwed mother' and 'illegitimate children' instead of 'single mother' and 'children'. As the representative of the only world religion to have permanent observer status in the United Nations, the Vatican has set out to oppose reproductive rights and reproductive health as phrases, and even to challenge the use of the word 'gender' in United Nations documents. Clearly, the decision of what words we may use determines what dreams we are able to express.

Consider the changes already made or still to come in your own language. They are a good indication of where we are and where we need to go.

—1995

# THE THIRD WAY: AN END OF TRAFFICKING AND PROSTITUTION, A BEGINNING OF MUTUAL SEXUALITY*

There are three million females trapped in prostitution in India, of which 1.4 million are girls between the ages of nine and thirteen according to estimates made by the Central Bureau of Investigation. Even the adult women were originally brought into prostitution as children, according to the National Human Rights Commission of India.

Sonagachi in Kolkata is one of the biggest red-light areas in Asia. Prostitution and sex trafficking have got more entrenched in India as the sex industry has gained legitimacy in the wake of AIDS-control programmes funded by the Bill and Melinda Gates Foundation. These programmes have funded pimps and brothel managers as 'peer educators' and overlooked the slavery and control in the brothel system. They have also created a false notion of 'ethical demand', which promotes the concept that it is all right to purchase sex if you use a condom. Buyers and traffickers have enjoyed impunity for the repeated buying and selling of girls in brothels.

Some women's groups who do not differentiate between sex and sexual exploitation have supported these AIDS-control programmes. They have accepted the inevitability of the sexual exploitation and prostitution of girls and women who are poor

---

*This essay includes passages adapted from Gloria Steinem's speeches after visits to Sonagachi in Kolkata, during the tenth anniversary of Apne Aap Women Worldwide at Jawaharlal Nehru University, New Delhi, in 2012 and to groups of survivors of trafficking and prostitution in the US and Forbesgunge, Bihar in 1997.

and of low caste. They are lobbying with the government to decriminalize pimps and brothel owners.

It is important to note that many in these groups were marching on the streets to end male impunity for all other forms of rape. Steinem analyses the possible outcomes of legalizing prostitution as a form of work, in which poor or migrant women may be asked to try prostitution before being given dole or be told that their visa is dependent on remaining in prostitution. She suggests a third way which will protect women from being through the criminal justice system and end the impunity of male perpetrators by penalizing the purchase of sex and having no punishment for the selling of sex.

—Ruchira Gupta

Since I am here to talk about a life-or-death change that is thought to be impossible—ending sex trafficking, prostitution and the demand for unequal sex that creates a market for both—let's talk about other deep changes that have happened in my own lifetime.

For instance, when I was auditing classes at the University of Delhi, there were many students who had never before been in classrooms with members of the so-called 'opposite sex'. Tension and self-consciousness were palpable and painful. Some young women sat in the back and said not a word. A professor told me that it was unnatural and impossible to teach amid such sexual tension, that co-education might work in other cultures, but not here.

Now, I think it's possible in both our countries for women and men to study and argue and learn together, to actually be friends, whether or not there is any sexual or romantic vibe between them. That is a huge step towards recognizing each other's full humanity.

When I was living here at the end of the 1950s, there were still instances of sati that were viewed as chosen or even romantic. Despite brave protests against enforced sati, and laws against it passed during the British Raj, some still considered it an inevitable and honourable part of culture—even of human nature. After all, a woman's identity came entirely from the man she married, and there was no other way she could make an honourable living or be other than a burden. Then in the 1980s, under pressure from a brave feminist movement, India passed its own laws against sati, and remaining instances became rare and deplored. Feminists also began to take on the police, the courts and the more concealed crime of dowry murders.

When I was a student here, both of our countries viewed some wife-beating as inevitable, even deserved, since wives were supposed to obey their husbands, and men might be justified in physically disciplining their wives. In pre-feminist America, the police might be called to intervene, but domestic violence was the one crime in which they defined success as getting the criminal and the victim back together again. Indeed, the terms 'domestic violence' and 'battered woman' hadn't been coined yet, there was no visible women's movement, and no shelters to escape to. The most common questions were: *What did you do to anger him?* Or: *Why don't you just leave?*

Now, there is still a long way to go—an American woman is more likely to be injured or killed by a man she knows than by a stranger—but at least there are laws against domestic violence, shelters are tax-funded, police can bring charges—even if the woman is too terrified to testify—and escaping 'masculine' control is understood to be the time a woman is most likely to be murdered; thus it must be carefully planned.

When I was a student here, both of our countries kept quiet about rape and sexual assault, or blamed it on the woman, or assumed it had some relationship to sex. Now, a critical mass in both our countries understand that rape is the fault of the aggressor, not the victim, and that it's about violence, not sex. 'Masculinity' requires superiority to females, and since that is a lie, it can only be maintained by violence or the threat of violence. Rapes are often carried out by groups of men or boys who are proving their 'masculinity' to each other. Rapists often use objects to penetrate and tear apart female bodies—no erection or ejaculation involved—and they may also rape the very old or very young—even infants. Nor does the number of raped women necessarily reflect the number of men who rape. In the US, one study showed that the average rapist had raped fourteen times.

Finally, we're beginning to understand that a male-dominant

culture tries to addict males to dominance in order to perpetuate itself, and to persuade men to risk their lives in wars that have nothing to do with their own self-interest, which is why female bodies are in special danger in war zones. But at least we now know about the mass rapes and evisceration with objects in Bosnia and Rwanda and the Congo. If the evidence of sexualized violence against Jewish women during the Holocaust hadn't been suppressed at the Nuremberg Trials some seventy years ago, we might have been better prepared for sexual violence in war zones now.[1]

It was a huge step forward when Judge Navanethem Pillay, a South African judge of Indian descent, became the first woman of colour in the judiciary in her own country, and then the first on the Rwanda Tribunal and the International Criminal Court. She was the main force behind legally defining rape as a war crime. 'Rape has always been regarded as one of the spoils of war,' as she said. 'Now it is a war crime, no longer a trophy.'

It was an even bigger step forward when, in both our countries, we began to reform rape laws that required a third-party eyewitness—so mistrusted were women—and to contest laws based on the idea that only virgins or married women of the right race or caste could be raped. Our respective women's movements agitated for laws against sexual assault that put the victimizer on trial, not the victim, and we ourselves took to the streets to protest sexualized violence.

This year, 2012, I watched with admiration as outrage reached a peak in massive and continuing demonstrations against the brutal gang rape, evisceration and murder of a paramedical student on a bus in New Delhi. This angry fire lit the dry tinder of sexualized violence in general, and forced government action. Soon, I was reading the final report of the Verma Commission. It recommended new punishments for gang rapes, acid attacks, stalking and trafficking, and new support for gender equality and equal political participation. It even recommended *against* the teaching of patriarchy and male supremacy in schools. When Gopal Subramaniam, one of its three Commission members, visited New York in 2013, he explained that now, sexualized violence was out in the open, and the victimizers were shamed, not the victims. Indeed, people fighting *against* this extreme form of inequality were looked upon as heroes. This was a sea change.

Like all such examples of changing consciousness that I've seen in my lifetime, I can imagine that prostitution or 'survival sex'— plus sex trafficking by force or fraud—could gradually diminish and die out. Even now, wherever there is *more* equality between males and females, there is *less* trafficking and prostitution. Wherever there is *less* equality, there is more of both. Just as the colonial era sent men without women into countries where they created or increased prostitution, male-superior cultures are now creating a son surplus and a daughter deficit. This also is increasing the buying, selling and kidnapping of women.

Prostitution isn't the oldest profession. It's the oldest oppression.

\*

One barrier to fighting both prostitution and sex trafficking is the false notion that there has always been this kind of inequality. In a patriarchy, some women are sexually restricted to child-bearing and keeping the ruling race or caste 'pure', while others are sexually exploited for sex only or for producing more workers. But when European colonists arrived among the five hundred or so tribes of North America, they wrote home about their shock that 'these savages' didn't rape, not even their female prisoners. Columbus himself wrote home his complaints when conquered Native women fought against becoming sexual slaves to his crew.

It's true that patriarchy has existed for five hundred to five thousand years, depending on the part of the world, but at most, that's 5 per cent of human history. From Kerala to Kenya, there still are remnants of matrilineal cultures in which women controlled agriculture, understood the means to decide when and whether to have children, and lived in a balance of authority with men. In my country, Cherokee and other original languages don't even have gendered pronouns, nor did many other languages with ancient roots; for instance, Persian, Bengali, Finnish, Yoruba, Basque and many more. They may have absorbed concepts of gender after colonists arrived, as Tagalog absorbed Spanish. But they were still a long way from, say, French, that attributes gender to everything, from pens and forks to tables and chairs.

In truth, gender roles are elaborate cultural inventions of subject/object, active/passive, that rose up over centuries to allow male control of reproduction by controlling women's bodies and freedom.

Even in our modern imaginations, gender and prostitution seem to be inevitable parts of human nature. Prostitution can also only be dealt with in only two ways: legal or criminal. Once again, duality conceals the full circle of possibilities, but it was the only choice I'd ever heard.

*

When I began to travel as a feminist organizer, as I had learned in India, legalization seemed more humane. Otherwise, prostituted women only had a choice between a pimp who protected them from arrest or got them out on bail—then took their earnings and forced them to work—and a literal prison cell. Given a choice between two prisons, eliminating one seemed like a good idea.

I did run into a few enlightened authorities who invented choices in between. For instance, an African American woman judge in night court refused to book a prostitute unless her customer was arrested, too. It was amazing how fast her charges melted away. But mostly, prostituted women agreed that legalization might be better, though some feared their pimps too much to care, others didn't see much difference since they had to have sex with their arresting officer, and a few said days in prison felt like a rest.

Then I got an emergency call from Johnnie Tillmon of the National Welfare Rights Organization. The daughter of a black sharecropping family, she had become a fierce organizer, arguing to increase the level of welfare payments, especially for single mothers. She was raising small children and, as she pointed out, it would cost the state infinitely more if she stopped doing it at home; yet payments were so slight that the end of each month brought Kool-Aid and potatoes. For *Ms.* magazine, she also wrote a lethal analysis of the welfare system as a gigantic jealous husband who looked under your bed for other men's shoes, controlled your life with endless paperwork, and doled out an inadequate allowance.

On the phone, she explained that Nevada, the only state in which prostitution was legal, had come up with a double whammy. Since prostitution was being described by a powerful combination of academics, pimps and some prostituted women themselves as 'sex work', a job like any other, women were being told that either they tried it or lost their welfare payments, unemployment cheque or other benefits meant for the jobless. The state was saving money and creating a tourist attraction at the same time.

It took two days of protest marches on the strip outside Las Vegas hotels by the full membership of the NWRO, outrageous speeches about 'body invasion' by my speaking partner Flo Kennedy, celebrities who attracted national press, and general disruption of the carefree atmosphere cultivated for tourists.

It also took a surrealistic few hours marching outside the Mustang Ranch, the first legal brothel of Nevada, looking at the occasional woman who peered out at us curiously while women peered out at us from the window of a house trailer that was an individual brothel. In the end, media attention forced the state to withdraw its threat.

\*

Women's movements around the world have been fighting the criminal and global sex-trafficking industry for as long as I can remember. In Germany, I heard that the same pressure had been put on women recipients of unemployment and other government programmes. There, prostitution was called 'hospitality work'. There must not have been many takers in that prosperous country. When the 2006 World Cup in soccer was held there, about 40,000 women and children were trafficked in, mostly from the surrounding and poorer countries of the former Soviet Union; all to service athletes and fans gathered from around the world.

In 2008, I went back to Nevada and its county of legalized prostitution with an experienced activist who thought she could gain entry into one of the new brothels. No such luck. Because it is legal, illegally trafficked women from other countries had probably been taken there to be 'broken in', the owner, a man with a gun in his belt, was being cautious. He was also said to be the single biggest contributor to the campaigns of judges in the state of Nevada, and he refused us even a drink at an empty bar.

Since this brothel, too, consisted of many house trailers lined up behind a high storm fence, we went to its farthest side where there was a restaurant and saloon run by a woman who had been living there for years. She told us that she saw the owner buying cartons of ramen noodles at a shopping centre, so she knew that's what he fed 'his girls'. She, too, bought soup and threw individual cartons over the fence. 'I know those girls don't get enough to eat,' she said, 'and this way, he won't know.'

So much for better conditions that are supposed to come with being legal.

Some enforcement of laws against trafficking of children have been successful. Even those who still believe that legalization creates better conditions probably don't want this life for children. But since the average age of entry into prostitution is between twelve and thirteen in the US—and between nine and twelve in India—how successful can they be? Even if they were, how could one look at an eighteen-year-old? It would mean saying, 'I'm sorry, I could have offered you a help and a way out yesterday, but today you are on your own.'

And what is happening globally is that females are being pulled into the sex trade ever younger—partly because of the idea that they are less likely to have AIDS or, most surrealistic of all, that sex with a virgin will cure AIDS. Also son preference in, say, China has resulted in a skewed sex ratio, and that has resulted in using deception and force to bring girls and women from, say, North Korea.

Indeed, this importation of women takes place from south to north within India.

And there are still the two opposite forces of criminalization and legalization. The first is supported by patriarchal religious power that condemns as sinful all sexual expression that cannot end in conception, and doesn't take place within patriarchal marriage. The second is the equally patriarchal but secular idea that freedom and democracy and even human rights are defined as the maximum sexual availability of females to males—under male terms. For instance, there are groups that talk about 'the human right to be a sex worker', but not the human right *not* to be a sex worker. This view doesn't have religion behind it, but it does have the huge sums of money of the sex industry, plus the increasing power of pornography that normalizes the sexual domination of women. *Porne* means female slaves, while *eros* means love, and implies mutual pleasure and free choice. Pornography is as different from erotica as rape is different from sex.

Most women's movements have fought for the Third Way: for make a living outside prostitution, for safe places to live in or at least meet outside brothels, for schools for children so girls needn't be prostituted and boys needn't become pimps, healthcare, safety from corrupt police, and just as important, respect, listening, friendship. Yet because women's movements have generally fought prostitution and sex trafficking, they are sometimes condemned as anti-sex by secular groups. Because they emphasize pleasure, not just reproduction, they are often condemned by the patriarchal religious world.

But this Third Way of listening and offering alternatives—of educating buyers about the cruelty and reality of the world they are supporting—is lessening demand and saving lives from Chicago to Sweden. Even some of the countries once most devoted to legalizing prostitution are discovering that it just doesn't work. For instance, the mayor of Amsterdam admitted in an editorial in *Het Parool* in 2003 that his city had become a magnet for trafficking, and 'it appeared impossible to create a safe and controllable zone for women that was not open to abuse by organized crime'.

None of this is easy. It is a huge global industry, and interfering with its profits can be dangerous. Many prostituted women, children, and men, too, have their own Stockholm Syndrome to overcome. A woman may have been sexually abused as child and come to believe she has no other value, or she may belong to a group that has been prostituted for generations. But it is a tribute to the human spirit— both among activists and among prostituted people—that in my country, groups like GEMS (Girls, Education and Mentoring Service), and in yours, groups like Apne Aap, are seeing women transform from objects to self-willed human beings.

And we are finding out that many myths are wrong: indoor prostitution is no less traumatizing than outdoor, and buzzers in rooms prevent injury by sadistic customers. The overall rate of life expectancy for prostituted women is comparable to men in combat. Indeed, body invasion is even more traumatizing than external beatings. Our skin is our defence, and our body is our domain, our sense of self.

It also hasn't been possible to independently document any diminishing of AIDS or child prostitution, despite payment to brothel owners to distribute condoms, and despite declarations of so-called unions that claim to bar children. When I have been to Sonagachi, for instance, I have looked inside open doorways and seen the children. But then, unlike Bill Gates, I didn't announce that I was coming.

And I also have seen signs all in Bengali—except for two large English words: SEX WORKERS. Though I've often been ashamed of the foreign policy of my country, I've never been ashamed of my own women's movement until I saw those words so clearly imported from the US. Having one's body invaded by strangers is not just any job. The term sex workers can be and has been used to deny unemployment and welfare and other benefits to those who refuse such 'work'. I hope this term was once invented by women in search for at least verbal dignity, but now it has become the property of sex-traffickers and brothel profiteers seeking unlimited demand. As I watch women being lined up in the street like cattle next to that 'sex workers' sign, and see children sitting inside a doorway under those words, I realize that I, for one, can never say them again. Except to apologize.

While it may or may not be legal for an individual adult woman or man to sell her or his sexual services, it should not be legal to sell the bodies of others. Thus pimps, brothel-keepers and certainly traffickers should be pursued with the full force of the law. In Scandinavian countries, it is not illegal to sell sex, but it is illegal and subject to a fine to buy it. France has also passed a law to fine customers. This is not irrational; it is simply a recognition of unequal power and thus unequal responsibility. And arrest does not mean jail for men who have committed no other crime; it means a fine and learning the human cost of this industry that sells the right to dominate other humans. For the first time, attention is shifting from the powerless and no longer criminalized supplier to the powerful demand.

We have reached a crucial place in history. We know that prostitution is not inevitable, that it is a function of unequal power. Yet, in my country, there are girls and women—especially women of colour and Native American women—who are tattooed with a pimp's distinguishing mark so other pimps will be warned away; sometimes even a tattoo that is itself a price code. This is hard and inhuman to see.

Remember that the key is listening, and change happens from the bottom up. For instance, I went to Zambia for a conference on sex trafficking. Afterwards, I visited friends who live on the Zambezi River and I ended up sitting on a tarpaulin in the middle of a hot and dusty field, in a circle with twenty or so village women. They were shy, our languages were diverse, and I thought: This is one time when the magic of women in a circle isn't going to work.

Then one woman began to say the unsayable—that her husband was beating her and she did not know what to do. The others supported her and began to tell the truth, too.

Gradually, I learned that what sent the women to Lusaka to be sex trafficked was the need for money to buy food and pay their children's school fees. Crops had been cut by two-thirds because the World Bank had built a dam in the Zambezi River to produce electricity, promised irrigation systems but never delivered. The women were carrying water in buckets to grow maize, yet once it grew, the elephants ate it.

I asked what they needed, and they said they wanted an electric fence to keep the elephants out. Then they could grow enough maize for themselves, and also to sell.

So I went home and raised a few thousand dollars for a fence. It wasn't much.

When I went back the next year, the women had pulled up acres of weeds by hand, carried buckets of water from the river, and raised a bumper crop of maize, enough for their own family food security for a year, and also to pay school fees.

They sang songs to the maize. We danced to the maize.

If you had asked me how to stop women from those villages going to Lusaka and being sex-trafficked, I never would have said, 'An electrified fence.' But that was just what it was.

We have to listen to each other. We have to be together in fields like that, and in rooms like these. We can go both back and forward to a time when sexuality was about mutual pleasure—and procreation if you chose. It will again be our human bond. Sex will be its own reward.

—2013

# SISTERHOOD

Wherever we are, women are unequal to men—from the feminization of our poverty, to the loss of control over our bodies, to the lack of access to capital or other resources, to being looked over even in the very political movement that we stand shoulder to shoulder with men. The good news is that we are organizing across cultures and countries to challenge the commonalities of our inequalities. In the work against sex trafficking, female genetic mutilation, child marriage and the rights for migrant workers, we stand united and collectively put pressure on world bodies and our governments to create fairer policies and practices. Inside our own countries, too, we have found strength in sitting in small circles or marching in big rallies, sharing our stories and building common strategies.

After the rape of 16 December 2012, woman after woman marched on the streets asking to change weak laws that gave impunity to men responsible for sexual violence. They were joined in solidarity by voices across the globe. The Verma Commission was able to submit its recommendations in record time because of the massive organizing by women and some men in India which provided more than 80,000 submissions and best practices sent in by sister lawyers in Africa, Europe and the US.

In India, young women found a voice in their sisterhood which is amplified every day with a courage that cannot be denied.

—Ruchira Gupta

A very, very long time ago (about three or four years), I took a certain secure and righteous pleasure in saying the things that women are supposed to say. I remember with pain:

'My work won't interfere with marriage. After all, I can always keep my typewriter at home.'

Or:

'I don't want to write about women's stuff. I want to write about foreign policy.'

Or:

'Black families were forced into matriarchy, so I see why black women have to retreat behind their men.'

Or:

'I know we're helping Chicano groups that are tough on women, but *that's their culture.*'

Or:

'Who would want to join a women's group? I've never been a joiner, have you?'

Or (when bragging):

'He says I write like a man.'

I suppose it's obvious from the kinds of statements I chose that I was secretly non-conforming. I wasn't married, I was earning a living at a profession I cared about, and I had friends outside my racial group. I had basically—if quietly—opted out of the 'feminine' role. But that made it all the more necessary to repeat the conventional wisdom, even to look as conventional as I could manage, if I was to avoid some of the punishments reserved by society for *not* doing as society says. I, therefore, learned to pretend conformity with subtlety, logic and humour. Sometimes, I even believed it myself.

If it weren't for the women's movement, I might still be dissembling away. But the ideas of this sea change in women's views of themselves are contagious and irresistible. They hit women like a revelation, as if we had left a dark room and walked into the sun.

At first my discoveries seemed personal. In fact, they were the same ones so many millions of women have made and are continuing to make. Greatly simplified, they go like this: Women are human beings first, with minor differences from men that apply largely to the single act of reproduction. We share the dreams, capabilities and weaknesses of all human beings, but our occasional pregnancies and other visible differences have been used even more pervasively, if less brutally, than racial differences have been used to create an 'inferior' group and an elaborate division of labour. This division is continued for a clear if often unconscious reason: the economic and social profit of patriarchy, males as a group.

Once this feminist realization dawned, I reacted in what turned out to be predictable ways. First, I was amazed at the simplicity and obviousness of a revelation that made sense, at last, of my life experience. I couldn't figure out why I hadn't seen it before. Second, I realized how far this new vision of life was from the system around us, and how tough it would be to explain a feminist realization at all, much less to get people (especially, though not only, men) to contemplate so drastic a change.

But I tried to explain. God knows (*she* knows) that women try. We make analogies with other groups marked for subservient roles in order to assist blocked imaginations. We supply endless facts and statistics of injustice, reeling them off until we feel like human information-retrieval machines. We lean heavily on the device of reversal. (If there is a male reader to whom all my pre-realization statements seem perfectly logical, for instance, let him read each sentence with 'men' substituted for 'women'—or himself for me—and see how he feels: 'My work won't interfere with marriage'; 'Chicana groups that are tough on men...' You get the idea.)

We even use logic. If a woman spends a year bearing and nursing a child, for instance, she is supposed to have the primary responsibility for raising that child to adulthood. That's logic by the male definition, but it often forces women to accept raising children as their only function, keeps them from doing any other kind of work, or discourages them from being mothers at all. Wouldn't it be just as logical to say that a child has two parents, therefore both are equally responsible for child-rearing, and the father should compensate for that extra year by spending *more* than half the time caring for the child? Logic is in the eye of the logician.

Occasionally, these efforts at explaining actually succeed. More often, I get the feeling that most women are speaking Urdu and most men are speaking Pali.

Whether joyful or painful, both kinds of reaction to our discovery have a great reward. They give birth to sisterhood.

First, we share the exhilaration of growth and self-discovery, the sensation of having the scales fall from our eyes. Whether we are giving other women this new knowledge or receiving it from them, the pleasure for all concerned is very moving.

In the second stage, when we're exhausted from dredging up facts and arguments for the men whom we had previously thought advanced and intelligent, we make another simple discovery: many women understand. We may share experiences, make jokes, paint pictures and describe humiliations that mean little to men, but *women understand.*

The odd thing about these deep and personal connections among women living under patriarchy is that they often leap across barriers of age, economics, worldly experience, race, culture—all the barriers that, in male or mixed society, seem so impossible to cross.

I remember meeting with a group of women in Missouri who, because they had come in equal numbers from a small town and from its nearby campus, seemed to be split between wives with white gloves welded to their wrists and students wearing boots who used words like 'imperialism' and 'oppression'. Planning for a childcare centre had brought them together, but the meeting seemed hopeless until three of the booted young women began to argue among themselves about a young male professor. The leader of the radicals on campus, he accused all women unwilling to run mimeograph machines of not being sufficiently devoted to the cause.

As for childcare centres, he felt their effect of allowing women to compete with men for jobs was part of a dreaded 'feminization' of the American male and American culture.

'He sounds just like my husband,' said one of the white-gloved women. 'He wants me to have bake sales and collect door-to-door for his Republican party.'

The young women had sense enough to take it from there. What difference did boots or white gloves make if they were all getting treated like servants and children? Before they broke up, they were discussing some subjects that affected them all (like the myth of the vaginal orgasm) and planning to meet every week.

'Men think we're whatever it is we do for men,' explained one of the housewives. 'It's only by getting together with other women that we'll ever find out who we are.'

Even racial barriers become a little less formidable once we discover this mutuality of our life experiences as women. At a meeting by black women domestics who had formed a job cooperative in Alabama, a white housewife asked me about the consciousness-raising sessions or 'rap groups' that are often an organic path to feminism. I explained that while men, even men from the 'wrong' groups, usually had some place—a neighbourhood, a bar, a street corner, something—where they could get together and be themselves, women of all groups tended to be isolated in their houses and families; isolated from other females. We had no street corners, no bars, no offices, no territory that was recognized as ours. Rap groups were an effort to create something of our own, a free place—an occasional chance for total honesty and support from our sisters.

As I talked about isolation, about the feeling that there must be something wrong with us if we aren't content to be housekeepers and mothers, tears began to stream down the cheeks of this dignified woman—clearly as much of a surprise to her as to us. For the black women, some distance was bridged by seeing this white woman cry.

'He does it to us both, honey,' said the black woman next to her, putting an arm around her shoulders. 'If it's your own kitchen or somebody else's, you still don't get treated like people. Women's work just doesn't count.'

The meeting ended with the housewife organizing a support group of white women who would extract from their husbands a living wage for domestic workers, and help them fight the local authorities who opposed any such pay raises; a support group without which the domestic workers felt their small and brave cooperative could not survive.

As for the 'matriarchal' argument that I swallowed in pre-feminist days, I now understand why many black women resent it, and feel that it's the white sociologists' way of making the black community feel inferior to a white patriarchal lifestyle. 'If I end up cooking grits for revolutionaries,' explained a black woman poet from Chicago, 'it isn't my revolution. Black men and women need to work together. You can't have liberation for half a race.' In fact, some black women wonder if criticism of the strength they were forced to develop isn't a way to keep half the black community working at lowered capacity and lowered pay, as well as to attribute some of black men's sufferings to black women, instead of to their real source, racism.

Looking back at all those white male-approved things I used to say, the basic hang-up seems clear—a lack of esteem for women, whatever our race, and for myself.

This is the most tragic punishment that society inflicts on any second-class group. Ultimately, the brainwashing works and we ourselves come to believe that our group is inferior. If we achieve a little success in the world, we think of ourselves as 'different' and don't want to associate with our group. We want to identify up, not down (clearly my problem in not wanting to join women's groups). We want to be the only woman in the office, or the only black family on the block, or the only Jew in the club.

The pain of looking back at wasted, imitative years is enormous. Trying to write like men. Valuing myself and other women according to the degree of our acceptance by men—socially, in politics and in our professions. It's as painful as it is now to hear two grown-up female human beings competing with each other on the basis of their husbands' status, like servants whose identity rests on the wealth or accomplishments of their employers.

And this lack of esteem that makes us put each other down is still the major enemy of sisterhood. Women who are conforming to society's expectations view the non-conformists with understandable alarm. Those noisy, unfeminine women, they say to themselves. They will only make trouble for us all. Women who are quietly non-conforming, hoping nobody will notice, are even more alarmed, because they think they have more to lose. And that makes sense, too.

The status quo protects itself by punishing all challengers, especially women whose rebellion strikes at the most fundamental social organization: the sex roles that convince half the population that its identity depends on being first in work or in war, and the other half that it must serve worldwide as unpaid or underpaid labour.

In fact, there seems to be no punishment of white males that quite equals the ridicule and personal viciousness reserved for women who rebel. Attractive or young women who act forcefully are assumed to be either unnatural or male-controlled. If they succeed, it could only have been sexually, through men. Old women or women considered unattractive by male standards are accused of acting out of bitterness, because they could not get a man. Any woman who chooses to behave like a full human being should be warned that the armies of the status quo will treat her as something of a dirty joke. Ridicule is their natural and first weapon, with more serious opposition to follow. She will *need* sisterhood.

All of that is meant to be a warning, but not a discouragement. There are more rewards than punishments.

For myself, I can now begin to admit anger and use it constructively, where once I would have submerged it and let it fester into guilt, or accumulate for some destructive explosion.

I have met brave women who are exploring the outer edge of human possibility, with no history to guide them, and with a courage to make themselves vulnerable that I find moving beyond the words to express it.

I no longer think that I do not exist, which is my version of the lack of self-esteem afflicting many women. (If male standards weren't natural to me—and they were the only standards—how could I exist?) This means that I am less likely to need external values and approval, and am less vulnerable to classic arguments. ('If you don't like me, you're not a real woman': said by a man who is coming on sexually. 'If you don't like me, you can't relate to other people': said by anyone who understands blackmail as an art.)

I can sometimes deal with men as equals, and therefore, can afford to like them as individual human beings.

I have discovered politics that are not intellectual or superimposed. They are organic. I finally understand why for years I inexplicably identified with 'out' groups: I belong to one, too. And I know it will take a coalition of such groups to achieve a society in which, at a minimum, no one is born into a second-class role because of the visible difference of race, sex or anything else.

I no longer feel strange by myself, or with a group of women in public. I feel just fine.

I am continually moved to discover I have sisters.

I am beginning, just beginning, to find out who I am.

—1972

# IF MEN COULD MENSTRUATE

Steinem illustrated a lesson in this essay: that anything a powerful group has is perceived as good, no matter what it is, and anything a less powerful group has is not so good, no matter how intrinsically great it might be. Thus menstruation, something even self-respecting and otherwise body-proud women are often made to feel ashamed of, would suddenly become terrific—provided only men had it.

Role reversals of all kinds create empathy and are great detectors of bias, in ourselves as well as in others, for they expose injustices that seem normal and so are invisible. In fact, the deeper and less visible the bias, the more helpful it is to take some commonly accepted notion/notions about one caste, religion, sex, class, race, ethnicity, sexuality, ability, whatever—and see how it/they sounds when transferred to another.

—Ruchira Gupta

Living in India made me understand that a white minority of the world has spent centuries conning us into thinking that white skin makes people superior, even though the only thing it really does is make them more affected by ultraviolet rays and wrinkles.

Reading Freud made me just as sceptical about penis envy. The power of giving birth makes 'womb envy' more logical, and an organ as external and unprotected as the penis makes men very vulnerable indeed.

But listening recently to a woman describe the unexpected arrival of her menstrual period (a red stain had spread on her dress as she argued heatedly on a public stage) still made me cringe with embarrassment. That is, until she explained that, when finally informed in whispers of the obvious event, she had said to the all-male audience, 'And you should be proud to have a menstruating woman on your stage. It's probably the first real thing that's happened to this group in years!'

Laughter. Relief. She had turned a negative into a positive. Somehow her story merged with India and Freud to make me finally understand the power of positive thinking. Whatever a 'superior' group has will be used to justify its superiority, and whatever an 'inferior' group has will be used to justify its plight. Black men were given poorly paid jobs because they were said to be 'stronger' than white men, while all women were relegated to poorly paid jobs because they were said to be 'weaker'. As the little boy said when asked if he wanted to be a lawyer like his mother, 'Oh no, that's women's work.' Logic has nothing to do with oppression.

So what would happen if suddenly, magically, men could menstruate, and women could not?

Clearly, menstruation would become an enviable, boast-worthy, masculine event.

Men would brag about how long and how much.

Young boys would talk about it as the envied beginning of manhood. Gifts, religious ceremonies, family dinners and stag parties would mark the day.

To prevent monthly work loss among the powerful, Congress would fund a National Institute of Dysmenorrhea. Doctors would research little about heart attacks, from which men were hormonally protected, but everything about cramps.

Sanitary supplies would be federally funded and free. Of course, some men would still pay for the prestige of such commercial brands as Paul Newman Tampons, Muhammad Ali's Rope-a-Dope Pads, John Wayne Maxi Pads and Joe Namath Jock Shields—'For Those Light Bachelor Days'.

Statistical surveys would show that men did better in sports and won more Olympic medals during their periods.

Generals, right-wing politicians and religious fundamentalists would cite menstruation ('men-struation') as proof that only men could serve God and country in combat ('You have to give blood to take blood.'), occupy high political office ('Can women be properly fierce without a monthly cycle governed by the planet Mars?'), be priests, ministers, God Himself ('He gave this blood for our sins.'), or rabbis ('Without a monthly purge of impurities, women are unclean.').

Male liberals or radicals would insist that women are equal, just different; and that any woman could join their ranks if only she were willing to recognize the primacy of menstrual rights ('Everything else is a single issue.') or self-inflict a major wound every month ('You must give blood for the revolution.').

Street guys would invent slang ('He's a three-pad man.') and 'give fives' on the corner with some exchange like, 'Man, you lookin' good!'

'Yeah, man, I'm on the rag!'

TV shows would treat the subject openly. (*Happy Days*: Richie and Potsie try to convince Fonzie that he is still 'The Fonz', though he has missed two periods in a row. *Hill Street Blues*: The whole precinct hits the same cycle.) So would newspapers (Summer Shark Scare Threatens Menstruating Men. Judge Cities Monthlies in Pardoning Rapist.) And so would movies (Paul Newman and Robert Redford in *Blood Brothers*!).

Men would convince women that sex was more pleasurable at 'that time of the month'. Lesbians would be said to fear blood and therefore, life itself, though all they needed was a good menstruating man.

Medical schools would limit women's entry ('they might faint at the sight of blood').

Of course, intellectuals would offer the most moral and logical arguments. Without that biological gift for measuring the cycles of the moon and planets, how could a woman master any discipline that demanded a sense of time, space, mathematics—or the ability to measure anything at all? In philosophy and religion, how could women compensate for being disconnected from the rhythm of the universe? Or for their lack of a symbolic death and resurrection every month?

Menopause would be celebrated as a positive event, the symbol that men had accumulated enough years of cyclical wisdom to need no more.

Liberal males in every field would try to be kind to women. The fact that 'these people' have no gift for measuring life, the liberals would explain, should be punishment enough.

And how would women be trained to react? One can imagine right-wing women agreeing to all these arguments with a staunch and smiling masochism. ('The Equal Rights Amendment would force housewives to wound themselves every month': Phyllis Schlafly.[1] 'Your husband's blood is as sacred as that of Jesus—and so sexy, too!': Marabel Morgan.[2]) Reformers and Queen Bees would adjust their lives to the cycles of the men around them. Feminists would explain endlessly that men, too, needed to be liberated from the false idea of Martian aggressiveness, just as women needed to escape the bonds of 'menses-envy'. Radical feminists would add that the oppression of the non-menstrual was the pattern for all other oppressions. ('Vampires were our first freedom fighters!') Cultural feminists would exalt a bloodless female imagery in art and literature. Socialist feminists would insist that once capitalism and imperialism were overthrown, women would menstruate, too. ('If women aren't yet menstruating in Russia,' they would explain, 'it's only because true Socialism can't exist within capitalist encirclement.')

In short, we would discover, as we should already have guessed, that logic is in the eye of the logician. (For instance, here's an idea for theorists and logicians: If women are supposed to be less rational and more emotional at the beginning of their menstrual cycle when the female hormone is at its lowest level, then why isn't it logical to say that, in those few days, women behave the most like the way men behave all month long? I leave further improvisations up to you.)[3]

The truth is that, if men could menstruate, the power justifications would go on and on.

If we let them.

—1978

# HITLER AND THE CULT OF MASCULINITY

In this essay, Steinem analyses that a tolerance of, or desire for, strong 'top-down' leadership was also a hallmark of the Weimar Republic in which National Socialism grew, and not all such longings came from the traditional right wing.

The impatience with our own national situation—the growing inequality between the rich and the poor, the continued sexual violence against women and girls, the housing shortage, the price of food and fuel, the breakdown of law and order for the weak and the marginalized—should not allow us social-justice-loving-Indians to be seduced by right-wing rhetoric. Today's religious ultra-rightists can obscure the difference between the individual's right to choose and the state's right to impose—whether the imposition is about the clothes we wear or the places we go to.

—Ruchira Gupta

'True idealism,' as Adolf Hitler wrote in *Mein Kampf*, 'is nothing but the subordination of the interests and life of the individual to the community... The sacrifice of personal existence is necessary to secure the preservation of the species.'[1]

Hitler's National Socialist Movement preached against and punished contraception, homosexuality, any women whose main purpose was not motherhood, men who did not prove their manhood by fathering many children, and anything else that failed to preserve and expand the 'Aryan' people and the German state.

The Nazi doctrine he created was unequivocally opposed to any individual rights. In *Mein Kampf*, Hitler wrote: 'We must also do away with the conception that the treatment of the body is the affair of every individual.'[2]

Those words were a direct slap at the feminist movement of Germany in the late-nineteenth and early twentieth centuries, an influential force for, among other things, divorce, contraception and abortion—in short, for a woman's right to control her own body.

Not only did German feminists share these goals of their sisters in other countries, but they had won some earlier and greater successes. They achieved the vote in 1918, for instance, as part of the Weimar Constitution that followed World War I.

By 1926, moderate feminists had elected thirty-two women deputies to the Reichstag, the national parliamentary body that politically symbolized this brief burst of democracy, just as it was culturally symbolized by the great German novelists, the Bauhaus and the between-the-wars flowering of literature and art. (In the same era, there were only fifteen women members of the British Parliament, and women in the US Congress had reached a total of three.)

Radical German feminists had also begun to organize against the protective legislation that kept women out of many jobs, and to work towards such international goals as alliances with their counterparts in other countries, demilitarization and pacifism.

German families had become much smaller, married women had gained the legal right to keep their own salaries, and both married and single women were joining the paid-labour force in record numbers.

Precisely because such changes were both obvious in daily lifestyles and profound in their potential effect, they were often resented by those who longed for the old male supremacist, hierarchical, 'undefeated' days before the war.

As unemployment and inflation grew worse, feminists in particular and women in the workforce in general were scapegoated, along with Marxists, Jews and any group that challenged the Aryan idea of power based on race and sex.

Because of right-wing pressure, the Weimar Republic began to ban married women from competing with men for government jobs. Because of that pressure plus alarm at the declining birth rate, access to contraception was also restricted. But the Nazi party promised much more. And much worse.

'The right of personal freedom,' Hitler explained in *Mein Kampf*, 'recedes before the duty to preserve the race.'[3] The Nazi leaders said they would not deprive women of the vote, but they ridiculed feminists, liberals and socialists who were 'masculinizing' women by treating them the same as men. Their own answer to women was *gleichwertig aber nicht gleichartig*—equivalent but not the same.

A return to a strong family life; women's primary identity as mothers; tax penalties for remaining single; loans for young married couples and subsidies for child-bearing; prohibition of prostitution, homosexuality, contraception and abortion: all these were positions that the Roman Catholic Church, the Catholic Centre Party and the Nazi Party could and did agree on. True, they disagreed bitterly on which patriarchy should prevail, the church or the state, but the place of women and the need for the authoritarian family was a shared platform, bond and reason for coalition.

As British historian Tim Mason wrote: 'This type of partial or apparent consensus on a basic issue among different sectional interests and elite groups was one of the most important foundations of Nazi rule... Antifeminism was not a minor or opportunistic component of National Socialism, but a central part of it.'[4]

Whether moderate or radical, feminist organizations were disbanded. Feminist publications were closed down or censored. At the same time, traditional women's organizations like the Evangelical Women's Association or the National Association of German Housewives were strengthened by being welcomed into Frauenfront, the Nazi women's association. In 1933, feminists were removed by law from teaching and other public posts: the same law that removed all 'non-Aryans' from such jobs. All women, feminist or not, were banned from the Reichstag, from judgeships and from other decision-making posts.

To the extent that labour needs allowed, married women were persuaded or forced to stay at home and leave paid jobs to men. Propaganda portrayed the ideal woman as healthy, blond, no make-up; a chaste and energetic worker while single, a devoted wife and mother as soon as possible. The magazine advertisements for contraception that had been commonplace were outlawed as pornographic (as many right-wing groups suggest today). Birth control and abortion clinics were padlocked (as some anti-abortion groups are demanding today).

Under Hitler, choosing abortion became sabotage—a crime punishable by imprisonment and hard labour for the woman and a possible death penalty for the abortionist. It was an act of the individual against the state; an exaggeration in degree, but not kind, of current fundamentalist arguments that women must have children 'for Jesus and the church'; or, as the Supreme Court ruled in denying poor women the choice of Medicaid-funded abortion, for 'legitimate government interest'.

As Hitler wrote, 'It must be considered as reprehensible conduct to refrain from giving healthy children to the nation.'[5]

The keyword was, of course, healthy. Since non-Aryans were 'racially impure' and thus unhealthy, Jews, gypsies, Poles and victims of serious handicaps and diseases (Hitler was, for instance, obsessed with syphilis) were all discouraged or prevented from reproducing by methods that varied from segregation of the sexes, threats, labour camps and forced abortion or sterilization, to imprisonment or death in a concentration camp. The choice of method depended largely on whether and for how long the 'unhealthy' were needed as workers. It also depended on convenience. A pregnant worker was easier to gas than to coerce into an abortion.

Interestingly, Hitler also supported capital punishment, 'because of its deterrent effect'.

The only argument among authoritarians is what level and kind of patriarchal power will be supreme—national or international, secular or religious. What all seem to agree on, however, is that the patriarchal family is the basis and training ground for any authoritarianism. It was the basic cell (Keimzelle) of the state for Germany's National Socialism. In the more mixed philosophy of the Eagle Forum, it is just 'the basic unit of society'.

If we're to identify authoritarianism in all its forms, we must study a three-step progression of authoritarian units—'the family, the nation, the very laws of God'.

But at that first level of the family—and the resistance to any self-determination for women within it—authoritarian preachings sound alike. For that matter, even some civil libertarians who cherish individual rights against the state will not guarantee individual and equal rights to women within either state or family. Individuals are men, the family is their basic unit of security in which the state has no right to interfere, and women are nowhere. It's as if a basic right of men is to dominate women and the family.

'Supposing Bach's mother, after her fifth or sixth or even twelfth child, had said, "That'll do, enough is enough"—the works of Bach would never have been written.'

That last quote comes from Heinrich Himmler, founder of the SS, head of all concentration camps and originator of the Lebensborn homes where Aryan pregnant women who were unwed, deserted or having children by lovers other than their husbands were encouraged to have the children Himmler feared might otherwise be illegally aborted. They could choose to keep the child and be supported by the state, or give it up for adoption to a good Aryan family of carefully matched social background.

What they couldn't do was to choose not to have the child, and thus seize control of the means of reproduction, their own bodies, in defiance of the patriarchal state.

In Germany before World War I, when Adolf Hitler himself was still a child, nineteenth-century feminism was already accomplishing a great deal. Women in industry, offices and the professions weren't oddities anymore, and politicians and the press were gradually becoming more sympathetic to their goals. Unlike feminist movements in most other Western countries, this one was giving organizational support to radical feminist demands for sexual and economic equality, the same rights for 'illegitimate' children as for those of married parents, an end to the idea that child-bearing was the only purpose of women or of marriage, and a 'new morality' that required equal rights and consideration for women and men in or outside marriage.

In addition, most activist women were focused on issues that seemed more immediate than achieving the right to vote. Top-down change always seems remote at best, and in Germany before

World War I, parliamentary democracy was a very new and limited possibility. But German feminists had won public support for their unprecedented campaign to decriminalize prostitution (its illegality created the familiar result of brothels protected or run by the police), and they almost succeeded in their careful lobbying effort to delete abortion from the criminal code completely by arguing that 'the competence of the modern State...is limited by the necessity of preserving the freedom of the individual over his [or her] own body'.

This challenge to the sexual caste system met with great resistance from the more agricultural, religious and military parts of German society, as well as reservations from some reformist or religious women who worked to replace radical feminist leaders of national organizations with those who cited motherhood and 'superior morality' as reasons that women should be given more (but not equal) rights. The national obsession with a declining birth rate, combined with new Darwinian theories on who should or should not be encouraged to reproduce, encouraged these non-feminist reformers to cite healthy German motherhood as their justification for education and other rights.

Nonetheless, feminists in the early 1900s were changing minds and eroding public hostility by the end of a half-century or so of activism. They were, that is, until 1912 when a small group of military officers, conservative politicians, racist geneticists and academics resentful of female competition (all of whom, as the press noted, shared the distinction of being unknown or so out-of-date as to be 'among the living dead') formed the League for the Prevention of the Emancipation of Women.

For the first time, there was an organized anti-feminist group turning out anti-equality propaganda. As a tribute to both German conservatism and feminist successes, the 'Anti-League' felt compelled to issue an anti-feminist manifesto. In a press report of its first congress, an ultra-right-wing aristocrat explained: 'The German Empire was created with blood and iron. That was man's work! If women helped, [they] stood behind their men in battle and fired them on to kill as many enemies as possible. (Fervent applause.)'

By 1913, the Anti-League had gained support from a white-collar union of male clerks who were convinced that Jews, the lower classes and 'the invasion of female elements into the profession' were taking their jobs away. Union leaders condemned feminists as 'men-women', 'degenerate' and 'perverse'.

In 1914 the Anti-League imported Lady Griselda Cheape, an English anti-suffrage leader—perhaps the Phyllis Schlafly of her day—to give lectures in Berlin and to tour the country.

Though feminists were divided on whether to take this challenge seriously or to ignore it (some thought it ridiculous enough to be inadvertently helpful), its theme of woman-hating struck a deep chord in patriarchal society. Groups such as the Anti-League never had many members (just as the Eagle Forum or Beal Women and other anti-equality groups spawned in the 1970s did not), but they did publicly scapegoat feminists in particular and active women in general for all that was difficult in modern life. This was something that the military, the church and other traditionalists could agree on, even when they could agree on nothing else.

As Richard Evans, one of the few male scholars to take women's history seriously, explained in *The Feminist Movement in Germany: 1894–1933*, 'these antifeminist arguments were based on the belief that Germany was subject to growing hostility and danger from forces inside the country and without.... The women's movement was creating fresh divisions by...destroying the family...by encouraging married women to take jobs, by supporting unmarried mothers, and by urging women in general to be more independent. It was endangering Germany's military potential by discouraging marriage plus encouraging family planning and thus lowering the birth rate. It was outraging nature by campaigning for the systematic equalization of the sexes and by inciting women to do things they were unsuited for. It was international in spirit and unpatriotic.'[6]

In other words, the later Nazi post-World War I campaign against feminism as anti-German, subversive—and, therefore, an obvious product of a Communist–Jewish conspiracy—was not invented by Hitler or by the philosophy of National Socialism. His promise to return women to 'Children, Cooking, Church' (Kinder, Küche, Kirche), and thus to restore the male-dominant family as the model of an authoritarian society, was an appeal to religious and other ultra-right-wing discontent that had been around since the early twentieth century. True, that discontent was deepened into bitterness by Germany's humiliation during and after World War I, but the atavistic elements of this obsession with male supremacy and restoration of 'the Fatherland' were already there. It just took a national leader willing to pander to such desires, by adding the respectability of a party platform in which they were key emotional planks.

Hitler presented himself as a champion of the lower classes against inherited wealth and power (hence his 'Socialism'), as well as against the 'international conspiracy' of powerful Jews. From a working-class family himself, he replaced upper-class superiority with race superiority, thus justifying his own right to rise to the top. Basic texts like *The Nazi Primer* emphasized hard work and talent as the ways any real German—that is, any Aryan-German—could succeed (hence, 'National Socialism').

A repressed would-be architecture student shocked by the sinfulness of Munich; a vegetarian who didn't smoke or drink and was obsessed by imagined sexual attacks on nice German girls (though only if the attacks came from 'the black-haired Jewish youth [who] lurks in wait', as Hitler wrote in *Mein Kampf*); an obscure and angry worker who felt exploited by the rich and powerful—this was Adolf Hitler when he entered the city's beer halls and workingmen's clubs. His gift for emotional speechmaking unlocked dreams of revenge.

Evil is obvious only in retrospect. It's important to remember that Hitler, champion of the everyman against the rich and the aristocratic, often seemed both selfless and charming. 'The Führer comes to greet me with outstretched hand,' a woman journalist for *Paris-Soir* wrote in 1936. 'I am surprised and astonished by the blue of his eyes, which look brown in photographs, and I prefer the reality—the face that brims with intelligence and energy and lights up when he speaks. At this moment, I comprehend the magical influence...and his power over the masses.'

The message of the interviewer's own second-class status as a female was sugar-coated and was a parallel to the National Socialist description of non-Aryans: 'No real differences in quality, but rather differences in kind.'

'I grant women the same right as men, but I don't think they're identical,' Hitler explained jovially. 'Woman is man's companion in life. She shouldn't be burdened with the tasks for which man was created. I don't envisage any women's battalions...women are better suited to social work.'

However sugar-coated, every form of authoritarianism must start with a belief in some group's greater right to power, whether that right is justified by sex, race, class, religion, or all four. However far it may expand, the progression inevitably rests on unequal power and airtight roles within the family.

'If the man's world is said to be the State...[the woman's] world is her husband, her family, her children, and her home... Every child that a woman brings into the world is a battle, a battle waged for the existence of her people...It is not true...that respect depends on the overlapping of the spheres of activity of the sexes; this respect demands that neither sex should try to do that which belongs to the sphere of the other,' said Hitler in his speech to the National Socialist Women's Organization in September 1934.

If we grow callous in our earliest, most intimate world to a power difference among our own family members, how much easier is it to accept all other hierarchies? If one sex is born to greater power, then why not one race? If women were allowed to marry and have children with men of their own choosing, how could race and class be kept 'pure'? If a man is not allowed to dictate to a wife and children beneath him, how is he to tolerate the dictation he must accept from above?

'The slogan "Emancipation of Women" was invented by Jewish intellectuals...Our National Socialist Women's Movement has in reality but one single point,' Hitler told women in his 1934 speech, 'and that point is the child.' In *Mein Kampf,* a copy of which was presented to every newly married Aryan couple in Germany, he wrote, 'Just as [the Jew] himself systematically ruins women and girls...it was and is Jews who bring Negroes into the Rhineland...ruining the hated white race by the necessarily resulting bastardization...rising [himself] to be its master.'[7]

The belief that men must control women—if men are to maintain race and class divisions, control the supply of workers and soldiers for the state, and keep ownership of their own children—is the root injustice from which all these flowers of evil grow.

In pleading for women's freedom seventy years ago, one German feminist said, 'Woman has often been reduced—callously, if unconsciously—to the level of a child-bearing machine, her children regarded as the property of the State while still in the womb.' Another said angrily, 'If we women do not take a stand for our own responsibility for ourselves here, in the most female of all tasks in life, that of "giving life", if we do not take a stand against our being regarded merely as the involuntary producers of cannon fodder, then in my opinion, we do not deserve to be regarded as anything else!'

Many women in Hitler's Germany did take a public stand against his sexual caste system, as well as against the anti-Semitism that, as a punishment from which many men also suffered, was better understood as an injustice. 'National Socialism has grown big in its fight against Jews and women,' said a leader of Germany's largest feminist organization. 'Today, I am for struggle.'

Many demonstrated in the streets against Hitler's closing of family planning clinics, an act that one German feminist, now a resident of this country, remembers as 'the first thing Hitler did'. The individual right to abortion was so suppressed that even women who miscarried had to prove they had not tried to abort or else risk criminal prosecution.

Other activist women tried unsuccessfully to save their organizations by becoming less 'political', by fighting the Nazi diatribe against them with dry 'factual corrections', or even by using Hitler's own racist arguments to get Aryan women into positions of influence where they might reform from within.

Jewish women in Germany were not only purged from any important jobs, but often abandoned by their own non-Jewish husbands or friends. First discouraged from marriage or having children, then forced out of both, they were eventually used as forced labour or sent to concentration camps. (Ravensbrüch, the one camp exclusively for women, was also the site of most Nazi 'medical experiments'. Though Jewish men underwent similar atrocities elsewhere, Aryan male doctors seemed better able to disassociate from bodies so different and despised.)

Meanwhile, Hitler assumed that women were or should be attracted to his military image. He stayed single partly to inspire the devotion and romantic fantasies of women followers. (Privately, he was reported as saying that he would not have children because no son of his, being partly the product of a woman, could be as great as he.) Though some National Socialists claimed 'it was the women's vote that brought Hitler to triumph', that was no truer than the current argument that women voters defeated the ERA. Hindenburg, president of Germany from 1925 to 1934, got more women's votes in 1932 than did Hitler, both in absolute numbers and percentage.

But some women did vote for National Socialism. Most were the young who knew little or nothing of past feminist struggles, and were excited by the romance of Hitler's heroine-goddess images of German womanhood. Others wanted to stay at home as housewives instead of being poorly paid workers and housewives. Still others were attracted by Hitler's promise of a bridegroom for every young woman, a seductive if unlikely campaign promise in a country where World War I had decimated the male population.

Ironically, women's traditional workload and their scepticism about getting help from any men, including National Socialists, saved many from Nazi involvement. 'The mass of German women did not want to be organized,' wrote historian Jill Stephenson, 'and their passive resistance to attempts to involve the housebound housewife, above all in the "women's work of the nation", ensured that the Nazi women's organization remained a minority concern.'

There can be no doubt that feminists would have been more effective in opposing Hitler if they had possessed local centres as did the churches, or work communities as did the unions, or an international network as did both.

As it was, their major organizations were dependent on public meeting places and communications, so they were easily outlawed or taken over. And their diverse, multi-issue approach was no match for the simple, driving emotionalism of the opposition.

'Whereas the cause of women's emancipation,' explained historian Tim Mason, '[was] promoted by a very wide range of small and normally uncoordinated groups with different partial goals and political outlooks, the cause of the restoration of men's pre-eminence could be made to appear a relatively simple single issue and could be pre-empted by a single political movement of incomparably greater power.'[8]

The result was tragic for men as well as women, not only in Germany, but in every area decimated by German expansion. Feminists had been virtually alone in challenging the patriarchal family as the basic unit of an authoritarian society, and in trying to replace its primacy with the primacy of the individual rights, and thus the possibility of democratic families. Many of the powerful religious groups supported Hitler's view of the family and of women—and supported the early growth of National Socialism because of it. True, they disagreed with state supremacy over the church—a development that came after Kinder, Küche, Kirche—but by then it was too late. Even liberal, radical and union groups that had supported women's rights in the marketplace and the voting booth had abandoned that support at the family door.

As in Germany, there is also a disquieting sameness between those who wish to enforce the traditional family, and those who want increased military spending and a more confrontational attitude towards the world. Most disquieting of all, this sameness is found in high places. A political cartoon of Ronald Reagan showed him in a Western hat, saying: 'A gun in every holster, a pregnant woman in every home. Make America a man again.' It was a brilliant summing up of the link between anti-feminism and militarism.

It all sounds a little too familiar. But at least we know that feminism has a history. It is the keystone of any lasting democracy.

—1980

# RUTH'S SONG
# (BECAUSE SHE COULD NOT SING IT)

Steinem wrote this essay soon after her mother's death. In writing about her mother she has transformed anecdotes into intensely felt anguish for all that her mother wanted and could not get, for all that she as a daughter never understood.

What would her life have been like if her mother had not been a journalist or Theosophist? What would her life have been like if her mother had not sunk into a depression and Steinem had to look after her, all alone in Toledo, Ohio?

And most importantly, what would her mother's life have been if she had been born after Steinem?

—Ruchira Gupta

Happy or unhappy, families are all mysterious. We have only to imagine how differently we would be described and will be described, after our deaths, by each of the family members who believe they know us. The only question is: Why are some mysteries more important than others?

The fate of my Uncle Ed was a mystery of importance in our family. We lavished years of speculation on his transformation from a brilliant young electrical engineer to the town handyman. What could have changed this elegant, Lincolnesque student voted 'Best Dressed' by his classmates to the gaunt, unshaven man I remember? Why did he leave a young son and a first wife of the 'proper' class and religion, marry a much less educated woman of the 'wrong' class and religion, and raise a second family in a house near an abandoned airstrip; a house whose walls were patched with metal signs to stop the wind? Why did he never talk about his transformation?

For years, I assumed that some secret and dramatic events during a year he spent in Alaska had made the difference. Then I discovered that the trip had come after his change, and probably been made because of it. Strangers he worked for as a much-loved handyman talked about him as one more tragedy of the Depression. It was true that Uncle Ed's father, my paternal grandfather, had lost his money in the stock market crash of 1929, and died (depending on who was telling the story) of pneumonia or a broken heart. But the crash also had come long after Uncle Ed's transformation. Another theory was that he was afflicted with a mental problem that lasted most of his life. Yet he was supremely competent at his work, led an independent life, and asked for help from no one.

Perhaps he had fallen under the spell of a radical professor in the early days of the century, the height of this country's romance with socialism and anarchism. That was the theory of another uncle on my mother's side. I do remember that no matter how much Uncle Ed needed money, he would charge no more for his work than materials plus 10 per cent, and I never saw him in anything other than ancient boots and overalls held up with strategic safety pins. Was he really trying to replace Socialism-in-one-country with Socialism-in-one-man? If so, why did my grandmother, a woman who herself had run for the school board in coalition with anarchists and socialists, mistrust his judgement so much that she left his share of her estate in trust, even though he was over fifty when she died? And why did Uncle Ed seem uninterested in all political opinions and acts? Was it true instead that, as another relative insisted, Uncle Ed had chosen poverty to disprove the myths of Jews and money?

Years after my uncle's death, I asked a son in his second family if he had found the key to this family mystery. No, he said, he had never known his father any other way. For that cousin, there had been no question. For the rest of us, there was to be no answer.

For many years I also couldn't imagine my mother any way other than the person she had become before I was born. She was just a fact of life when I was growing up; someone to be worried about and cared for; an invalid who lay in bed with eyes closed and lips moving in occasional response to voices only she could hear; a woman to whom I brought an endless stream of toast and coffee, bologna sandwiches and dime pies, in a child's version of what meals should be. She was a loving, intelligent, terrorized woman who tried hard to clean our littered house whenever she emerged from her private world, but who could rarely be counted on to finish one task. In many ways, our roles were reversed: I was the mother and she was the child. Yet that didn't help her either, for she still worried about me with all the intensity of a frightened mother, plus the special fears that came from her own world full of threats and hostile voices.

Even then, I suppose I must have known that years before she was thirty-five and I was born, she had been a spirited, adventurous young woman who struggled out of a working-class family and into college, who found work she loved and continued to do, even after she was married and my older sister was there to be cared for. Certainly, our immediate family and nearby relatives, of whom I was by far the youngest, must have remembered her life as a whole and functioning person, She was thirty before she gave up her own career to help my father run the Michigan summer resort that was the most practical of his many dreams, and she worked hard there as everything, from bookkeeper to bar manager. The family must have watched this energetic, fun-loving, book-loving woman turn into someone who was afraid to be alone, who could not hang on to reality long enough to hold a job, and who could rarely concentrate enough to read a book.

Yet I don't remember any family speculation about the mystery of my mother's transformation. To the kind ones and those who liked her, this new Ruth was simply a sad event, perhaps a mental case, a family problem to be accepted and cared for until some natural process made her better. To the less kind or those who resented her earlier independence, she was a wilful failure, someone who lived in a filthy house, a woman who simply refused to pull herself together.

Unlike the story of my Uncle Ed, exterior events were never suggested as reason enough for her problems. Giving up her own career was never cited as her personal parallel of the Depression.

(Nor was there discussion of the Depression itself, though my mother, like millions of others, had made potato soup for her family, and cut up blankets to make my sister's winter clothes.) Her real fears of dependency and poverty were no match for my uncle's possible political beliefs. The real hopes inspired by newspaper editors who praised her reporting were not taken as seriously as the possible influence of one radical professor.

Even the explanation of mental illness seemed to contain more personal fault when applied to my mother. She had suffered her first 'nervous breakdown', as she and everyone else called it, before I was born, when my sister was about five. It followed years of trying to take care of a baby, be the wife of a kind but financially irresponsible man with show-business dreams, and still keep her much-loved job as reporter and newspaper editor. After many months in a sanatorium, she was pronounced recovered. That is, she was able to take care of my sister again, to move away from the city and the job she loved, and to work with my father at the isolated rural lake in Michigan he was trying to transform into a resort worthy of the big dance bands of the 1930s.

But she was never again completely without the spells of depression, anxiety and visions into some other world that eventually were to turn her into the non-person I remember. And she was never again without a bottle of dark, acrid-smelling liquid she called 'Doc Howard's medicine', a solution of chloral hydrate that I later learned was the main ingredient of 'Mickey Finns' or 'knockout drops', and that probably made my mother and her doctor the pioneers of modern tranquilizers. Though friends and relatives saw this medicine as one more evidence of weakness and indulgence, to me it always seemed an embarrassing but necessary evil. It slurred her speech and slowed her coordination, making our neighbours and my school friends believe she was a drunk. But without it, she would not sleep for days, even a week at a time, and her feverish eyes began to see only that private world in which wars and hostile voices threatened the people she loved.

Because my parents had divorced and my sister was working in a faraway city, my mother and I were alone together in these years, living off the meagre fixed income that my mother got from leasing her share of the remaining land in Michigan. I remember a long Thanksgiving weekend spent hanging on to her with one hand and holding my eighth-grade assignment of *A Tale of Two Cities* in the other, because the war outside our house was so real to my mother that she had plunged her hand through a window, badly cutting her arm in an effort to help us escape. Only when she finally agreed to swallow the medicine could she sleep, and only then could I end the terrible calm that comes with crisis and admit to myself how afraid I had been.

No wonder that no relative in my memory challenged the doctor who prescribed this medicine, or asked if some of her suffering and hallucinating might be due to overdose or withdrawal, or even consulted another doctor about its use. It was our relief as well as hers.

But why was she never returned to that first sanatorium? Or to help that might have come from other doctors? It's hard to say. Partly, it was her own fear of returning to that pain. Partly, it was too little money, and a family's not-unusual assumption that mental illness is an inevitable part of someone's personality. Or perhaps other family members feared something like my experience when, one hot and desperate summer between the sixth and seventh grade, I finally persuaded her to let me take her to the only doctor from those sanatorium days whom she remembered without fear.

Yes, this brusque old man told me after talking to my abstracted, timid mother for twenty minutes: She definitely belongs in a state hospital. I should put her there right away. But even at that age, *LIFE* magazine and newspaper exposés had told me what horrors went on inside those hospitals. Assuming there to be no other alternative, I took her home and never tried again.

In retrospect, perhaps the biggest reason my mother was cared for but not helped for twenty years was the simplest: her functioning was not that necessary to the world. Like women alcoholics who drink in their kitchens while costly programmes are constructed for male executives who drink, or like homemakers subdued with tranquilizers while male patients get therapy and personal attention instead, my mother was not an important worker. She was not even the caretaker of a very young child, as she had been when she was hospitalized the first time. My father had patiently brought home the groceries and kept our odd household going until I was eight or so and my sister went away to college. Two years later, when wartime gas rationing closed his summer resort and he had to travel to buy and sell in summer as well as in winter, he said: 'How can I travel and take care of your mother? How can I make a living?' He was right. It was impossible to do both. I did not blame him for leaving once I was old enough to be the bringer of meals and answerer of my mother's questions. ('Has your sister been killed in a car crash?' 'Are there German soldiers outside?') I replaced my father, my mother was left with one more way of maintaining a sad status quo, and the world went on undisturbed.

That's why our lives, my mother's from forty-six to fifty-three, and my own from ten to seventeen, were spent alone together. There was one sane winter in a house we rented to be near my sister's college in Massachusetts, then one bad summer spent house-sitting in suburbia while my mother hallucinated and my sister struggled to hold down a summer job in New York. But the rest of those years were lived in Toledo where both my mother and father had been born, and on whose city newspapers an earlier Ruth had worked.

First we moved into a basement apartment in a good neighbourhood. In those rooms behind a furnace, I made one last stab at being a child. By pretending to be much sicker with a cold than I really was, I hoped my mother would suddenly turn into a sane and cheerful woman bringing me chicken soup à la Hollywood. Of course, she could not. It only made her feel worse that she could not. I stopped pretending. I almost never got sick again.

But for most of those years, we lived in the upstairs of the house my mother had grown up in and that her parents left her—a deteriorating farmhouse engulfed by the city, with poor but newer houses stacked against it and a major highway undermining its sagging front porch. For a while, we rented the two downstairs apartments to a newlywed factory worker and his wife, and a local butcher's family. Then the health department condemned our ancient furnace for the final time, sealing it so tight that even my resourceful Uncle Ed could not break it open to produce illegal heat.

In that house, I remember:

...lying in the bed my mother and I shared for warmth, listening to the early morning live radio broadcast of the royal wedding of Princess Elizabeth and Prince Philip, while we tried to ignore and thus protect each other from the unmistakable sounds of the factory worker downstairs beating up and locking out his pregnant wife.

...hanging paper drapes I had bought in the dime store; stacking books and papers in the shape of two armchairs and covering them with blankets; evolving my own dishwashing system (I waited until all the dishes were dirty, then put them in the bathtub); and listening to my mother's high praise for these housekeeping efforts to bring order from chaos, though in retrospect I think they probably depressed her further.

...coming back from one of the Eagles' Club shows where I and other veterans of a local tap-dancing school made ten dollars a night for two shows, and finding my mother waiting with a flashlight and no coat in the dark cold of the bus stop, worried about my safety walking home.

...in a good period, when my mother's native adventurousness came through, answering a classified ad together for an amateur acting troupe that performed biblical dramas in churches, and doing several very corny performances of *Noah's Ark* while my proud mother shook metal sheets backstage to make thunder.

...on a hot summer night, being bitten by one of the rats that shared our house and its back alley. It was a terrifying night that turned into a touching one when my mother, summoning courage from some unknown reservoir of love, became a calm, comforting parent who took me to a hospital emergency room despite her terror at leaving home.

...coming home from a local library with the three books a week into which I regularly escaped, and discovering that for once there was no need to escape. My mother was calmly planting hollyhocks in the vacant lot next door.

But there were also times when she woke in the early winter dark, too frightened and disoriented to remember that I was at my usual after-school job, and so called the police to find me. Humiliated in front of my friends by sirens and policemen, I would yell at her, and she would bow her head in fear and say, 'I'm sorry, I'm sorry, I'm sorry,' just as she had done so often when my otherwise kind-hearted father had yelled at her in frustration. Perhaps the worst thing about suffering is that it finally hardens the hearts of those around it.

And there were many, many times when I badgered her until her shaking hands had written a small cheque to cash at the corner grocery, and I could leave her alone while I escaped with my girlfriends to the comfort of well-heated dime stores that smelled of fresh doughnuts, or to air-conditioned Saturday-afternoon movies that were windows on a very different world.

But my ultimate protection was this: I was just passing through; I was a guest in the house; perhaps this wasn't my mother at all. Though I knew very well that I was her daughter, I sometimes imagined I had been adopted and that my real parents would find me, a fantasy I've since discovered is common. (If children wrote more and grown-ups less, perhaps being adopted might not be seen only as a fear, but also as a hope.) Certainly, I didn't mourn the wasted life of this woman who was scarcely older than I am now. I worried only about the times when she got worse.

Pity takes distance and a certainty of surviving. It was only after our house was bought for demolition by the church next door, and after my sister had performed the miracle of persuading my father to give me a carefree time before college by taking my mother with him to California for a year, that I could afford to think about the sadness of her life. Suddenly, I was far away in Washington, living with my sister who shared a house with several of her friends. While I finished high school and discovered to my surprise that my classmates felt sorry for me because my mother *wasn't* there, I also realized that my sister, at least in her early childhood, had known a very different person who lived inside our mother, an earlier 'Ruth'.

She was a woman I met for the first time in a mental hospital near Baltimore, a humane place with gardens and trees where I visited her each weekend of the summer after my first year away in college. Fortunately, my sister hadn't been able to work and be our mother's caretaker, too. After my father's year was up, my sister had carefully researched hospitals, and found the courage to break the family chain of simply tolerating our mother's condition.

At first, this Ruth was the same abstracted, frightened woman I lived with all those years, now all the sadder for being approached through long hospital corridors and many locked doors. But gradually, she began to talk about her past life, and to confide memories that doctors there must have been awakening. I began to meet a Ruth I had never known:

...A tall, spirited, auburn-haired high-school girl who loved basketball and reading; who tried to drive her uncle's Stanley Steamer when it was the first car in the neighbourhood; who had a gift for gardening and who sometimes wore her father's overalls in defiance of convention; a girl with the courage to go to dances even though her church told her that music itself was sinful, and whose sense of adventure almost made up for feeling gawky and unpretty next to her daintier, dark-haired sister.

...A very little girl, just learning to walk, discovering the places on her body where touching was pleasurable, and being punished by her mother who slapped her so hard she was pushed across the kitchen floor.

...A daughter of a handsome railroad engineer and a school teacher who felt she had married 'beneath her'; the mother who took her two daughters on Christmas trips to faraway New York on an engineer's free railroad pass, and showed them the restaurants and theatres they should aspire to—even though they could only afford to stand outside them in the snow.

...A good student at Oberlin College whose freethinking traditions she loved, where friends nicknamed her 'Billy'; a student with a talent for both mathematics and poetry, who was not above putting an invisible film of Karo syrup on all the toilet seats in her dormitory the night of a big prom; a daughter who had to return to Toledo, live with her family, and go to a local university when her ambitious mother—who had scrimped and saved, ghostwritten a minister's sermons, and made her daughters' clothes in order to get them to college at all—ran out of money. At home, this Ruth became a part-time bookkeeper in a lingerie shop that catered to the very rich, commuting to classes and listening to her mother's harsh lectures on the security of becoming a teacher; but also a young woman who was still rebellious enough to fall in love with my father, the editor of their university newspaper, a funny and charming young man who was a terrible student, had no intention of graduating, put on all the campus dances, and was unacceptably Jewish.

I knew from family lore that my mother had married my father twice: once secretly, after he invited her to become the literary editor of the campus newspaper, and once a year later in a public ceremony, which some members of both families refused to attend because it was the 'mixed marriage' of its day.

And I also knew that my mother had gone on to earn a teaching certificate. She had used it to scare away truant officers during the winters when, after my father closed the summer resort for the season, we lived in a house trailer and worked our way to Florida or California and back by buying and selling antiques.

But only during those increasingly adventurous weekend outings from the mental hospital in Baltimore—going shopping, to lunch, to the movies—did I realize that she had taught college calculus for a year in deference to her mother's insistence that she have teaching 'to fall back on'. And only then did I realize that she had fallen in love with newspapers along with my father. After graduating from the university, she wrote a gossip column for a local tabloid, under the name 'Duncan MacKenzie', since women weren't supposed to do such things. Soon after, she had earned a job as society reporter on one of Toledo's two big dailies. By the time my sister was four or so, she had worked her way up to the coveted position of Sunday editor.

It was a strange experience to look into those brown eyes I had seen so often and realize suddenly how much they were like my own. For the first time, I realized that she really was my mother.

I began to think about the many pressures that might have led up to her first nervous breakdown: leaving my sister whom she loved so much with a grandmother whose values my mother didn't share; trying to hold on to a job she loved but was being asked to leave by her husband; wanting very much to go with a woman friend to pursue their own dreams in New York but punishing herself for even the thought; falling in love with a co-worker at the newspaper who frightened her by being more sexually attractive, more supportive of her work than my father, and perhaps the man she should have married; and finally, nearly bleeding to death with a miscarriage because her own mother had little faith in doctors and refused to get help.

Did those months in the sanatorium brainwash her in some Freudian or very traditional way into making what were, for her, probably the wrong choices? I don't know. It almost doesn't matter. Without extraordinary support to the contrary, she was already convinced that divorce was unthinkable. A husband could not be left for another man, and certainly not for any reason as selfish as a career. A daughter could not be deprived of her father, and certainly not be uprooted and taken off to an uncertain future in New York. A bride was supposed to be virginal (not 'shopworn', as my euphemistic mother would have said), and if your husband turned out to be kind, but innocent of the possibility of a woman's pleasure, then just be thankful for his kindness.

Of course, other women have torn themselves away from work and people they loved and still survived. But a story my mother told me years later has always symbolized for me the formidable forces arrayed against her.

'It was early spring, nothing was open yet. There was nobody for miles around. We had stayed at the lake that winter, so I was alone a lot while your father took the car and travelled around on business. You were a baby. Your sister was in school, and there was no phone. The last straw was that the radio broke. Suddenly it seemed like forever since I'd been able to talk with anyone–or even hear the sound of another voice.

'I bundled you up, took the dog and walked out to the Brooklyn road. I thought I'd walk the four or five miles to the grocery store, talk to some people and find somebody to drive me back. I was walking along with Fritzie running up ahead in the empty road when suddenly a car came out of nowhere and down the hill. It hit Fritzie head-on and threw him over to the side of the road. I yelled and screamed at the driver, but he never slowed down. He never looked at us. He never even turned his head.

'Poor Fritzie was all broken and bleeding, but he was still alive. I carried him and sat down in the middle of the road, with his head cradled in my arms. I was going to make the next car stop and help.

'But no car ever came. I sat there for hours, I don't know how long, with you in my lap and holding Fritzie, who was whimpering and looking up at me for help. It was dark by the time he finally died. I pulled him over to the side of the road and walked back home with you and washed the blood out of my clothes.

'I don't know what it was about that one day—it was like a breaking point. When your father came home, I said: "From now on, I'm going with you. I won't bother you. I'll just sit in the car. But I can't bear to be alone again."'

I think she told me that story to show she had tried to save herself, or perhaps she wanted to exorcise a painful memory by saying it out loud. But hearing it made me understand what could have turned her into the woman I remember: a solitary figure sitting in the car, perspiring through the summer, bundled up in winter, waiting for my father to come out of this or that antique shop, grateful just not to be alone. I came along, too, because I was too young to be left at home, and I loved helping my father wrap and unwrap the newspaper around the china and small objects he had bought at auctions and was selling to dealers. It made me feel necessary and grown-up. But sometimes it was hours before we came back to the car again, and to my mother who was always patiently, silently waiting.

At the hospital and in later years when Ruth told me stories of her past, I used to say: 'But why didn't you leave? Why didn't you take the job? Why didn't you marry the other man?' She would always insist that it didn't matter, she was lucky to have my sister and me. If I pressed hard enough, she would add: 'If I'd left, you never would have been born.'

I always thought but never had the courage to say: But you might have been born instead.

I'd like to tell you that this story has a happy ending. The best I can do is one that is happier than its beginning.

After many months in that Baltimore hospital, my mother lived on her own in a small apartment for two years while I was in college and my sister married and lived nearby. When she felt the old terrors coming back, she returned to the hospital at her own request. She was approaching sixty by the time she emerged from there and from a Quaker farm that served as a halfway house, but she confounded her psychiatrists' predictions that she would be able to live outside for shorter and shorter periods. In fact, she never returned. She lived more than another twenty years. For six of them, she was well enough to stay in a rooming house that provided both privacy and company. Even after my sister and her husband moved to a larger house and generously made two basement rooms into an apartment for her, she continued to have some independent life and many friends. She worked part-time as a 'salesgirl' in a china shop; went away with me on yearly vacations and took one trip to Europe with relatives; went to women's club meetings; found a multiracial church that she loved and attended most Sundays; took meditation courses; and enjoyed many books. She still could not bear to see a sad movie, to stay alone with any of her six grandchildren while they were young, to live without many tranquillizers, or to talk about those bad years in Toledo. The old terrors were still in the back of her mind, and each day was a fight to keep them down.

It was the length of her illness that had made doctors pessimistic. In fact, they could not identify any serious mental problem and diagnosed her only as having 'an anxiety neurosis': low self-esteem, a fear of being dependent, a terror of being alone, a constant worry about money. She also had spells of what now would be called agoraphobia, a problem almost entirely confined to dependent women: fear of going outside the house, and incapacitating anxiety attacks in unfamiliar or public places.

Would you say, I asked one of her doctors, that her spirit had been broken? 'I guess that's as good a diagnosis as any,' he said. 'And it's hard to mend anything that's been broken for twenty years.'

But once out of the hospital for good, she continued to show flashes of a different woman inside; one with a wry kind of humour, a sense of adventure and a love of learning. Books on maths, physics and mysticism occupied a lot of her time. ('Religion,' she used to say firmly, 'begins in the laboratory.') When she visited me in New York during her sixties and seventies, she always told taxi drivers that she was eighty years old ('so they will tell me how young I look'), and convinced theatre-ticket sellers that she had difficulty in hearing long before she really did ('so they'll give us seats in the front row'). She made friends easily, with the vulnerability and charm of a person who feels entirely dependent on the approval of others. After one of her visits, every shopkeeper within blocks of my apartment would say: 'Oh yes, I know your mother!' At home, she complained that people her own age were too old and stodgy for her. Many of her friends were far younger than she. It was as if she were making up for her own lost years.

She was also overly appreciative of any presents given to her—and that made giving them irresistible. I loved to send her clothes, jewellery, exotic soaps and additions to her collection of tarot cards. She loved receiving them, even though we both knew they would end up stored in boxes and drawers. She carried on a correspondence in German with our European relatives, and exchanged letters with many friends, all written in her painfully slow, shaky handwriting. She also loved giving gifts. Even as she worried about money, saved pennies and took home sugar from restaurants, she would buy or make carefully chosen presents for grandchildren and friends.

Part of the price she paid for this much health was forgetting. A single reminder of those bad years in Toledo was enough to plunge her into days of depression. There were times when this fact created loneliness for me, too. Only two of us had lived most of my childhood. Now, only one of us remembered. But there were also times in later years when, no matter how much I pleaded with reporters *not* to interview our friends and neighbours in Toledo, *not* to say that my mother had been hospitalized, they published things that hurt her very much and sent her into another downhill slide.

On the other hand, she was also her mother's daughter, and so had a certain amount of social pride and pretension. Some of her objections had less to do with depression than with false pride. She complained bitterly about one report that we had lived in a house trailer. She finally asked angrily: 'Couldn't they at least say "vacation mobile home"?' Divorce was still a shame to her. She might cheerfully tell friends: 'I don't know *why* Gloria says her father and I were divorced—we never were.' I think she justified this to herself with the idea that, having gone through two marriage ceremonies, one in secret and one in public, they had been divorced only once. In fact, they were definitely divorced, and my father had briefly married someone else.

She was very proud of my being a published writer, and we generally shared the same values. After her death, I found a mother–daughter morals quiz I had written for a women's magazine. In her unmistakably shaky writing, she had recorded her own answers, her entirely accurate imagination of what my answers would be, and a score that concluded our differences were less than those 'normal for women separated by twenty-odd years'. Nonetheless, she was quite capable of putting a made-up name on her name tag when going to her conventional women's club where she feared our shared identity would bring controversy or even just questions. When I finally got up the nerve to tell her I was signing a 1972 petition of women who publicly said we had had abortions and demanded the repeal of laws that made them illegal and dangerous, her only reply was sharp and aimed to hurt back. 'Every starlet says she's had an abortion,' she said. 'It's just a way of getting publicity.' I knew she agreed that abortion should be a legal choice, but I also knew she would never forgive me for embarrassing her in public.

In fact, her anger and a fairly imaginative ability to wound with words increased in her last years when she was most dependent, most focused on herself and most likely to need the total attention of others. When my sister made a courageous decision to go to law school at the age of fifty, leaving my mother in a house that not only had many loving teenage grandchildren in it, but a kindly older woman as a paid companion, my mother reduced her to frequent tears by insisting that this was a family with no love in it, no home-cooked food in the refrigerator and not a real family at all. Since arguments about home cooking wouldn't work on me, she devised a punishment that was creative and different. She was going to call up the *New York Times*, she said, and tell them that this was what feminism did: it left old sick women all alone.

Some of this bitterness brought on by failing faculties was eventually solved by a nursing home near my sister's house where my mother not only got the twenty-four-hour help her weakening body demanded, but the attention of affectionate nurses besides. She charmed them, they loved her, and she could still get out for an occasional family wedding. If I ever had any doubts about the debt we owe to nurses, those last months laid them to rest.

When my mother died just before her eighty-second birthday in a hospital room where my sister and I were alternating the hours in which her heart wound slowly down to its last sounds, we were alone together for a few hours while my sister slept. My mother seemed bewildered by her surroundings, and by the tubes that invaded her body, but her consciousness cleared long enough for her to say: 'I want to go home. Please take me home.' Lying to her one last time, I said I would take her. 'Okay, honey,' she said. 'I trust you.' Those were her last understandable words.

The nurses let my sister and me stay in the room long after there was no more breath. My mother had asked us to do that. One of her many fears came from a story she had been told as a child about a man whose coma was mistaken for death, and who was nearly buried alive. She also had made out a living will requesting that no extraordinary measures be used to keep her alive, and that her ashes be sprinkled in the same stream as my father's.

Her memorial service was in the Episcopalian church that she loved because it fed the poor, let the homeless sleep in its pews, had members of almost every race, and had been sued by the Episcopalian hierarchy for having a woman priest. Most of all, she loved the affection with which its members had welcomed her, visited her at home and driven her to services. I think she would have liked the Quaker-style informality with which people rose to tell their memories of her. I know she would have loved the presence of many friends. It was to this church that she had donated some of her remaining Michigan property in the hope that it could be used as a multiracial camp, thus getting even with those neighbours who had snubbed my father for being Jewish.

I think she also would have been pleased with her obituary. It emphasized her brief career as one of the early women journalists, and asked for donations to Oberlin's scholarship fund so others could go to this college she loved so much but had to leave.

I know I will spend the next years figuring out what her life has left in me.

I realize now why I've always been more touched by old people than by children. It's the talent and hopes locked up in a failing body and unsure mind that get to me—a poignant contrast that reminds me of my mother, even when she was strong.

I've always been drawn to any story of a mother and a daughter on their own in the world. I saw *A Taste of Honey* several times as both a play and a film, and never stopped feeling its sadness. Even *Gypsy* I saw over and over again, sneaking in backstage for the musical and going to the movie as well. I told myself that I was learning the tap-dance routines, but actually my eyes were full of tears.

I once fell in love with a man only because we both belonged to that large and secret club of children who had 'crazy mothers'. We traded stories of the shameful houses to which we could never invite our friends. Before he was born, his mother had gone to jail for her pacifist convictions. Then she married the politically ambitious young lawyer who defended her, stayed home, raised many sons and went slowly mad in a different kind of jail. I fell out of love when my friend wished I wouldn't smoke or swear, and hoped I wouldn't go on working. His mother's plight had taught him self-pity but nothing else.

For many years, I was obsessed with the fear that I would end up in a house like that one in Toledo. Now, I'm obsessed instead with the things I could have done for my mother while she was alive, or the things I should have said to her.

I still don't understand why so many, many years passed before I saw my mother as a person, and before I understood that many of the forces in her life were patterns women share. Like a lot of daughters, I couldn't afford to admit that what had happened to my mother was not all personal or accidental. It would have meant admitting it could happen to me.

One mystery has finally cleared. I could never understand why my mother hadn't been helped by Pauline, her mother-in-law, a woman she seemed to love more than her own mother. This paternal grandmother had died when I was five, before my mother's worst problems began, but long after that 'nervous breakdown'. I knew Pauline was once a suffragist who addressed Congress, marched for the vote and was the first woman elected to a school board in Ohio. She must have been a courageous and independent woman, yet I could find no evidence in my mother's reminiscences of her that Pauline had encouraged or helped my mother find a life of her own.

I finally realized that my grandmother had never changed the politics of her own life. She was a feminist who kept a neat house for a husband and four anti-feminist sons, a vegetarian among five male meat-eaters, and a woman who felt so strongly about the dangers of alcohol that she used only paste vanilla, yet she served both meat and wine to the men of the house. She made sure their lives and comforts continued undisturbed. After the vote was won, Pauline seemed to stop all feminist activity. My mother greatly admired the fact that her mother-in-law kept a spotless house and prepared a week's meals at a time. Whatever her own internal torments, Pauline was to my mother a woman who seemed able to 'do it all'. 'Whither thou goest, I shall go,' my mother used to say to this much-loved mother-in-law, quoting the Ruth of the Bible. In the end, her mother-in-law may only have added to my mother's burden of guilt.

Like many later suffragists, my grandmother seems to have been a public feminist and a private isolationist. That may have been heroic in itself and the most she could be expected to do, but the vote and a legal right to work were not the only kind of support my mother needed.

So the world still missed a unique person named Ruth. Though she longed to live in New York and travel in Europe, she became a woman who was afraid to take a bus across town. Though she drove the first Stanley Steamer, she married a man who never let her drive at all.

I can only guess what she might have become. There are clues in her moments of spirit and humour.

After all the years of fear, she still came to Oberlin with me when I was giving a speech there. She remembered everything about its history as the first college to admit blacks as well as the first to admit women, and responded to students with the dignity of a professor, the accuracy of a journalist and the charm that was all her own.

When she could still make trips to Washington's wealth of libraries, she became an expert genealogist, delighting especially in finding the rogues and rebels in our family tree.

There was a story she told with great satisfaction. Before I was born, when she had cooked one more enormous meal for all the members of some famous dance band at my father's resort and they failed to clean their plates, she took a shotgun down from the kitchen wall and held it over their frightened heads until they had finished every last crumb of strawberry shortcake. Only then did she tell them that the gun wasn't loaded.

Though sex was a subject she couldn't discuss directly, she had a great appreciation of sensuous men. When a friend I brought home tried to talk to her about cooking, she was furious. ('He came out in the kitchen and talked to me about *stew*!') But she forgave him when we went swimming. She whispered: 'He has wonderful legs!'

On her seventy-fifth birthday, she played softball with her grandsons on the beach, and took pride in hitting home runs into the ocean.

Even in the last year of her life, when my sister took her to visit a neighbour's new and luxurious house, she looked at the vertical stripes of a very abstract painting in the hallway, and said tartly: 'Is that the price code?'

She worried terribly about being socially acceptable herself, but she never withheld her own approval for superficial reasons. Poverty or style or lack of education couldn't stand between her and a new friend. Though she lived in a mostly white society and worried if I went out with a man of the 'wrong' race, just as she had once married a man of the 'wrong' religion, she always accepted each person as an individual.

'Is he *very* dark?' she once asked worriedly about a friend. But when she met this very dark person, she only said afterwards: 'What a kind and nice man!'

My father was the Jewish half of the family, yet it was my mother who taught me to have pride in this tradition. It was she who encouraged me to listen to a radio play about a concentration camp when I was little. 'You should know that this can happen,' she said. Yet she did it just enough to teach, never enough to frighten.

It was she who introduced me to books and a respect for them, to poetry that she knew by heart, and to the idea that you could never criticize someone unless you 'walked miles in their shoes'.

It was she who sold that Toledo house, the only home she had, with the determination that the money be used to start me in college. She gave both her daughters the encouragement to leave home for the four years of independence she herself had never had.

After her death, my sister and I found a journal she had kept of her one cherished and belated trip to Europe. It was a trip she had described very little when she came home perhaps because she always deplored people who talked boringly about their personal travels and showed slides. Nonetheless, she had written a narrative essay called 'Grandma Goes to Europe'. After all those years, she still thought of herself as a writer. Yet she showed this long journal to no one.

I miss her—but perhaps no more in death than I did in life. Dying seems less sad than having lived too little. But at least we're now asking questions about all the Ruths in all our family mysteries.

If her song inspires that, I think she would be the first to say: It was worth the singing.

—1981

# NOTES

## PREFACE

1. Valerie M. Hudson, Bonnie Ballif-Spanvill, Mary Caprioli and Chad F. Emmett, *Sex and World Peace* (New York: Columbia University Press, 2012).
2. Ibid.
3. Ibid.
4. Marianne E. Lien and Brigitte Nerlich, *The Politics of Food*, (London: Bloomsbury Publishing, 2004).
5. Diana E.H. Russell and Roberta A. Harmes (eds.) *Femicide in Global Perspective* (New York: Teachers College Press, 2001).
6. United Nations Office on Drugs and Crime, 'Global Report on Trafficking in Persons', February 2009. The full report is available online at <http://www.unodc.org/documents/Global_Report_on_TIP.pdf>.
7. As quoted on the website of the Polaris Project: A Life without Slavery. The statistics are available on <http://www.polarisproject.org>.

## THE INDIA THAT SHAPED ME

1. Manabendra Nath Roy, *The Russian Revolution*, (Calcutta: Renaissance Publishers, 1949), p. x.
2. Gandhi's response to a reader in *Hind Swaraj*, a newspaper of which he was editor, quoted in *The Collected Works of Mahatma Gandhi* Volume 10 (New Delhi: Government of India, 1958–1984), p. 43
3. Anne Koedt, 'The Myth of the Vaginal Orgasm', reprinted in *Radical Feminism*, Anne Koedt, Ellen Levine and Anita Rapone (eds.) (New York: Quandrangle Books, 1973), pp. 198–207.
4. Steinem travelled with other feminist organizers to meetings and rallies and they would often address audiences in pairs or in groups.
5. To contact the recently formed Prathisthan or coordinating body for

266

these grassroots groups, write to the Principal Coordinator, Nirmala Deshpande, A-233 Pandara Road, New Delhi, India.
6. Devaki Jain, 'Remembering Kamaladevi', *The Indian Express*, 11 March 1988.

## THE MASCULINIZATION OF WEALTH

1. 'India's Richest', *Forbes*, available online at <http://www.forbes.com/india-billionaires/list/>.
2. Susan A. Ostrander, *Women of the Upper Class* (Philadelphia: Temple University Press, 1984), p. 151.
3. Robin Morgan, *The Demon Lover: The Roots of Terrorism* (New York: W.W. Norton, 1989), p. 159
4. This fifteen-year old study began in 1981. A ten-year report has now been published. Karen D. Arnold, 'Academic Achievement—A View from the Top: The Illinois Valedictorian Project', North Central Regional Education Library, 1900 Spring Road, Suite 300, Oak Brook, IL 60521. 'Higher Education: Colder by Degrees', Myra and David Sadker, *Failing at Fairness: How Our Schools Treat Girls* (New York: Charles Scribner's Sons, 1994), pp. 161–196.
5. Joan Jacobs Brumberg, *Fasting Girls: The History of Anorexia Nervosa* (Cambridge, Mass.: Harvard University Press, 1988), pp. 12–13.
6. Linda Tschirhart Sanford and Mary Ellen Donovan, *Women and Self-Esteem: Understanding and Improving the Way We Think and Feel about Ourselves* (New York: Anchor Press/Doubleday, 1984), p. 74.
7. Ibid., p. 47.
8. 'Relating to Our Family, Money, and Communities', Selected Highlights of the Third Annual Women Managing Wealth Conference, 1990. A programme of the Ms. Foundation for Women, 141 Fifth Avenue, New York, NY 10010
9. G. William Donhoff, *Who Rules America Now?* (New York: Simon & Schuster/Touchstone, 1983), p. 42.
10. Ibid., p. 27.
11. Ibid., p. 77.
12. Ann D. Gordon (ed.) *The Selected Papers of Elizabeth Cady Stanton and Susan B. Anthony, Volume II: An Aristocracy of Sex, 1866-1873* (New Jersey: Rutgers, the State University of New Jersey, 2000).
13. Gunnar Myrdal, *An American Dilemma: The Negro Problem and Modern Democracy* (New York: Harper and Brothers, 1944).
14. Library of Congress. The Learning Page. *Lesson Two: Changing Methods and Reforms of the Woman's Suffrage Movement, 1840-1920.*

15. Aileen S. Kaditor, *The Ideas of the Woman Suffrage Movement: 1890–1920* (New York: W.W. Norton, 1981), pp. 153–54.
16. Ibid., p. 153.
17. Madeleine B. Stern, *Queen of Publisher's Row: Mrs. Frank Leslie* (New York: Messner, 1965), p. 186.
18. For information about local or national meetings of women managing wealth, contact: Resourceful Women, 3543 18th Street #9, San Francisco, CA 94110, 415-431-5677, fax 415-431-9634.; National Network of Women's Funds, 1821 University Avenue, Suite 409 North, St. Paul MN 55104, 612-641-0742, fax 612-647-1401; Funding Exchange, 666 Broadway, Suite 500, New York, N.Y. 10012, 212-529-5300.
19. Tracy Gary and Nancy Adess, *Inspired Philanthropy: Your Step by Step Guide to Creating a Giving Plan and Leaving a Legacy* (San Francisco: Jossey-Bass, 2007).

## THE IMPORTANCE OF WORK

1. The Reserve Bank of India, 'Handbook of Statistics on the Indian Economy', 2012–2013. The full report is available online at <http://rbidocs.rbi.org.in/rdocs/Publications/PDFs/FHB160913FLS.pdf>.
2. Howard Spodek, 'Shramshakti: Report of the National Commission on Self Employed Women and Women in the Informal Sector', *Economic Development and Cultural Change*, Volume 38, Number 4 (Chicago: The University of Chicago Press, July 1990), pp. 896–901.
3. Ibid.
4. World Economic Forum, 'The Global Gender Gap Report 2012'. The full report is available online at <www3.weforum.org/docs/WEF_GenderGap_Report_2012.pdf>.
5. Ibid.
6. The Reserve Bank of India, 'Handbook of Statistics on the Indian Economy', 2012–2013.
7. Ibid.
8. This turned out to be an underestimation. By 1990, females of all races made up 57.5 per cent of the labour force. According to the US Bureau of Labor Statistics, this had increased slightly in the 1990s, and is projected to reach 63 per cent by the year 2005. Nonetheless, more media attention has been paid to a statistically insignificant trend of women leaving paid work to raise children—something parents, women or men, should be able to choose, especially in the absence of flexible work schedules and adequate childcare—than to women's positive reasons for staying in the paid labour force.

9. Francine S. Hall and Douglas T. Hall, *The Two-Career Couple* (Boston: Addison-Wesley Pub. Co., 1979).
10. Now the representative of the District of Columbia in the US Congress.

## THE POLITICS OF FOOD

1. United Nations Population Fund, 'Adolescents in India: A Profile'. The full report is available online at <http://web.unfpa.org/focus/india/facetoface/docs/adolescentsprofile.pdf>.
2. United Nations Children's Fund, 'Progress for Children: A Report Card on Adolescents', 2012. The full report is available online at <http://www.unicef.org/media/files/PFC2012_A_report_card_on_adolescents.pdf>.
3. Amol Sharma, 'In Slowing India, a Fast-Growing Star', *The Wall Street Journal*, 29 August 2012. The report is available online at <http://online.wsj.com/news/articles/SB10000872396390444432720 4577616060613980088>.
4. International Institute for Population Sciences (IIPS) and Macro International 'National Family Health Survey (NFHS-3), India, 2005–06' (Gujarat.Mumbai: IIPS, 2008). The full report is available online at <http://www.rchiips.org/nfhs/NFHS-3%20Data/gujarat_state_report_for_website.pdf>.

## MARILYN MONROE: THE WOMAN WHO DIED TOO SOON

1. Martin Amis, 'Diana Trilling at Claremont Avenue', *The Moronic Inferno: And other Visits to America* (London: Jonathan Cape, 1986).

## WHAT IS SELF-ESTEEM?

1. Watch the video in which Kavita Krishnan expresses this sentiment on YouTube at <http://www.youtube.com/watch?v=fD6YlpgxdYI>.
2. Susanne K. Langer (tr.) *Language and Myth* (London: Harper and Brothers, 1946).
3. Susan Sontag, 'Illness as Metaphor', *Illness as Metaphor and AIDS and Its Metaphors* (New York: Picador, 1988), p. 57.
4. Barbara Boggs Sigmund, 'I Didn't Give Myself Cancer', *The New York Times*, 30 November 1989.
5. The 1971–72 Virginia Slims Poll, the first national survey of women's opinions on women's issues. Designed by Carolyn Setlow, Louis Harris and Associates, 630 Fifth Avenue, New York.
6. Ryszard Kapuscinski, ' Revolution', William R. Brand and Katarzyna Mcoczkowska-Brand (trans.), *The New Yorker*, 4 and 11 March 1985.

7. Stendhal, *The Red and the Black*, Roger Gard (trans.), (London: Penguin, 2002).
8. Alice Walker, *The Color Purple* (New York: Harcourt Books, 1970).
9. W. Hugh Missildine, *Your Inner Child of the Past* (New York: Simon and Schuster, 1963).
10. Gloria Steinem, *Marilyn: Norma Jeane* (New York: Henry Holt, 1986).
11. Missildine, p 222.
12. Ibid., p 224.
13. Marilyn Murphy, *Are You Girls Travelling Alone?: Adventures in Lesbianic Logic*, (Los Angeles: Clothespin Fever Press, 1991), p. 20. For her current columns, write to *The Lesbian News*, P.O. Box 1430, Twenty-nine Palms, California 92277.
14. Mohandas Karamchand Gandhi, *An Autobiography or The Story of My Experiments with Truth*, Mahadev Desai (trans.) (Ahmedabad: Navajivan Publishing House, 1982), p. 14.
15. Mohandas Karamchand Gandhi, *Harijan*, 3 October 1936.
16. Gandhi, *An Autobiography*, p. 31.
17. Ibid., p. 20.
18. Ibid., p. 162.
19. Kalima Rose, *Where Women Are Leaders: The SEWA Movement in India* (New Delhi: Sage Publications, 1991).

## ROMANCE VERSUS LOVE

1. Simone de Beauvoir, *The Second Sex*, H.M. Parshley (trans.) (New York: Knopf, 1989), p. 667.
2. G.D. Klingopulos, 'The Novel as Dramatic Poem', quoted in Emily Brontë, *Wuthering Heights* (New York: Random House, Modern Library Edition, 1978), p. xvii.
3. Royal A. Gettmann, 'Introduction', (New York: Random House, Modern Library Edition, 1950) *Wuthering Heights*, p. ix.
4. Charlotte Brontë, 'Biographical Notice of Ellis and Acton Bell', *Wuthering Heights* (London: Smith, Elder & Co. 1850), pp. xxv-xxvi.
5. Ibid., p. xxv.
6. Ibid., p. xx.
7. Ibid., p. xxiv-xxv.
8. Adrienne Rich, 'Jane Eyre: The Temptations of a Motherless Woman,' *On Lies, Secrets, and Silence* (New York: W.W. Norton, 1979), p. 90.
9. Emily Brontë may have had in mind a racial distance greater than that between the gently bred Catherine and a 'dark-skinned gypsy', as Heathcliff was described. Jamaican-American writer Michelle Cliff

points out in her unpublished essay, 'Caliban's Daughter', that Liverpool was a centre of the slave trade, where discarded Africans, perhaps also children fathered by slave traders, lived in the streets. Catherine's father brought home this boy who was 'dark as if it came from the devil' and speaking 'some gibberish that nobody could understand' only after he had unsuccessfully 'enquired for its owner'. Later, when Heathcliff runs away to become rich enough to marry Catherine, what trade other than slave ships could have earned him such a fortune in three years? And if that self-betrayal was the source of his wealth, no wonder he was in such pain when he returned to find even this blood money couldn't give him Catherine. Perhaps Emily Brontë, wandering over moors she must have known were part of a slave trader's estate, was drawing parallels between a Heathcliff who could be bought (and forced to see others) and a Catherine who could be sold in marriage. Or perhaps as an outsider by sex who had written imaginary stories about Africa as a child, she was simply finding within herself the emotions of an outsider by race—just as Aphra Behn, the first professional woman writer in England had done almost two hundred years earlier.

10. 'Survey: Sex and Self-Esteem', *Medical Aspects of Human Sexuality*, Volume 17, Number 5, May 1983, pp. 197–211.

11. Mary McCarthy, *The Company She Keeps* (Boston: Houghton Mifflin Harcourt, 2003).

12. Helen Handley (ed.), *The Lovers' Quotation Book* (New York: Pushcart Press, 1986), p. 63.

13. Linda Sanford and Mary Ellen Donovan, *Women and Self-Esteem* (New York: Anchor/Doubleday, 1984), p. 123.

14. Virginia Goldner, Peggy Penn, Marcia Sheinberg and Gillian Walker, 'Love and Violence: Gender Paradoxes in Volatile Attachments', *Family Process*, December 1990, Volume 20, Number 4, p. 343.

15. Handley, *Lovers' Quotation Book*, p. 45.

16. Charlotte Davis Kasl, *Women, Sex, and Addiction: A Search for Love and Power* (New York: Ticknor & Fields, 1989) p. 130.

17. Frank Pittman, *Private Lies: Infidelity and the Betrayal of Intimacy* (New York: W.W. Norton, 1989) p. 183.

18. Q.D. Leavis, 'Introduction', Charlotte Brontë, *Jane Eyre* (London: Penguin, 1966), p.11.

19. Rich, 'Jane Eyre', p. 96.

20. Ibid.

21. For a view of this story as it might have looked through the mad wife's eyes, see the Jean Rhys novel, *Wide Sargasso Sea*.

22. Robin Morgan, *The Anatomy of Freedom: Feminism in Four Dimensions* (New York: W.W. Norton & Co., 1982).

23. Albert Camus, *The First Man*, (New York: Vintage International, 1995).

24. Clare Boothe Luce, *Stuffed Shirts*, (New York: Horace Liveright. Inc, 1931), p. 78.

25. Simone de Beauvoir, *The Second Sex*, Constance Borde and Sheila Malovany-Chevallier (trans.) (New York: Vintage, 2009).

26. Margaret Caroline Anderson, *Forbidden Fires*, Mathilda M. Hills (ed.) (Missouri: Naiad Press, 1996).

27. Phyllis Rose, *Woman of Letters: A Life of Virginia Woolf* (Oxford University Press, 1978).

28. For a critical look at measures of masculinity and androgyny, see Joseph Pleck, *The Myth of Masculinity* (Cambridge, Mass.: MIT Press, 1983).

29. For conditions of creativity in our children and ourselves, see Teresa M. Amabile, *Growing Up Creative: Nurturing a Lifetime of Creativity* (New York: Crown, 1989).

30. For more about the case for and tradition of androgyny, see Carolyn G. Heilbrun, *Toward a Recognition of Androgyny: A Search into Myth and Literature to Trace Manifestations of Androgyny and to Assess Their Implications for Today* (New York: Harper Colophon Books, Harper & Row, 1974).

31. Barbara Risman, 'Intimate Relationships from a Microstructural Perspective: Men Who Mother', *Gender and Society*, Volume 1, 1987, pp. 6–32.

32. Dorothy Dinnerstein, *The Mermaid and the Minotaur*, (New York: Other Press, 1999).

33. Rainer Maria Rilke, *Letters to a Young Poet*, Mark Harman (tr.), (Library of the Congress, USA, 2011).

34. Marilyn French, 'Self-respect: A Female Perspective', *The Humanist*, November/December, 1986, p. 22.

35. Alice Walker, *Revolutionary Petunias and other Poems*, (New York: Harcourt Brace Jovanovich, 1973), p. 66.

## EROTICA VERSUS PORNOGRAPHY

1. Melinda Tankard Reist and Abigail Bray (eds.) *Big Porn Inc: Exposing the Harms of the Global Porn Industry* (North Melbourne: Spinifex Press, 2011), pp. 239–49.

2. Some of Tiger's works have included controversial concepts, including the biological origins of social interactions. Tiger published a work, *The Imperial Animal*, with Robin Fox in 1972 which advocated a 'social

carnivore theory' of human evolution. Tiger has predicted the higher status of women within society in books such as *The Decline of Males* and *Men in Groups*. He has also written books such as *The Pursuit of Pleasure*, which discussed the concept that evolution has established the biological mechanisms of pleasure and that they have survival origins. Lionel Tiger lives in New York City, and regularly contributes to mainstream media such as *Psychology Today* and *The New York Times*.

3. Kinsey's research went beyond theory and interview to include observation of and participation in sexual activity, sometimes involving co-workers. The data published in the *Kinsey Reports* as his *Sexual Behavior* books later revealed that Kinsey used data from a single paedophile and presented it as being from various sources. Kinsey collected sexual material from around the world, which brought him to the attention of US Customs when they seized some pornographic films in 1956—he died before this matter was legally resolved.

4. For a history of this controversial and misunderstood ordinance that was passed by the City Council of Minneapolis but vetoed by its Mayor—as well as a compendium of research on pornography—see Franklin Mark Osanka and Sara Lee Johann, *Sourcebook on Pornography* (Lexington, Mass.: Lexington Books, 1989).

### THE REAL LINDA LOVELACE

1. Catharine MacKinnon and Andrea Dworkin, *Pornography and Civil Rights: A New Day for Womens' Equality* (Minneapolis: Organizing against Pornography, 1988).
2. Linda Lovelace, *Ordeal: The Truth behind Deep Throat* (New York: Citadel Press, 1980).

### I WAS A PLAYBOY BUNNY

1. 'Chiffon Drapes India's Bunnies', *Mumbai Mirror*, 3 January 2013.

### THE THIRD WAY: AN END OF TRAFFICKING AND PROSTITUTION, A BEGINNING OF MUTUAL SEXUALITY

1. Sonja Hedgepeth and Rochelle Saidel (eds.), *Sexual Violence against Jewish Women during the Holocaust*, (Massachusetts: Brandeis University Press, 2011).

### IF MEN COULD MENSTRUATE

1. Phyllis McAlpin Stewart Schlafly, born 15 August 1924, is an American constitutional lawyer, conservative activist, author, and founder of

the Eagle Forum. She is known for her opposition to modern feminism and for her campaign against the proposed Equal Rights Amendment. Schlafly argued that the ERA would take away gender specific privileges currently enjoyed by women, including 'dependent wife' benefits under Social Security and the exemption from Selective Service registration.

2. Marabel Morgan is an American author of self-help books for married women, including *The Total Woman* (1973), *Total Joy* (1983), *The Total Woman Cookbook* (1980) and *The Electric Woman* (1986). *The Total Woman* reportedly sold more than ten million copies and was the bestselling non-fiction book of 1974. Grounded in evangelical Christianity, it taught that 'a total woman' caters to her man's special quirks, whether it be in 'salads, sex or sports', and is perhaps best remembered for instructing wives to greet their husbands at the front door wearing sexy outfits, or draped in transparent saran wrap, with nothing (but herself) underneath. 'It's only when a woman surrenders her life to her husband, reveres and worships him and is willing to serve him, that she becomes really beautiful to him,' Morgan wrote.

3. With thanks to Stan Pottinger for many of the improvisations already here.

## HITLER AND THE CULT OF MASCULINITY

1. Adolf Hitler, *Mein Kampf*, The Noontide Press: Books On-Line. The full text of the book is available online at <http://www.angelfire.com/folk/bigbaldbob88/MeinKampf.pdf>.

2. Ibid.

3. Ibid.

4. Tim Mason, 'Women in Germany, 1925-1940: Family, Welfare and Work. Part I', *History Workshop*, Number 1, Spring 1976, pp. 73–113.

5. Hitler, *Mein Kampf*.

6. Richard Evans, *The Feminist Movement in Germany: 1894-1933* (London: Sage Publications, 1976).

7. Hitler, *Mein Kampf*.

8. Tim Mason, 'Women in Germany, 1925-1940', *Nazism, Fascism and the Working Class: Essays by Tim Mason* (Cambridge: Cambridge University Press, 1995).

# ACKNOWLEDGEMENTS

In alphabetical order, the people without whom this book would not have been possible:

Abhilasha Kumari, Amelia Richards, Anuradha Joshi, Ashley Lott, Bob Levine, Francesca Tarrant, Jennifer Buffet, Kanishka Gupta, Laura Fischer, Madhu Prasad, Md Kalam, Pamela Shifman, Peter Buffet, Rajni Gupta, Rakshanda Jalil, Ranjan Prasad, Samantha Oddi, Samta Gupta, Sujata Prasad, Sunil Narula, Tinku Khanna and Vidyasagar Gupta.

\*

The author and the publisher wish to acknowledge the following for permission to reproduce copyright material:

Bloomsbury Publishing Plc. for 'The Masculinization of Wealth' and 'The India That Shaped Me' (originally published as 'Doing Sixty') which first appeared in *Moving beyond Words: Age, Rage, Sex, Power, Money, Muscles: Breaking the Boundaries of Gender* (1995).

Henry Holt and Company, Inc. for 'The Importance of Work', 'The Politics of Food', 'In Praise of Women's Bodies Again', 'Marilyn Monroe: The Woman Who Died too Soon', Erotica versus Pornography', 'The Real Linda Lovelace', 'I Was a Playboy Bunny', 'Words and Change: Who Were You before This Wave of Feminism Began?' 'Sisterhood', 'If Men Could Menstruate', 'Hitler and the Cult of Masculinity' (originally published as 'If Hitler Were Alive, Whose Side Would He Be On?') and 'Ruth's Song (Because She Could Not Sing It)' which first appeared in *Outrageous Acts and Everyday Rebellions* (1983).

Little, Brown Book Group for 'What Is Self-esteem?' and 'Romance versus Love' which first appeared in *Revolution from Within: A Book of Self-Esteem* (1992).

Ruchira Gupta for 'The Third Way: An End of Trafficking and Prostitution, a Beginning of Mutual Sexuality'.

CPSIA information can be obtained
at www.ICGtesting.com
Printed in the USA
LVHW111013070920
665225LV00002BA/505

9 788129 131034